ALIAS JUNGLE DOCTOR

In mid-safari—Honolulu Airport, 1955

ALIAS JUNGLE DOCTOR

An Autobiography
by
PAUL WHITE

EXETER
THE PATERNOSTER PRESS

ISBN: 0 85364 205 2
Copyright © 1977 The Paternoster Press Ltd.

No part of this publication may be reproduced, stored in a retrieval system or transmitted, in any form or by any means, electronic, mechanical, photocopying, recording or otherwise, without the prior permission of The Paternoster Press Limited

AUSTRALIA:
Emu Book Agencies Pty., Ltd.,
63 Berry Street, Granville 2142, N.S.W.

SOUTH AFRICA:
Oxford University Press,
P.O. Box 1141, Oxford House, 11 Buitencingle St., Cape Town

This book is sold subject to the condition that it shall not, by way of trade or otherwise, be lent, re-sold, hired out, or otherwise circulated without the publisher's prior consent, in any form of binding or cover other than that in which it published and without a similar condition including this condition being imposed on the subsequent purchaser

British Library Cataloguing in Publication Data

White, Paul Hamilton Hume
  Alias Jungle Doctor.
  1. White, Paul – Biography
  I. Title
  823'.9'14   PR6045.H/

ISBN 0–85364–205–2

Made and printed in Great Britain for
The Paternoster Press Ltd., Paternoster House,
3 Mount Radford Crescent, Exeter, Devon,
by Butler and Tanner Ltd., Frome, Somerset

To
RUTH

Contents

1	Come in!	1
2	Small boy with Father	3
3	Boy without Father	7
4	Junior Schoolboy	19
5	December Revolution	27
6	Look for Facts, White	34
7	University	42
8	Love	64
9	Junior Doctor	73
10	The Adventure Begins	93
11	Doctor Meets Jungle	107
12	Doctor with Pen	122
13	Doctor at Work	138
14	Committees	148
15	Houses	152
16	Radio to Television	161
17	Fables	174
18	Bathrooms	183
19	A Time to Play	187
20	Mary	196

21	Secretaries and More	205
22	Cars and Dogs	212
23	Changing Jobs	218
	List of Publications	225

List of Illustrations

In mid-safari – Honolulu Airport	*frontis*
	facing page
The author, aged 1 yr. 9 mths, and 4 years	6
Bong-bong Street, Bowral, in 1920s and today Early cottage home in Bowral	7
26 Roseville Avenue, Roseville William P. Nicholson	20
Sydney Grammar School: Sydney University	21
Running practice on Sydney University Oval Inter-Varsity Athletics Team, 1930	54
Graduation Day: the new Doctor Sydney University Medical School	55
Medical Hazard? Floods at St. George, Queensland	86
Jungle Surgery: Cataract operation in progress	87
Daudi and his wife and tumour	136
Witchdoctor's handiwork	137
Home again: the family, 1948	154
The family at Beecroft, 1957	155
Return to Tanganyika: greeting an old friend	166
Return to Tanganyika: Danieli with Gospel recording	167
Rosemary and David, Wanganui, N.Z., 1963 With Rev. Dan Mbogoni at Mvumi, 1967	172
Television: BBC "Meeting Point" programme, 1967 Television: with Clifford Warne and puppet "Toto"	173

Mary and David, 1959	204
With Ruth in Switzerland, 1973	205
"The funniest thing I've read since Darwin"	224

We acknowledge the kindness of friends who have supplied illustrations including the Balonne Shire Council (facing p. 86), Jean-Luc Ray of Lausanne (cover, and facing pp. 173, 205), Agent-General for N.S.W., London (facing p. 21), and Pilgrim International and O.F. Emery (facing pp. 7, 21, 55, 155, 166, 167, 173 and 224).

Chapter One:

Come In!

Welcome to my personal jungle

HYAENAS MAKE UNLOVELY NOISES WHICH SOUND PARTICULARLY eerie between midnight and the hour before dawn.

The African night nurse at the hospital in Tanzania was making tea while we waited for a baby to arrive. She chuckled as almost outside the window the jungle scavenger howled again.

"Mbisi, the hyaena, mocks you, Bwana doctor. He knows you have no joy in those of his tribe."

"He's right, and the closer he is the less I like him."

"You would prefer to be in bed?"

I yawned, "Indeed I would."

"So you wish the child would arrive soon?"

"I certainly do. This is a most inconsiderate time of the night to start life."

"Hongo!" she exclaimed, putting down the teapot. "And what time did you yourself select to arrive?"

"At *saa mbili*, the second hour of the day. Eight a.m. as we call it in Australia."

She smiled. "After the doctor had had his breakfast?"

"Truly. And on a fine Saturday morning in the summer."

She raised her eyebrows, "Truly you have a memory of strength."

"That was among a number of things my mother told me."

Urgent voices broke in. I scrubbed and gloved-up and ushered the baby into the world. Then, avoiding the hyaenas, I went to bed.

That was in 1938, and twenty-eight years after my voice had first come into action in a weatherboard house round which was my father's bulb nursery. As some of the less kindly of my friends have often pointed out, this was next door to the local gas works.

Nothing is more warming and cheery than a pine log blazing on a wide open hearth. Add to this a high wind and rain driving in gusts against the window and you have an ideal situation for the birth of an idea.

I sat relaxed in front of the fire. Beside me was a large man who possessed a deep, warm, musical voice. He had a wide view and experience of life. A draftsman – unemployed in the depression of the 1930s – almost a policeman – a soldier – a clergyman – a Bishop and Chaplain-General to the forces.

He kicked the great log. Sparks rocketed up the chimney. "Write up your life one day, Paul. Intimate stuff. What made you tick, what you felt at the time. Take the lid off. Dialogue it. What you thought when you were patted on the back and kicked in the teeth. What you did as a kid. Go right back and give us a verbal filmstrip of your failures – what made you chuckle, the things that twisted your heart and pounded your soul.

"A lot has happened to you as a boy, an undergraduate, a doctor, a writer. Pass on some of the African experiences that you told us about in the Cathedral tonight here in Nelson; that sort of thing."

I watched little flames spurt out of the log and the red coals underneath it, and after a long pause nodded and said, "M-m-m!"

But the idea was sold and a loose-leafed folder started to hold a collection of scribbled pictures of things as they happened. A dilapidated concertina-file slowly bulged with clippings, letters, pamphlets and my special weakness – odd bits of paper with ideas and happenings scribbled on them.

Chapter Two:

Small Boy with Father

BOWRAL, A BEAUTIFUL COUNTRY TOWN IN THE SOUTHERN Highlands of New South Wales, is a most congenial place in which to be born. Towering over a neat and mellow township is a hill, two hundred metres high, strikingly like the rock of Gibraltar. The Gib, as it is known locally, gives character and poise to Bowral.

We lived in Jasmine Street, most suitably named. Here the old world seemed linked with the new. Gum trees and tall pines made the air aromatic with their scent. Hawthorn grew side by side with wattle, honeysuckle and roses. Violets in profusion added their subtle fragrance.

We lived in a small weatherboard, corrugated-iron-roofed cottage directly beneath the Gib. It was separated from the gas works by a pastel-shaded wall of willow and silver poplars. My first memory was when I was about two years old and propelling myself round the house on a cylindrical-shaped waste paper basket.

My father was a farmer. He specialised in growing peonies and daffodils. He would sit me in the barrow and wheel me round to where he was at work, telling me about birds and animals and insects. He understood the art of telling a story and had a most nimble sense of humour.

When I appeared on the scene my father, Richard Sibford White, was thirty-three. He was a man of many parts. In his boyhood he had travelled widely in Europe with his family and spoke fluent German. He had been one of the Australian contingent to fight in the Boer War.

In South Africa he had picked up a smattering of Zulu and could pass the time of day in Cantonese with the local Chinese gardener, Koon Sing. This cheerful old man always called him

Governor General and me, to my intense satisfaction, Little Governor General.

In common with most of his family my father was quick to see the funny side of any situation and if I am to believe sundry uncles he had a strong urge to play practical jokes. One of my mother's sisters had a sense of humour on the same wavelength. She told me hilarious stories of his exploits.

Two things stand out in my memory: a bout of whooping cough – a frightening experience. Dad seemed very close beside me. He would quieten me down by telling me stories.

Then again, when Mother was losing her appendix in hospital Dad looked after me. Suddenly there was a change in the quality of the food and the house looked different. But life was full of new interests.

Dad could throw a clasp knife and a tomahawk like a Red Indian. He showed me how to build houses for the neighbourhood cats with logs of wood and old pieces of timber. He took me down to the creek (a forbidden area) and caught crayfish with a dangling lump of meat and picked them up with his bare fingers. This I thought an outstanding piece of courage.

One of my father's favourite exploits was to collect lizards of various sizes. They had an uncomfortable habit of coming to light when we had visitors who either did not impress him or whom he regarded as pompous.

Those days by the creek he collected all manner of grubs, beetles and beasties for my interest and intrigued me by his ability to mimic bird song, which brought magpies, thrushes and peewees to the back door. At night his owl noises were delightfully eerie.

He tried manfully to sing me to sleep with songs such as I had nevery heard before. I can now recognise *The Wild Colonial Boy*, and army ditties that went back to the beginning of the century. When I should have been asleep and he slowly moved away from my bed I spoiled the effect my asking, "Why do you have whiskers when Mummy doesn't?"

In 1915 when I was five years old, he enlisted in the Australian Infantry Forces. I remember my father coming home one day with his army uniform, his rifle and bayonet. He perched me in the barrow and wheeled me off to the maize paddock where he slashed down corn-stalks with the bayonet blade and told me stories of his soldiering in South Africa during the Boer War. He told me how he had cooked and eaten mealies and milked goats into his helmet. I listened spellbound as he told me yarns of Africa, of the animals of the veldt and of Zulus with ostrich feathers in their hair.

A few weeks later I stood at the front door with mother and waved goodbye as my father walked through the front gate, dressed in his A.I.F. slouch hat and army uniform.

A month later I went to the same front door and felt important to take a telegram to my mother as she lay sick in bed. As I watched, her face went deadly white. My father had died of meningitis in the military camp.

Mother was a courageous woman with great independence of outlook. Her maternal grandfather was one of the pioneers and the brother of Hamilton Hume, the famous explorer, who discovered the Murray River. She had been brought up in the house of a horse-and-buggy doctor and had tasted the loneliness of the Australian bush as a farmer's wife on the upper reaches of the Hawkesbury River. Though she did not relish emergencies, she well knew how to deal with them and did so without fuss.

Her father, Alan Bradley Morgan, was an active Christian man and the Christian way was no empty formality in either his life or his household.

Mother was last but one in a family of eight. As a child she had visited England in the days when sailing ships were the fastest means of overseas transport and the route of choice had been round the Cape of Good Hope. She had gone to boarding school in Derbyshire. Her stories of these years made me think of Dickens.

Later at the Croydon (New South Wales) Presbyterian Ladies' College she had finished her schooling; a highlight of which was a gold medal inscribed:
        Sydney College of Music, 1903
          Organ-Playing Honours
            Rose Morgan

Her childhood was lived in Queen Victoria's reign and in many ways her outlook reflected this period. She had and passed on a deep sense of loyalty to the Crown.

Mother liked people. The girls who were or had been in her Sunday School class really mattered to her. She had a deep concern for them and followed their activities carefully. One thing she did supremely well was to listen and quietly and persistently to pray.

Missionary enterprise was a deep concern to her. She read widely and wrote newsy letters to people at work overseas after finding out their interests. She backed this up by giving to the limits of her rather slim purse.

Life as the only son of my mother who was a widow had its problems, especially for her. We hadn't much money apart from a war pension and our weatherboard cottage. I was a sickly child and with great ease would develop bronchitis. Mother blamed the westerly winds and was probably right. As I lay wheezing she would read to me by the hour: adventure stories, fairy tales, books on animals and birds and always stories from the Bible.

At night she played the piano as I went to sleep: Mendelssohn's Songs without Words, Liszt's Rhapsodies, children's hymns, bits from Handel and Haydn.

At Bowral the westerly winds of late winter were particularly bleak. Once mother took me to a beach a few miles north of Sydney in an attempt to dodge bronchitis. I celebrated the event by falling off a verandah and acquiring a "Green-stick fracture of the right humerus." X-rays were rare at that time. The doctor was genial and said, "Nothing to worry about." He set my arm by putting it in a sling in a way that would have failed him in a surgery examination. The result – a twisted and weakened right arm, usable but weak. A "something" that marked me out as a child with an abnormality.

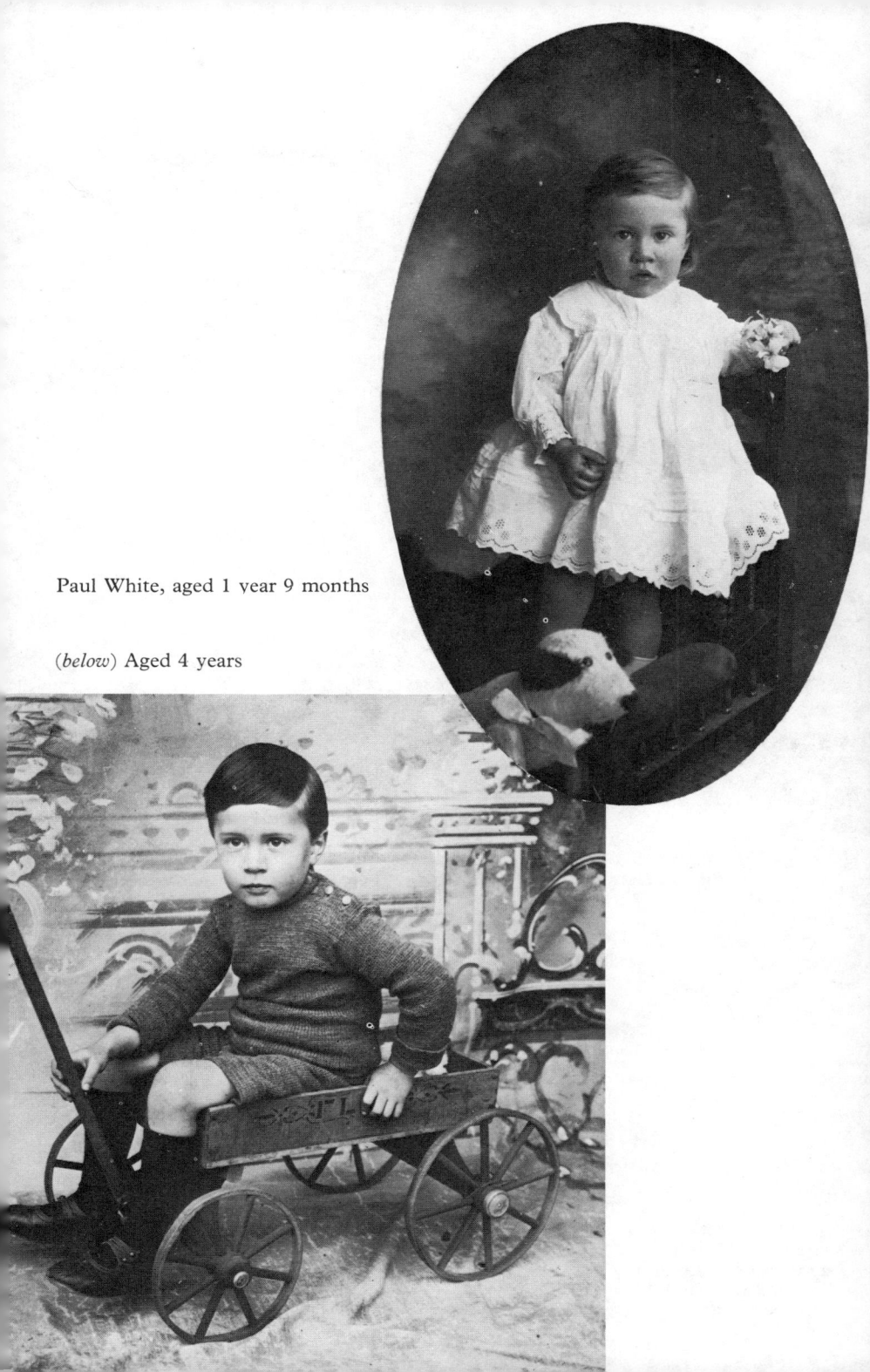

Paul White, aged 1 year 9 months

(*below*) Aged 4 years

"Advance, Australia!"—Bong-Bong Street, Bowral, in the 1920s, and the same street today

Cottage home in Jasmine Street, Bowral, where Paul White spent some years of his early boyhood with his widowed mother

Chapter Three:

Boy Without Father

WHEN WE RETURNED TO BOWRAL WE MOVED HOUSE. I think there was an acute shortage of cash. We went to live in half of the colonial-type house where my grandfather and his family of eight had lived. The rental was made very nominal.

The house, "St. Helens," was interesting to me. There were wide verandahs with pillars to support the roof. These were decorated with wrought-iron. The windows and doors were of cedar, the ceilings high and the rooms large. They had open fireplaces which it was my task to keep stocked with wood. The inside was cool, excessively so in the winter.

In the garden were huge gum trees. Ivy climbed over the fences and fell in bunches over the roof of a building which had once been the stables. Great dark green clusters dangled over the narrow pathway which led to what mother called the W.C.

Certainly it was no water closet. Fridays started dramatically with the noisy arrival of a shadowy figure at or before dawn. He would make his way through the back gate and take the leading role in what is known in Public Health circles as the "pan-and-fly system" of hygiene. This most useful individual combined the office of Mayor with his professional activity. There was time in the dawning, as I watched the sun light up The Gib, to meditate on how he managed to appear spruce and shining on official occasions, resplendent in his robes of office and with what looked to me like a necklace of medals.

My pulse-rate would always go up as I covered this sinister twenty-five yard safari at night time, holding a guttering candle. The lament of the boobook owl, whose cry is *mopoke*, sounded most ghostly in that ivy-draped retreat. In the daytime the candle was still required because of the dim light of this so-called convenience.

Apart from all his other activities, the Mayor in his sanitary capacity used annually to leave a Christmas greeting-card with a poem inscribed. I felt sure it was all his own work. The wording intrigued me so I learned it off by heart.

At a Christmas afternoon tea party given by some of mother's most conservative friends it was suggested that I recite a seasonal poem.

At once I complied with:

> Although the police keep order
> There's no more useful man,
> Than the bloke who comes at sunrise,
> And juggles with the pan.

The paralysed silence that greeted this offering discouraged me from producing the other verses! Later, when mother explained the ethics of the situation to me, her carefully-worded reproof was somewhat spoiled by laughter which quickly turned into a spasm of coughing.

Being an only child can be a very lonely affair. In many ways I learned to entertain myself. I slept on the verandah and had a fine view of the stars, especially on the cold crisp nights of winter when I coughed into the pillow so that mother wouldn't hear. The Kookaburras, the largest of the kingfisher family, would greet the first light with their laughter and wake me. Very quietly I would dress and hurry to the railway station. Here was a feast of action for one who found trains and the then rarity, aeroplanes, a high attraction.

Three times within an hour at the station there was drama, opening with the arrival of the two divisons of the Melbourne Express. I would sit entranced on a fence-post and watch the distant cloud of steam turn into a black powerful engine dragging a long line of silent carriages at over a mile a minute — to me an incredible speed. Ten minutes later the performance would be repeated and finally my favourite, the 6.00 a.m. fast passenger train, left Bowral for Sydney, eighty-five miles away. I had the opportunity of sitting within ten yards of the great engine, seeing the furnace and watching carefully the manoeuvres of the driver when he pulled the whistle and opened the throttle. I discovered a host of interesting facts from the kindly and understanding stationmaster, who in his uniform with its cap, braid and badges seemed to me the most important man in the town.

When the train disappeared round the end of The Gib, I would walk briskly home, quietly undress, and go to bed. At seven o'clock I would be called, and dress. Then I would cut the wood for the fire and feed our dozen or so hens. I don't think mother was ever aware of my early morning entertainment.

When the time came for me to start school we moved again, this time a mile further out along the street with the cheerful-sounding name, Merrigang Street. The stress of moving house influenced mother to arrange a holiday, which to me was most adventurous.

Holidays which did not involve a visit to the dentist were always exciting events. First there was the ritual of packing substantial suit-cases and the finding of keys to fit them. There was a large cardboard box which had once held jewellery and in this was a vast, heterogeneous tangle of keys which must have represented half a century of collection. I found it amusing that so many of these keys would open the same suit-case. Then there were straps and labels kept in a hessian bag which also housed longer lengths of cord and string.

This specially notable journey was to my careful calculations the nearest thing to a hundred miles — at that time I had never heard of a kilometre. The impressive trip involved travelling first by a horse-drawn hansom cab from our home to the Bowral railway station (one mile). Then the train. What anticipations. Would there be a window seat ? How would we get the luggage on to the rack ? I was not sturdy-looking but managed a large suit-case somehow with frequent stops and hand-changing. There was the excitement of tunnels and closing windows at the right time, the pungent, sulphurous fumes that swirled in if you were not quick enough. The smuts which you must not get into your eye.

Then there was the excitement of arriving in the suburbs. Sydney was a special experience. To me, Central Station was the heart of the metropolis. There was the opportunity of looking at closest quarters into the cab of the locomotive. The huge departures board with exotic names of stations like Coonabarabran, Gwabegar, Wagga Wagga, Gerringong. Just through the arches were the trams — those intriguing linked-together, toast-rack trams with the conductor acrobatically making his way along a footboard. They bucked deliciously on corners and small hills. Twopence for adults, a penny for children, to Circular Quay.

Here wharves were lined with mail steamers from Britain, the East and America. I imagined myself as an overseas passenger as I boarded the Manly ferry. I was soon to know them intimately: the Barrenjoey, the Burrabra, the Barragoola, the Belubra, the Bingarra and the Kuringai with its small funnel. I didn't fancy this ferry. It was the runt, the poor relation. I would rather wait half an hour than travel in her. I was all eyes as the sharp steel bows of the Barrenjoey – always my favourite – cut their shapely way through the blue waters of the harbour and we rounded Bennelong Point – then a huge khaki shed from which trams emerged. The same neck of land now supports the Sydney Opera House. On the port side (I was careful to think in nautical terms) was the romantic stone fort, Pinch Gut, built originally to foil any naval onslaught from the Russians. Over the stern I watched two vehicular ferries, laden with cars, making their way to and from the north side of the harbour – the Sydney Harbour Bridge at this time was nothing but a dream. I caught a glimpse of Government House before feasting my eyes on a bevy of battleships, cruisers, destroyers, and that sinister under-water killer, the submarine. Then there was the Zoo and the Heads, with Barrenjoey riding magnificently through the heavy swells that came in from the Pacific Ocean. I scorned the thought of sea sickness but was thankful to see Manly Wharf not far ahead – Manly, so-called because of the behaviour of the aborigines in Captain Cook's day. It is now a prestige suburb, largely built on a sand spit with a mere quarter of a mile separating the Pacific Ocean from the Harbour, and shaded by tall Norfolk Island Pines. I imagined a tidal wave sweeping these and Manly away and opening up a second entrance to Port Jackson.

My safari ended in a highlight: a short but exciting journey over the blue metal road in a taxi, a Dodge, 1914 model. The driver wore goggles, a peaked cap and a dust coat. Mother paid him the sum of two shillings – heavy expense for so short a journey I thought, but worth it. As I struggled with the suitcases I thought of this romantic journey with its five different means of transport. It had been a notable day for a six-year-old.

Our new house was an inconspicuous weatherboard home with three large tanks fed from its tin roof. I was impressed with the fact that we had three tanks and our immediate neighbours two only. There was a brass plate screwed to the wall near the front door on which was inscribed *Canberra*. This was some years before the country town of the same name became Australia's Federal Capital. We were in a strategic location, for directly opposite was the Church of England Grammar School for Girls, an institute of which I am proud to be, technically, an "old girl".

Again I slept on an enclosed verandah and lying in bed at night I made up stories about all sorts of things including my "sister." We had amazing adventures and discussed the strange and illogical behaviour of adults. None of these epics was ever transferred to paper. I was acutely lonely, and in my secret prayers, I asked God again and again to send me a real sister.

To me, mother seemed to have some formidable friends, many of them unmarried, who took a considerable interest in my welfare and my behaviour. Later I was to realise how the prayers of these good folk had been a most positive factor in my life.

There was a sense of security in our home. It was a house with books and music and pets. We had canaries and a parrot and, for a time, a guinea pig. This turned out to be a lady and very soon we had five of the species but only for a very short time.

I was always interested in collecting things: stones, all manner of geological specimens about which I knew very little, African curios, tapa cloth and weapons from New Guinea and the South Sea islands, spoils from a trip mother had made years before. I collected shells, tadpoles, butterflies, birds' eggs and feathers, coins, pressed and dried flowers, cigarette cards, match box tops and, pre-eminently, stamps. I set up my "museum" under the house and spent hours labelling, cataloguing and thinking out stories about my various specimens.

Then I was given a cricket ball, an event to me of the highest importance. The sons of the family where I was later to milk cows hacked a cricket bat out of a piece of wood. I supplied the ball and the sticking plaster to cover over the splinters of the handle. We spent hours digging out and levelling an earth wicket. Then one golden day I tasted the joys of cricket from the participant's angle.

It was a mile from our house at the top of the hill to the railway station and also to St. Simon and St. Jude's church. Mother and I walked it regularly every Sunday and in the spring and summer – twice. Being 1917, cars were somewhat unusual and the roads unruly tracks, covered with blue-metal.

I liked church. There were splendid stained-glass windows, one in memory of my grandfather, another, a real work of art, to my aunt. I always thought that the saints in the stained-glass windows looked old and wore the most impractical clothing. I had no ambition to be anything like them. I liked the angels at the empty tomb. They had good muscles. I liked the pipe organ. It was a two-manual affair and was powered by a donkey-engine that could be heard in the *pianissimo* patches of music panting away in its little shed behind the church.

The choirmaster and organist also conducted the town brass band and could sing very loudly. I sat in the back seat of the church with the Sunday School children who stayed on for church. My Aunt Margaret, a formidable lady, precise, neat and very proper, relaxed a little and encouraged us by quietly handing out jelly beans in the hymn before the sermon. It was a shameful thing to drop one and search for it under the seat.

Later I joined the choir. This was a salaried position. The first class choir boys received sixpence a Sunday, while second class songsters were given threepence.

In that choir sang Don Bradman, the famous cricketer. He was a notable batsman even as a ten-year-old and he was a first class choir boy. I was classified well down in the lower bracket. As I only attended in the morning my choral income amounted to sixpence a month. Mother didn't take kindly to my keeping this money. Rather reluctantly I put it into a missionary box shaped like a loaf of bread. The contents went to the British and Foreign Bible Society.

The boys used to laugh at me because mother felt I should wear stockings that covered the backs of my knees. Someone had passed on to her the apocryphal information that this place was the danger spot of the body. It's not amusing for a nine-year-old to be laughed at and chased and pelted with horse manure. My only comfort was that those black-encased legs seemed to carry me away from my tormentors most successfully.

I had a special treat every Wednesday when I purchased my copy of *Tiger Tim's Weekly* from the local newsagent, and later, schoolboy stories in the form of *The Gem*, *The Magnet* and *The Adventures of Nelson Lee, Schoolmaster and Detective*.

I financed my literary taste by not very skilfully milking cows, for which I was paid a penny a time. It was tedious work, particularly on cold frosty mornings when the only warm thing in sight was the cow. I was intensely proud of my ability to squirt milk into the face of an expectant dog. At this state of my life to have had a dog of my own would have done much to bring companionship into my life, but mother maintained that dogs dig up vegetable gardens and much of our food came from the vegetable garden.

For Christmas I was given a copy of either the *Boys' Own Annual* or *Chums*. Both were magnificent books, full of stories, puzzles, articles, games, stamps, interesting places and people.

I had on my bookshelf some prized possessions. Among them a dilapidated copy of H. M. Stanley's *How I found Livingstone*, Mungo Park's *Travels in East Africa*, *Mackay of Uganda*, and *The Man Eaters of Tsavo*. Particularly I liked to take Livingstone's diary and read it under the gum trees on The Gib. I needed these books seeing I spent one week in four in bed with a cough and someone's "bronchitis cure." At no time was a doctor called, but my back was very frequently rubbed with camphorated oil. To this day a whiff of camphor brings a cough to my throat.

I read and reread those *Chums* and the *Boys' Own Papers*; they filled a most important part of my bookshelf and my life. One book that I read again and again was called *Little Folks*. It contained stories that intrigued me greatly about Fitzi the Marmoset, Boobanda the Bear and other animals who lived in a magnificent forest. These lifted my imagination and peopled the bush for me.

There were stories of families including a little girl with long hair. Around her I built up a series of adventures which were a fine antidote for loneliness. I suspect she was the sister figure in my unwritten stories.

The Gib, solid and friendly, was a place to ramble over. There were many places where you could see and not be seen, and could feel the tranquillity of Bowral. You could look out over the panorama of the Southern Highlands and watch trains coming from miles away and traffic – mainly horse-drawn – winding its way along the dirt roads. You could sit quietly and watch the way birds behaved. There was the notable day when a wallaby grazed gently within yards of me.

Then and many times since I have felt completely at rest in this place. To the east of the town is a green hill, its skyline laced with gum trees. Tucked away in the green is the white colonial house built by John Oxley, the pioneer. Even visualising the shade and sunlight pattern on that grey warm rock where lizards basked makes my nose tingle to the smell of honeysuckle and wattle.

Sometimes the local paper would publish an announcement that an aeroplane was expected to fly over Bowral at a certain time on a certain day. I welcomed this exciting event by climbing The Gib and sitting on the grey rock and peering into the sky for hours.

In the *Boys' Own Paper* was an article on telescopes and the way they made things appear closer. How I wanted a telescope! Soon I convinced myself that I needed one, but how to buy it was quite another matter. Where to find the amount of money necessary was a particular problem. I worked hard at my milking. I became more skilful but at a penny a cow my savings seemed to grow very slowly.

The only time mother and I now went to Sydney was to visit the dentist. My teeth were a constant nuisance. I learned the value of oil of cloves. A sharpened stick dipped into this pungent medicine and pushed into an aching cavity really worked. To this day my choice is ginger and not cloves as a flavouring agent in stewed apple.

The only two bright spots in visiting Sydney were the possibility of buying a telescope and the opportunity of riding unaccompanied on a tram. Sometimes it was possible to sit so close to the driver that you didn't miss an item in his technique.

I concentrated on money-raising. A doctor uncle in Tasmania used from time to time to send me a postal note for a shilling, two shillings, or occasionally half a crown. His fee was in guineas and these postal notes came to make up the odd shillings above the pound. Two shillings came my way from him and I posted an immediate thank you letter telling him of my telescope plans. Two more letters with the mystic Tasmanian postmark arrived and four more shillings found their way into my cedarwood box.

An unexpected windfall was when I was asked to do some shopping for a neighbour who gave me a sovereign to pay for the goods. Vaguely I remembered my friend Koon Sing, the market gardener, saying something about gold. I consulted him at once. "Little Governor General," he said, "for every one of these I give you twenty-five shillings."

Bank notes those days were inscribed with a statement that upon demand a pound note would be exchanged for a sovereign. By visiting all the banks in the town I managed to come by three more sovereigns which I later learnt Koon Sing sent illicitly to relations in China.

When the fatal day came to go to Sydney and the dentist I had twenty-seven shillings. Two weeks of almost daily visits to the dentist with his vicious drill was a prospect to be faced without joy. Mother very understandingly spent a lot of time with me going to shops and patiently waiting as I examined telescopes and asked innumerable questions. I found one for thirty shillings. An advance in pocket money which was at that stage sixpence a week would mean none of my *Gems*, *Magnets* or *Nelson Lees* and certainly no *Tiger Tim's Weeklies*.

I had learned that you showed your thankfulness to God not by a mumbled thank you but in a concrete fashion. Mother called it "tithe." I understood it as one penny in every ten. There was a British and Foreign Bible Society Box on the shelf and into it I put my "thank yous." With threepence a week it was a problem to know just how to give. Sixpence was easier; a halfpenny was placed into the box at regular weekly intervals and then a penny.

Now I faced a heavy problem. Would I make God wait a bit? With this came the realisation that my milking money and my gold trading money had not been shared with God. This shook me. It meant waiting a year for my telescope.

The decision was made and I worked out that I owed God nearly five shillings. To my utter amazement a letter came only days later with a five shilling postal note and this brief letter:

DEAR PAUL,
This arrived today. Immediately I thought of you and hope it comes in usefully.

My Uncle Ted was tops, and, as I quietly thought about it, so was my God.

Six months later toothache took us to Sydney again. The excitement of buying the telescope almost cancelled out the misery of a record crop of cavities in my low-grade teeth.

Being an only child meant that of necessity I became adept at entertaining myself. I had a bird book given me on my third birthday. Perched high in an oak tree I would sit unseen and identify birds from the pictures in the book. Below was a path that led to The Gib. It passed through a fence at the foot of the oak tree. The ladies of 1919 wore long skirts. One day a nail caught and tore such a garment. The idea came to my mind that ripping a piece of calico might produce unsual and interesting results. I tried it, and it did. Under heavy-leafed cover I played my small joke with great effect a considerable number of times. This innocent amusement, I'm glad to say, never came to light.

Around this time, a boy I had been warned to have nothing to do with invited me into the loft of a local alderman's stables directly opposite the Police Station. He propounded a long list of adventurous ideas, like catapult shots at the policeman's horse, pulling a fire-bell after dark, putting a fire cracker into a pillar-box – he would supply all that was required if I did the posting.

I was then indelicately introduced to the subject of sex, via pages torn from an ancient medical book. My prayers for a sister ceased after that day. This rather sleazy boy also taught me some four-letter words and their polysyllabic relations and gave a terse description of their meaning. He then produced cigarettes. These I thought then, as I still think, are uncommonly irritating to the nose. I liked adventure but there was something about this whole project that repelled me.

It was a minor crossroad in my life – but a real one. A week later my mentor found himself in the Police Station because he had unwisely pulled up the alderman's prize dahlias. Years later he found himself behind bars.

At about this time I was told that a visiting speaker was coming to our church. I was very interested. Mother and I had "family prayers" daily. I found them not very significant, but I did like reading from the Bible, using the Scripture Union method, which is a systematic form of going through the Bible in five years. There were small explanatory notes which I found helpful.

Mother's reading to me had told of people who had become Christians. They had "given their hearts to Jesus." I wondered why He wanted their hearts. My soul to me was a rather vague, invisible, internal organ and I was frankly scared of the Holy Ghost. Perhaps this visiting speaker would be able to untangle the whole thing for me. But he proved to be deaf and talked in a very loud voice about "Spiritual Arithmetic." In spite of this I waited after the meeting was over and then shyly went to talk to him. He put his hand on my shoulder. "Are you a Christian, my boy?"

When anyone spoke to him he had a strange trumpet affair which he held, narrow end, into his ear and the lily-shaped part pointed to the speaker.

"I don't know, sir," I stammered. "But I want to become one."

"Beg your pardon, my boy?" he bellowed. Blushing all over I said it again. "Speak a little louder," came his booming voice.

By this time many heads were turned in our direction and a very devout lady came hurrying down the hall. She patted me on the head and said, "Run along now, Paul, you're a good little boy." I crept out of the parish hall more disappointed than I dared to say.

Months later I walked to the church one scorching summer day. It was a long, hot walk. Not long before the father of one of the choir boys had died. The grave stone was new. I sat on the roots of a pine tree while the wind made lonely noises through its branches. The smell of wet clay and pine needles will always be associated in my mind with cemeteries. I thought how my father had died and now this boy's father. I wanted the everlasting life that I had read about. I recited John 3:16. It was tough going for a nine-year-old to know what to do next; how to turn that verse into something that worked. I sat there for a long time then sadly and slowly I walked home.

Mother loved music but I only remember going to one concert. This meant a walk of over a mile to and from the Bowral School of Arts. On our way home progress was slowed down because gas lamps on occasional corners produced a mere puddle of light. Between two of these mother bumped into a moving object. To my huge enjoyment she said, "Oh, I beg your pardon." My night sight, being somewhat better than hers, made it very clear that she had collided with a wandering cow!

Band music was there for the listening on high days and festivals, played in the rotunda in the town gardens. I would regularly turn up and listen enthralled. Trombones and cornets intrigued me but I made no effort to learn to play. My talent for producing music was a sickly plant.

At this time mother bought a piano-player. I would pump away and particularly rejoice in the Gilbert and Sullivan rolls with words beside the slotted paper which produced the music. I spent hours and gained valuable exercise pedalling and singing about the Duke of Plaza Toro. There were Liszt's Rhapsodies and the Moonlight Sonata, a collection of Folk Songs, traditional British music and quite a bit of the Scandinavian musicians. I did not meet Mozart or Bach till much later. Such music as we had was played by me *fortissimo* with all the air I could force into the machine's bellows.

August came and with it bleak westerly winds. I went to bed with a top-class attack of bronchitis. It lasted so long that I was taken to see a certain professor of medicine. He made me strip and put a cold stethoscope on my chest, pushed my stomach with cold hands and looked grave.

Dressed again, I was put into a dreary waiting room, furnished with drab and uncomfortable chairs. While I sat on the very edge of one of these, from inside his consulting room his voice came clearly. "Madam, that child will be fortunate to survive his sixteenth year unless you move to a warmer climate." This no doubt confidential medical opinion lost much of its secrecy because of an open fanlight.

I was shocked to think of leaving Bowral but as far as survival was concerned I was all for it.

Chapter Four:

Junior Schoolboy

FOLLOWING THE DOCTOR'S ADVICE WE MOVED TO SYDNEY. My heart was heavy. I loved the Southern Highlands, the bush, the strong, rugged, friendly Gib, the tall gum trees, the oaks, the elms, the pines and the poplars – all of them well known, many of them much climbed.

Our new home was at Roseville, some eight miles north of the heart of Sydney. It was close to the station and had a big garden, fruit trees, roses and a fifteen-year mortgage. The sadness of leaving the country was overshadowed by novel and exciting happenings.

We had electricity. What a change from the task of standing on chairs, turning on the gas and lighting incandescent mantles! Then there was the hose. At Bowral we only had tanks, and water was used sparingly. Watering with a can had been a chore. What a change to squirt water from a hose! There are a series of primitive slap-stick jokes that a hose makes possible.

Early exploration showed me that Roseville also had its bush. An arm of Sydney Harbour wound its way into sandstone country which had even more birds and other creatures than Bowral. There were gum trees – new varieties of them – each with its own particular appeal.

I started making friends with boys who lived in our street and our suburb. They played cricket, read books and also looked forward to the weekly arrival of *Gems, Magnets* and *Nelson Lees*. We soon formulated a scheme of buying and lending which was a great help to the pocket.

My new friends had a taste for adventure and bush cookery. We would go down to Middle Harbour and have picnics, grilling sausages and chops and frying chip potatoes. These excursions were not without incident. Once we started a bush fire and spent a hectic hour putting it out. This taught me to clear away everything within a six foot range of any fire I lit in the bush.

We went swimming in a creek which I now know was infested with sharks. Once we had our clothes stolen by practical jokers. They had the charity to leave our shoes, but it is quite a problem to walk back home with nothing to wear but ancient newspaper, vines and gum branches. We hit on the idea of using charcoal and turning the whole incident into a game. For a few hours we became the original aboriginals of the district. The locals laughed. Mother was harder to convince!

Mother felt that I should go to a private school. She tightened her belt and I found myself at Heatford Grammar School in the rather select Sydney suburb of Killara. There was a walk of a mile from the station, pleasant under most circumstances, trying on a wet day. That year from the educational point of view was a write-off. The only thing that stands out in my mind was winning a silver-plated medal for running a hundred yards, and obtaining a Scripture prize.

It happened this way. The local clergyman who had given a series of extremely dull lessons, worked out the winner of the Scripture prize in that class of eleven-year-olds by the quiz and elimination method. I found myself at last with only one rival, a cherubic boy named Stephen Bradley, now still cherubic and a bishop in South Africa. We each were successful in question after question, then I was asked the names of the twelve apostles. I started off, "Peter, Andrew, James the son of Zebedee and John his brother, surnamed Boanerges, the sons of thunder."

"Stop!" said the reverend gentleman. "You win."

As we walked out Stephen said, "I knew that, and I could have done the whole twelve." I'm pretty sure that I would have managed only eleven!

Heatford Grammar closed down and I found myself at the Gordon Public School, a cold stone building, full of both girls and boys. I learned a lot there but some things still give me the creeps. A mistake in mental arithmetic was rewarded by a brisk cut with the cane. How I hated mental arithmetic!

The headmaster made his flock write out, in the lunch

On removal to Sydney, Mrs White and Paul lived here, at 26 Roseville Avenue, Roseville, from 1921 to 1934

William Patteson Nicholson, the Irish evangelist who was used to lead Paul White to Christ. His preaching was vivid, uncompromising and unconventional. He campaigned in Australia, New Zealand, and South Africa, and joined with William Temple and others in a united mission to Cambridge University, where large numbers were converted

The imposing façades of Sydney Grammar School (*above*) and Sydney University (*below*)

Junior Schoolboy

half-hour, any spelling mistakes made in dictation. I wrote word after word out thirteen times while he, within reach of both my eye and ear, enthusiastically consumed his food which generally included soup. The effectiveness in my case may be gauged by the fact that I am still unsure of the words I wrote out so reluctantly.

Generally, however, this was a better year. Some of my local friends went to the school and I made new ones. Though still not robust I was intrigued to find myself less sick than I had been at Bowral. But I could still produce a magnificent cough which was labelled by some of mother's friends as "graveyard." I was neither amused nor encouraged by the adjective.

Towards the end of the year mother took me to be interviewed at Sydney Grammar School and pointed out that both my uncle and my great-uncle were old boys of Grammar. This school was one of the earliest in the colony and is situated in the city itself, next door to the museum. It is termed one of the G.P.S. (Great Public Schools) which strangely enough means that it is one of the private schools! I was immensely proud to become a Grammar boy and mother was immensely relieved that there was at the same time a rise in widows' pensions.

Two milestones were passed the first day I arrived at this school, where I was extremely happy. I graduated into the variety of nether garments known as knickerbockers and had no more the burden of long socks to cover my knees. Then I had my first, and incidentally my only, fight. In the *Boys' Own Paper* I had read the advice given to one such as I, "When threatened by a bully, cover your chin and poke out your straight left." Another new boy, considerably bigger than myself, attacked me. Following out the *Boys' Own Paper* advice to the letter, I poked out my straight left. He ran into it and, to my amazement and horror, went down and out. Through the excited crowd of small boys the school Sergeant pushed his way. He took in the situation in a moment. He looked at the dazed boy on the ground, then turned to me and said, "What's your name, lad?"

"White, sir."

"Did you knock him down?"

"Yes, sir."

He turned to those who crowded round. "He may be thin

and skinny looking, but take my advice, don't ever touch young White. He's got poison in both hands."

No one ever bullied me or attempted anything in the way of aggression all the days that I was at school and twice at the University individuals apologised rather hurriedly because they heard the dread message that I had poison in both hands!

My penchant for collecting things reached its peak with the formation of the Roseville Philatelic Club of which I became president. At the advanced age of twelve we read papers to one another and had discussions on stamps, geography, lithography, watermarking, vagaries of perforations or the lack of them and many variations on the same theme.

At this stage I met a tough, muscular, but quiet boy, Marcus Loane, now Archbishop of Sydney. When it came to wrestling, none of my friends could put me on my back more quickly or expertly than he. From this group of a dozen boys came a lawyer, two accountants, a veterinary surgeon, a banker, two doctors and a very successful businessman.

Cricket intrigued me, especially as a friend's father was the slow bowler for the local first-grade club, Gordon. We played cricket in our garden for quite a time till a full-blooded and somewhat lofted shot in the direction of square leg neatly removed the dining room window! Price seven-and-sixpence. No more cricket was played in our garden.

There were other gardens, however, and later, Roseville Park, with its concrete wicket. The park keeper was a ferocious looking man named Crunkhorn – a lovely name, I thought. I discovered he was a rose-grower and an authority on the culture of this magnificent flower. Mother had books on the subject. I read them carefully, then rather deferentially asked Mr. Crunkhorn whether I should prune all types of roses at the same time of year. He snorted, thinking I was up to some prank. His cow had had its horns painted green a week before. Let me hasten to add that this was not my work. I hadn't even thought of it! When he realised I could tell a rambler from a hybrid tea, he relaxed and we became firm friends from then on.

Cricket was my great interest. I knew everybody who played in the Sheffield Shield, I had seen Charlie Kellaway in the train and watched (from a respectful distance) Charlie Macartney mowing his lawn. Armed with a bottle of lemonade and some sandwiches I had sat on "the Hill" at the Sydney Cricket Ground and watched everything that had happened from the first ball to the last. Going to the cricket involved cutting back sharply on lunch for a week but it was worth it.

Our house was set way back from the street. A privet hedge gave "privacy." How I hated that hedge! It was my task at least once a month to cut it. Every time I did I developed asthma, which, mother was assured, stemmed from my antipathy to the job. I certainly had no joy in it but later on as I learned a little more medicine I was to discover that privet is a prevalent cause of asthma and a variety of allergies.

Then there was the lawn. It was large, complicated, and full of paspalum − a grass excellent for cattle-feed but a curse amongst lawn grasses. To add to my problems was a vintage, hand-propelled mower that was considerably blunt. Sharpening was beyond my skills and our pocket. Mowing that lawn was a job that had no fun in the doing and no satisfaction in the completing. It had to be done strictly weekly.

Our garden was adorned with circular flower beds, star-shaped flower beds, half-moon and elliptical shapes, which added up to a horrible task, especially on the edges. There were ornamental shrubs, taps, standard roses and a lemon tree, all of which had to be skilfully avoided. It is hard to know which I detested more, the hedge or the lawn.

I thought it would be good to learn to play the piano. Unfortunately my imagination was at no time captured by my teachers. It was no easy matter for me to bring satisfying music from the ivory keyboard. Practice was tedious, uninteresting, and seemed to lead nowhere. Boredom was not relieved by pep talks. Lack of result led on to frustration and the feeling of acute inability.

In a way I was proud of my distorted right arm. But its weakness, coupled with my inability even to come near to touching my toes without bending my knees, made me the butt for comment from our physical education instructor, a bald man with a gravelly voice.

When I failed in back-bending exercise, his voice came, "Try harder, you Hercules in the third row − yes, you."

Ridicule is acid to anyone but it's corrosive to a fourteen-year-old. The next exercise was press-ups. I couldn't get off the ground as my right arm repeatedly collapsed. Again a snide remark, and inside me grew the idea of my extensive inabilities.

I tried hard with my school work and received lukewarm praise. The history master, a very proper and impeccably groomed elderly man, would read from the book to us in a cultured monotonous voice which was dull and quite uninspiring. No one would be unwise enough to attempt to misbehave in his class. I tried hard to absorb this dismal material but my efforts were greeted with the report, "Work unsatisfactory. Conduct fair."

A year before I had had a blow. The desire to know I had eternal life was great, but the time I chose to ask the one I loved most about it was when she was making gravy, just before serving our Saturday "half a leg of mutton." Mother looked up from her cooking and said brusquely, "Ask me about it later on, this isn't the time...." To me it was, and I didn't bring up the subject again; but I thought about it and lay awake wondering and worrying. I read books about all phases of the Christian faith but they didn't answer my question.

Being a member of the Church of England I was duly baptised a month or two after my birth and apparently screamed deafeningly when the answer to, "Name this child," was "Paul Hamilton Hume." In due course when I was fourteen I joined the Confirmation Class. I knew about the Faith and the Creeds and was more than familiar with the stories of the Bible. What I wanted to know was *how* to become a Christian.

I realised that eternal life was not automatic or obtainable by what I did or achieved; but how you asked for it, how you crossed the line, what you said to God – this eluded me AND I WANTED TO KNOW. Class followed class – I heard the facts that I already knew restated. Then I heard with satisfaction that our minister would interview each individual candidate. Here was my chance. He gave us a small project: to write an essay on salvation. This presented no problem and my efforts gained commendation and a book as prize. When it came to the interview the kindly old man put his hand on my shoulder and said, "It won't be necessary for you, Paul." Such was the shape of my reticence that I said nothing of what I so greatly wanted to ask. Again frustration.

To cap it all, one day I had struggled to cut the robustly growing lawn with the reluctant mower. Puffed and sweating I sat in the shade. Mother arrived on the scene and thought that I was loafing. When I tried to explain she said, "Oh, you're a weakling," and turned on her heel. I boiled inwardly but said nothing. Later, when I was cuttng the unending edges of those gardens, I thought of an article in the *Boys' Own Paper* which told how to train for athletics to reach a peak in three months.

It was January. I had nine months to the school sports, so I multiplied each month by three and drew up a programme which started with a two-mile run every day for six days in the week. This I did as unobtrusively as possible. Shod in sandshoes I plodded round and round the rough track of Roseville Park, encouraged by the good Mr. Crunkhorn. I became more and more determined to make a reasonable showing at the school sports to prove not only to mother but to everybody else that I was not a weakling. As I lost my initial stiffness I developed more enthusiasm for what I was doing. The mile was the longest run on the programme. The mile therefore would be the distance that I would run. It took more strength, will and guts, to run a mile than to sprint or high-jump or hurdle.

My interest in God started to wane. I read and thought and dreamed about running. I was careful with my diet and duly massaged methylated spirits into my toes — I am the proud possessor of what are known clinically as hammer-toes.

Mother's birthday was two days before my own. I was not a little disturbed to discover that she planned to give me the black and gold running shorts and singlet of the Grammar School, when I had purchased for her a copy of the current *Boys' Own Annual*! My savings were back to pence when I bought a small bottle of Eau-de-Cologne to go with it for her and a pair of spiked running shoes for myself.

At long last the sports came. I turned out looking very new. But all this glory did little to cover two very thin legs and a body in which the bony structure was no secret at all.

"*You're* not running the mile, White?" said the sports' master incredulously. I nodded, and did. But after only two hundred yards my shoelace broke. With a feeling of complete calamity I ran on, battling to keep the shoe on my foot. At the end of the first lap, although moving with a distinct limp I was still in the running. Half way I was convinced that not only could I keep the shoe in place but I could finish reasonably well. What an inward glow when runner after runner was overtaken and what deep satisfaction when I finished fourth and heard the same sports' master who had underlined my fragile look some five minutes before, saying, "Well done, White, you could become quite a useful middle distance runner. I want you to keep in training for the All-School Sports." This was the athletics event of the year, held on the famous Sydney Cricket Ground.

I was chosen to run the mile, and gained a second place, my school "colours," and incidentally a large slice of confidence.

Suprisingly I lost my cough. Bronchitis became a thing of the past and my muscles noticeably grew. Confidence is all very well but I still had not been able to solve my special problem. After the sports I was accepted at school in a new way and one morning arriving in the classroom had a copy of a popular, but now extinct, morning paper thrust into my hand. "Read that, Paul." I read and grinned.

Those dark headlines were the beginning of a complete change in my life.

Chapter Five:

December Revolution

THE PAPER WAS DATED NOVEMBER 26TH, 1926. MY SEVENTEENTH birthday was three months ahead.

I read the large black headlines IRISH EVANGELIST CALLS BISHOP STINKING POLECAT. I liked that. It appeared that the Bishop had a somewhat mature pipe and used a powerful brand of tobacco. The Irishman's nose had told him all about it and he told the Bishop, and the press, exactly what his nose had told him. I was determined to hear this man speak. He would be fun. A few days later I sat in a large tent and listened to William P. Nicholson. He started off with a string of amusing stories, mainly Irish. I liked that.

But I didn't like it when he hit me hard between the eyes with the words, "HOW WILL YOU ESCAPE IF YOU NEGLECT SUCH A GREAT SALVATION?"

I knew about God but I didn't know Him. This is what I had been looking for. I knew that sin was a malignant disease but I had not made use of the cure. I didn't know how to do so.

It was a hot summer night. I sat on a creaky, folding chair in the tent. He hit on a number of tender spots. I started to sweat. He said forcibly, "You can't sin and get away with it." He talked about God as a judge. He quoted a verse that talked about the goodness and the severity of God. Progressively I became more uncomfortable. These were things I liked to forget.

W. P. Nicholson bored in. Obviously he felt the tremendous importance of what he had to say and pulled no punches in getting it across.

He finished up by talking about the Cross and Jesus' love. He made it clear that there were two things I could do: either go God's way, or turn my back on Him.

He asked everyone to pray. My mind was in a turmoil. In front was an obvious crossroad.

With me at that meeting was my mother who fully believed that I was a Christian. There were a dozen people from our church who knew me as a Sunday School teacher, a rather inaccurate tenor in the choir and a regular attendant both at church and Communion.

I sat there with my eyes tightly shut, trying to pray and not knowing what to say. There was the hot smell of a tent full of people and grass trodden under foot. Crickets sang softly and in the distance came the rattle of an electric train. Nicholson's strong, aggressive voice broke into my thinking. "It's not enought to hear about Jesus and what He's done for you." I opened my eyes and saw him turning to those on the left. He paused, turned to those on his right. "And for you." Suddenly he shouted, "And what He's done for you, you there in the back, you who are taking no notice of my words."

I grinned and looked over my shoulder. The grin didn't last long for he started talking gently and compellingly. "This is your special chance. Listen. Everyone who knows he's a Christian, who knows he has everlasting life, who *knows* it, not just hopes it, stand up."

His voice was suddenly loud. "If you're not sure, remember God is here and He sees your soul as clearly as I see your body. If you're not sure, before God I urge you to stay seated."

My mouth was dry. My hands were clammy. What would mother think? What would the people from the church think if I stayed sitting down? I could hear people standing up all round. Chairs creaked. An ambulance drove by, its siren wailing. Be honest, my conscience urged. It doesn't matter what people think or say. Here's your chance. You've side-stepped before. Don't do it now. My stomach sank and then suddenly I realised that what I had been looking for was here for the taking.

"If you want Jesus to forgive you and you are prepared to put you're life in His hands and do what He tells you to do, then stand up. But before you do, wait a minute. You must consider the cost." He outlined starkly what it was.

I stood up feeling red all over. William Nicholson's Irish voice with a most friendly ring about it filled my ears, "Would those who have just stood up please come to the front of the tent, here in front of me." I was acutely embarrassed but equally determined to find out how to become a Christian and to take action when I found out.

My feet felt unusually large. I bumped into a chair and stumbled to the front not knowing what to do with my hands. With some twenty others I looked up into his rugged face. He smiled at us and said, "There is a smaller tent behind this one. I'd like you to go through to it. There are those there who will help you personally."

My particular helper was a middle-aged man dressed in a black coat and striped morning trousers. He looked severe and unsmiling. Under his arm was a large black-covered Bible. He piloted me to a squeaky chair and sat down opposite me. He talked earnestly and at length. When he stopped for breath, I said, "Sir, how do you ask Jesus to become your Saviour?"

At once he answered my question using a word formula with which he was obviously familiar. To me it was most difficult to understand. There was a sense of poetry and Shakespeare and hymn books about what he was saying.

Realising that he was not really helping me he started quoting Scripture again. It gave me inward glee to help him find the verses he wanted me to read when he was unsure of the reference. He handed me a card and the unsatisfying interview ended as he moved on to counsel another enquirer. The one positive thing that I did was to sign that card but I felt myself confused and still standing undecided at the crossroads. Clutching the card I slipped away from the tent unnoticed. Outside was my mother, some of my friends and a few people from the church. I didn't know what to say. Wisely mother started walking towards the station. Behind us I heard clearly a rather voluble lady from the church remark, "Well who would have thought that Paul White would have done that. Won't the Rector be interested? He always thought...."

Mother stepped out more briskly. The train journey home was silent as was the walk to our front gate when I said, "Mum, I'm glad that we went."

Home was exactly as we had left it. With considerable understanding mother said nothing she would not have said any other time. I found and consumed an apple and a glass of milk.

A score of times I had been told that the one would make the other curdle. Mother smiled at me and I smiled back and said, "Mum, its wonderful to have a stomach like a billygoat."

She kissed me and went to bed and I fiddled with our two-valved radio set. There was the ghostly screeching of static merging into hard-to-hear voices. One of them said, "This is 3LO, Melbourne."

I looked fondly at the large box with its great horn-like loud speaker and then switched if off and went to sit on my bed. My thinking was clear and went like this, "Why not make sure of what I've wanted to do for years? The clue is there in those verses: God understands what I'm thinking about and even if I don't pray exactly what I want to pray, He will understand."

It was vastly satisfying to realise this. I knelt down and prayed, "Lord Jesus, please come into my heart and take away my sin and give me everlasting life. Please show me what you want me to do with my life here and now." I knelt there for awhile but nothing happened so I undressed and went to bed and to sleep.

Next morning was like any other morning. Heaven above was the same coloured blue. The lawn was still growing and so was the hated hedge. The same people were walking up the street. The same people were on the station saying the same things. The 7.58 train left exactly at 7.58. At Chatswood station I looked through the window and was able to catch a glimpse of the W. P. Nicholson tent. Obviously something had happened to me but it hadn't done much to my feelings. I had done what I had wanted to do for years. That was clear and it had been worth doing.

I would take some of my friends to hear that Irishman. He was a straight shooter. I grinned to myself remembering how straight he'd been and some of the earthy things he had said. Why hadn't other people at church and in Sunday School been clear and direct and understandable and not talked in a jargon so different from ordinary conversation?

That night I took my special friend to hear W. P. Nicholson. He and I had been very close for years. We'd played games together and gone on to cricket and football. We had been on holidays together, exchanged books, swapped stamps and helped each other with Latin and Mathematics. On the two—

mile walk home that evening I asked him if he knew he had everlasting life. He said stiffly, "I have my own religion."

The conversation was closed at that point and the subject as well. Our lives drifted apart from that night. I tried getting others to find what I had found – one a mile runner, later to become a Rhodes Scholar and a militant Communist. He listened most attentively. Again we walked home a considerable distance. At his gate we talked, "Yes," he said, "I will ask Jesus into my life." I waited for him to talk to me again, and tried unsuccessfully to start a conversation but nothing ever came of it.

The Nicholson meetings finished a few days later. The tent was folded up and again there was a vacant allotment. I felt flat. The same old routine pressed in on me and the question cropped up day after day, was it all real?

Sunday morning came. A boy of my own age at church had been to these meetings and had done as I had done. As we talked he seemed to have much the same trouble. He asked me, "Did you make a decision?"

I nodded, "And I signed one of those cards. Do you feel different ?"

He shook his head. "I don't think so."

"Has anything happened?"

That jolted him. He looked up quickly. "It must have. God promised He would forgive us our sins and give us everlasting life if we meant what we said. It must have happened. Have you struck the verse that says, 'Without faith it is impossible to please God'?"

I shook my head. "Where did you get that one? The bloke who talked to me afterwards didn't even know where to find the verses that he was quoting to me."

My friend grinned, "Mine did. He was a parson named Begbie. Boy, he knew his way around. He told me that without faith it is impossible to please God and so I'm having faith." He walked away. I took the card that I had signed from my pocket. It said:

MY DECISION
"I take God the Father to be my God (I Thes. 1:9.)
"I take God the Son to be my Saviour (Acts 5:31.)

"I take God the Holy Ghost to be my Sanctifier (I Peter 1:2.)
"I take the Word of God to be my Rule (II Tim. 3:16-17.)
"I take the People of God to be my People (Ruth 1:16-17.)
"I likewise dedicate myself wholly to the Lord (Rom. 14:7-8.)
"And I do this prayerfully (Psalm 119:94.): deliberately (Joshua 24:15.): sincerely (II Cor. 1:12.): freely (Psalm 110, 3.): and for ever, (Rom. 8:35-39)"
                                        Signed:
Dated, 3rd December, 1926

The back steps of the parish hall in Roseville were not exactly a dramatic setting for realising one of the most important things of my life; but sitting there after most people had returned home from the morning service I realised that I *had* crossed the border. I *had* eternal life. I *was* a member of God's family and I *had* asked Him to take charge of my life. It would have helped greatly if I had felt different – a glow or some sort of spiritual effervescence. However, all I had was a promise from God which I had taken up.

Perhaps the clergyman my friend had been talking about could help me. I walked three miles to his church that evening. He preached a resounding, clear, understandable sermon, which explained crossing the line from death to life and the necessity for going on for God with purpose. I stayed behind afterwards and found that I had run the mile against one of his sons. They invited me to stay for supper and I discovered another new thing: Christian fellowship. I had found new friends travelling the same path. They suggested I should go to a camp after Christmas at a place called Austinmer, some forty miles south of Sydney. I gladly accepted. Things were beginning to work out.

Most of my thinking and planning was done in my bedroom which was an architectural after-thought in our house. It was a built-in verandah facing east, and was a room full of "things." There was a collection of ancient but workable furniture: a bookcase, sturdy but unaesthetic, an iron-framed bed with a kapok mattress (later two kapok mattresses), a plywood wardrobe with doors slightly warped and a table with a box screwed underneath for scribble paper. Not a thing nor a penny was wasted in number 26, Roseville Avenue, Roseville!

That particular Monday morning the roosters, as usual,

sounded off at dawn. It was a hot summer. The iron roof and the fibrous plaster walls ensured uncomfortable warmth from early morning. I got up, turned over the pages of a worn Bible I had won as a prize at Sunday School. Out of it tumbled a piece of poor quality paper – a third carbon copy and barely a quarter of a sheet. Up till then I had strong dislike for what was on that scrap of paper. The typed words had made me extremely uncomfortable. Again and again it had nearly been thrown into the waste paper basket (the same one I had rolled on aged two). I picked up that scrap of paper and read again:

> "When I am dying how glad I shall be,
> That the lamp of my life has been blazed out for Thee"

I hated the thought of death. My mind went back to the telegram that told of my father's death. I thought of Dick Wiseman, the schoolboy who had sat next to me in class, who had been killed in a football match. Suddenly, I realised that death had lost its power over me now. This was good but it was clear that God wanted live men to serve Him.

Here I was, sixteen, with life ahead of me. How could I best be useful for God? I hadn't much to offer. Then into my mind came the incident of the boy with the rolls and the small fish and what Jesus had done with them. In His hands a lunch could turn into a crowd-size picnic. There was value in blazing out your life for the Lord, Jesus Christ.

Chapter Six:

Look for Facts, White!

Senior School

I HAD DISCOVERED SOMETHING THAT I HAD WANTED VERY MUCH. For a long time I'd had a triple objective: to be a doctor, an athlete and a success. Now I had a motive: to do things for God, and to say "thank you" to Him. There was plenty of zeal and enthusiasm, but little knowledge of how to do it.

I decided to tell people about what had happened to me. One person who I felt sure would listen, was old Bill, the Chemistry master. While he delighted to talk about non-chemical matters in his chemistry class — things like oriental poetry, orchid culture and astronomy — he looked unhappy and purposeless. Surely he would be interested to know what I had found.

My reception was cold. "Look for facts, White. That all sounds very emotional. Now get on with your work."

This hit me like a bucket of cold water, but my next try was more successful. I had heard a whisper that David Grant — one of the most important boys in the school in my eyes — carried a New Testament in his pocket. He was full-back for the school Rugby team, a leading batsman in the cricket eleven and captain of athletics. I saw him walking past the tuckshop and said, "Er, excuse me, Dave, I-um-well, you see, I was converted the other day."

His face lighted up. "That's great. There are quite a few Christians about the place; chaps who want to get on with the job. Why don't you come to a houseparty we are running? There will be a lot of good blokes there from other schools as well."

I was vastly encouraged and then and there decided to go. This was the first big event of 1927 — a year I had dreaded ever since reading an article in a magazine to which mother subscribed. It has stated quite definitely that 1927 was to be the year of the Second Coming of the Lord. With the uncomfortable knowledge that I was outside God's family I had shrunk from the fast-moving calendar but now it was different and I faced the new year with confidence. January 3rd, the day on which the houseparty started, looked like putting me in touch with a lot of other people of my own age who would understand what I wanted to talk about.

This is exactly what happened. The big thing about that camp was that the boys I met there were normal, full of fun and good at games yet they surprised me by starting the day with what was called a "quiet time": half an hour reading quietly from the Bible and praying. Since this was the pattern of things I fitted in with it and found it a first rate idea. My soul thrived on system. In the afternoons they had meetings on the beach. A large pulpit was built out of sand, a banner with Children's Special Service Mission (white letters on a red background) was erected, a small foldable organ supplied music and short punchy tuneful choruses were sung; choruses which summarised facts of the Faith and practical details of living out what you believed.

I was scared at the beginning that someone would see me there, someone from school, someone who might laugh. But when I saw Dave Grant stand on that pulpit and read from the Bible I thought again and realised that if I was going to be an active member of God's family I would be so in the full light of day. A number of fellows of my own age took some active part in that beach mission. With some trepidation I did too, and found it was within my scope.

One chap who intrigued me was Geoff Young who had an eye and ear for engines. He had a motor bike, one of a series of devices he either rode, drove or flew. Much later on, in no small way he and a motor bike helped me to start book writing. At that camp I also met Maurice Deck, who became my closest friend. Maurice was a useful footballer, a good swimmer and very keen on sailing. One morning he asked me, "What are you going to do after camp?"

I shrugged, "Go home and muck around, I suppose."

"Would you like to come and stay with us at Katoomba in

the Blue Mountains? I had a letter from mother today suggesting I invite one of my friends."

I went gladly, and for the first time experienced life as part of a large family. Maurice's father was a doctor of dentistry and his mother a charming person. I found myself living in a family of six – the first five were boys and the youngest a girl. I was absorbed automatically into that family. It was a wonderful experience.

Those were notable Christmas holidays. In a matter of weeks my life had suddenly opened out. Then came a crisis – an official envelope with Repatriation Department printed on it. A month or two before another like it had arrived. Inside was a form to be filled in in my best handwriting. It had asked a number of blunt questions in the centre of which was, "When you leave school, what do you plan to do? First preference. Second preference."

I filled in these lines: 1) Doctor, 2) Analytical Chemist. I had put in the second because I liked doing things in laboratories. There was a special aura about Bunsen burners and test tubes. The words burettes, pipettes, titration, indicators, acids and alkalies had an intriguing ring about them. They played a little tune on the imagination. There were the men in white coats in large skylighted rooms with a smell which challenged the nostrils. Yes, I thought, analytical chemistry would be interesting.

The first form had gone on its way. I opened the second envelope. In it was a letter requesting me to present myself at the Repatriation Department, Chalmers Street, Sydney, at 10.30 a.m. on Tuesday next and signed by someone whose name I could not read on behalf of the Minister for Repatriation who termed himself, with amazing humility, "your obedient servant." I went with mother. We sat and waited for a considerable time on hard chairs in a long corridor from which opened numerous glass doors. Inside were men in their shirt sleeves, for the most part with green eye-shades. They sat at dull-looking desks and bookshelves on each side seemed crammed to the ceiling with manilla folders tied up with pink tape.

At last I was ushered into one of these rooms and stood behind mother's chair. The shirt-sleeved gentleman read through a folder which had my name on it. He picked up the form I had filled in a month before. In a most business-like fashion he said, "An opportunity has arisen for a pathology technician's job that has a certain amount of analytical chemistry in it and you work in a hospital. It's a good opening. It's not likely to occur again. I think you'd be wise to take it. Think about it for a few moments." He left the room.

Mother looked at me questioningly. The widow's pension wasn't all that we had. Only months before some "worthless" shares which a lawyer uncle had once bought and left to us had produced £400. However, here was security. My mother spoke quietly, "This would put an end to all your African hopes."

I nodded. When the repatriation offical came back I said, "Thank you sir, but I think I'll go on to be a doctor." He shrugged his shoulders and I watched my folder being retied with its pink tape and going back on its dusty shelf.

This interview started me thinking seriously. In the year ahead was the solid study necessary for passing the General Schools Leaving Certificate and obtaining Matriculation. It was very clear that if I was to graduate in medicine I would need to earn one of those two hundred spots which were known as Exhibitions – all fees being paid subject to my passing each and every examination. I worked reasonably hard and was acutely conscious of my teachers. Some were my friends and encouraged me. It was a pleasure to work at the subject they taught. Mathematics was not one of these subjects. At this gentle art I was a very moderate performer. I was informed of this not infrequently by the Maths master whose sarcastic voice was strangely in keeping with his small, waxed moustache. What a relief, probably to both of us, when I was relegated to the B form. There I was not subjected to the outpourings of verbal acid which to me was a sure way of paralysing my mental processes.

Toothache had been a bugbear for most of my life, probably due to a stong taste for sweets and underactivity of the toothbrush. I was both relieved and shattered when an authoritative dental voice said, "Have them all out on Thursday next under general anaesthetic."

Friday saw me at school enduring a relatively useless day but I was determined not to let my toothless state interfere with my routine. On the Saturday I packed my cricket gear and went to play against The King's School. A strangely swollen face and a blurriness of vision combined to give me the most successful bowling figures of my life – four wickets for one run. I can only imagine that the peculiarity of my visage destroyed the batsman's concentration. Two weeks later I arrived at school with "temporary dentures." Some used the word "plates" to describe these useful contrivances. To me they were flying saucers! I was destined to part company with them in front of the grandstand at the end of the third lap of the mile at the school sports. They stayed in place however as I won the half–mile and furlong to become the athletics champion. Any overgrowth in ego was smartly cut to size when the examination results came out and I scored four B passes which was the absolute minimum. The subjects in which I was successful were not those required for matriculation. In a kindly voice the headmaster advised me, "I think it would be a good thing if you repeated the year and worked a little harder and played a little less."

It was not only the muscles that developed that year. The Bible came to life for me. As I read it I could see how and where it applied to me. It was full of paths to follow and sign posts to direct me. I shall be unendingly grateful to the Scripture Union who supplied a systematic way of reading the Bible and to a gentleman named Battersby who produced a small book giving a method of praying regularly and systematically for people – daily, weekly or monthly. The statement that the weakest ink is better than the strongest memory is particularly true when it comes to remembering those for whom you want to pray.

Then came a set-back. I didn't *feel* the slightest bit different. Questions swirled dizzily in my head. Had anything happened that night in the tent? Was I back where I had started? Was it all a slab of wishful thinking?

The old temptations bombarded my mind. The familiar failures recurred. People who jeered seemed to do so more loudly. The less noisy who asked me things I could not answer seemed to do so more successfully.

"Drop the lot. Turn it in," came the thought.

System had started to creep into my living. Athletics training was severe and disciplined. Thinking about it I realised that in running a mile it was common to feel the pinch and, as early as halfway, the temptation was to drop out and sit on the side line. A man in training would recognise this as not worth a second thought and plug on. Determination was a highly important part of winning.

The temptation to throw in my faith, I realised, was another of these persistent but useless ideas.

"Train harder, White," had been the advice of the athletics coach.

"Keep at it," said my soul and I came up against the verse, "I can do all things through Christ who strengthens me" (Philippians 4:13).

I put my head down and studied not only my school work but the Bible as well.

In the train I sat next to a girl from the church – an undergraduate. I told her about my U-turn. She was an Arts student and at that stage not a Christian. She fired all sorts of questions at me. Some I could answer and did. Many of the others were answerable by seeing what the Bible had to say. A concordance and a commentary helped me to find the material I needed.

Mother had given me a reference Bible with thin paper. How much more attractive and useful than the "school" Bibles with their tiny print and funereal black covers. As I re-read the Bible closely and with a new interest, the Shakesperian language of the King James Version struck me as rather hard to understand. I liked the sound of it but when it came to meaning, I found it uphill.

Our talks in the train became more regular. The more I read the better I could answer her questions. One day at church Eileen told me she had given her life into God's hands. This was a considerable stimulus to me and a great step out of the gutter of doubts. Helping someone to find their way into the Kingdom of God is a very special experience. This to me was a first.

The school sports were at the end of August. My scales recorded seven pounds more weight than at the same time a year before. It could only be bone and muscle. Markings on the kitchen door showed an increase in height and it was a struggle to force my way into most of my shirts.

"You're doing well. I reckon you have the quarter, the half and the mile in the bag," smiled Jack Martin, my coach. "You could easily crack a record."

I tried to look indifferent, but felt warm inside. However, next morning in running down the steps at the railway station I sprained my ankle!

"You will hobble for three weeks," said the medical pundit, "and then perhaps you'll be able to walk normally."

I asked him about the sports in a month's time. He shook his head and smiled sadly. "What about October, the All School Sports?" This was particularly important to me.

"It is just possible." He opened the door and I limped painfully out. The number of sad stories about sprained ankles I had told to me in those first few days was legion. And then Maurice Deck came up with the idea. "Why not have regular massage for it? And keep your muscles in trim without putting your feet to the ground." I blinked. "Underwater exercises, or doing inverted bicycle exercises. Someone could show you just what."

Someone did and noticeable improvement occurred but I still hobbled. And then Dave Grant rang me up. "Are you going to the International Rugby match at the Sydney Cricket Ground?"

"No," I replied, but did not go into detail which included my reluctance to dig deep into my financial reserves to purchase a ticket.

He went on, "We are going out in the Chandler." This was a large and very robust American car which could hold an incredible number of school boys. "Bob Burns, who is playing lock for Australia is staying with us and he is coming to speak at the Crusader meeting that evening. Would you like to be in on it?"

Would I? "Too right."

"We'll pick you up outside the museum at ..." He mentioned a time.

That was a memorable match to me. To play lock in Rugby Union football you need to be big, strong, fast and have an active mind. Bob Burns fulfilled all the conditions. He had a fine game. I swelled with pride sitting in the same car as that muscular Christian international.

His talk that night was direct and uncomplicated. It came humbly and forcibly from a young man who was preparing to do whatever God told him. He was later to spend the major part of his life in South India with the Dohnavur Fellowship. Few men have had a greater influence on my life and thinking.

When the day for the sports arrived my ankle was firmly strapped up. I put on running shoes for the first time in three weeks and walked with a certain amount of difficulty on to the track. But once I was warm it was obvious that running would be possible. Instead of crouching in the block holes to start, I stood upright and to my own amazement managed to head the field in the half mile. Hours later I did the same thing in the mile. The times were very slow.

A few months earlier I had been appointed a prefect, as the headmaster was accustomed to saying, "The greatest honour that the school could confer on any of its pupils." But he went on to say that in my case the appointment was his own and not, as generally happened, on the advice of the other prefects. All of which boiled down to the fact that my popularity was not particularly high with my peers!

Once when I had reported coming across the son of a leading industrialist smoking a cigar in a restaurant famous for its milk shakes and waffles, the Senior Prefect, a very fine chap indeed, had said, "You're an odd bloke, Paul. The chaps don't go much on you. You're too religious." I raised my eyebrows questioningly. "Oh, you know what I mean. That talking down on Balmoral Beach on Sundays – that Sunday School affair. And don't be so tough on the kids when they get up to some of these harmless games. Let's face it, you'll get on much more smoothly in life if you keep religion for the church."

October came and the All School Sports. My ankle worked and I was second in both the half and quarter miles. Then it was November – examination time. I had worked hard and was delighted to find that I had scored the coveted Exhibition. Sadly I heard the school bell ring for the last time. Sadly I walked through the gate on to College Street. They had been good years at Sydney Grammar School. I was grateful to a lot of people but wondered what I had left behind me of a positive nature. Probably I would be remembered not as the winner of the mile but as Paul White who lost his false teeth in doing it!

Chapter Seven:

University

Medicine I – Student on the run

DIRECTLY AHEAD WAS THE TOWER OF SYDNEY UNIVERSITY AND beside it the less imposing one of the Medical School.

As I walked up the road the University carillon rang out. The sound of those great bells was full; a harmony rather than the brisk order of the school bell which I had obeyed over the last six years. Life would be very different as an undergraduate in the next six years. I was taking the second step of my ambition to be a medical missionary. Medicine was in my blood. A grandfather, a great uncle, an uncle and a veritable cohort of cousins were doctors. My grandfather on father's side was a Sea Captain with high adventure in his life.

In front the road forked. Across the way was a church notice-board. On it, in large letters, were the words:
IT'S BETTER TO BE IN A TIGHT CORNER
THAN IN A CORNER TIGHT.

This tickled my sense of humour. I thought it would be good to be able to juggle nimbly with words like that. My abilities were not all I would have liked. I had taken two years instead of one to matriculate. The first year I had passed the Leaving Certificate with the lowest possible score and succeeded reasonably well at athletics and cricket. At study I had done better at my second attempt and won an Exhibition. The significance of this was that I could proceed to do a university course without payment of fees. As an encouragement to hard work there was a sharp axe-blade poised above the neck of each exhibitioner. Failure on any occasion in even one examination, or part thereof, meant that the scholarship was automatically cancelled.

In what was then called the Leaving Certificate examination the results after my name were B passes in five subjects, a failure in French and second-class honours in English. I thought second-class seemed to sum me up. Here I was going to the university to be interviewed. Every thing was new and I was anxious not to make a fool of myself.

I glanced again at the notice-board — IT'S BETTER TO BE IN A TIGHT CORNER.... I had been in that uncomfortable position in the examinations and wondered if an average mind like mine could make it through six tough years in medicine. It was hard to escape from the salutary thought that if I failed in one subject the door to my career was closed.

Half an hour later I was sitting on the edge of a chair facing the University Registrar. He was very kind and informative. He looked at the long list of Exhibition winners and ran his finger down the first page. Diffidently I said, "Sir, you will find it quicker if you start at the other end."

He smiled and then laughed, "You are number one hundred and ninety eight in order of merit, White." He looked at me over his glasses. "But the thing that matters is, you're on the list."

I did a deal of thinking as I walked back to Sydney's Central Railway station. Outside the church with the notice-board I stopped. It informed me that the church was called St. Barnabas, Broadway and that the rector was Canon R. B. S. Hammond. I knew of him as a man of purpose and drive, a man who cared for others and who had absolutely no time for the liquor traffic. He was a magnificent speaker with a devastating gift for repartee. Once when campaigning for six o'clock closing of the hotels an interjector had shouted, "You're talking through your hat, Hammond. You've never been drunk and you don't know what you're talking about."

"True, I've never been drunk," flashed back the reply. "Also I've never laid an egg, but I know a bad one when I smell it."

Why couldn't I be like R. B. S. Hammond? The answer was easy. I didn't have the ability, the gifts, or the determination. A voice seemed to say, "Paul White, you're second-class material and not much use to anybody." Then across the screen of my mind again flashed one of those verses I had learnt as a child,

"I can do all things through Christ who strengthens me." The meaning of this verse exploded in my brain like a rocket. I was to experience this same burst of light again and again at various times in my life.

As I climbed up the steps of the station I had another thought. Canon Hammond had preached one day and I remembered the whole of his sermon. It was the only talk ever to have taken permanent residence. With punch and humour and a voice that carried you along he had told that the world's most dangerous biters were not snakes, sharks or crocodiles but the little ones: mosquitoes, fleas and flies. The meaning had stuck. The sins you brushed out of your mind as tiddlers did more overall damage than those that sent the creeps up your conscience.

Now I began to see my own personal insect pests. Doubting God's ability to make me into something that He could use was one of them. I took the necessary steps to deal with that situation as I sat in the train. I had learnt that it wasn't necessary to be down on my knees to pray. Then my thoughts went to the A, B, C, D, of becoming a Christian:

A – You *admit* that you're a sinner
B – You *believe* that God can and will forgive you. There are two steps here: something to believe, someone to receive
C – You *count the cost*
D – You *do* something about it

The adventure and the security of the steps taken appealed to me greatly, but counting the cost was a new idea. I remembered the words, "If any man will come after me let him deny himself and take up his cross daily and follow me."

Another verse hit me as I thought of being an active Christian at university. Jesus said, "If you follow me I will make you fishers of men." I would be fishing in new and turbulent waters in the days that lay immediately ahead. The time was March, 1929, and the financial depression was coming to a peak. A picturesque Sydney University quadrangle with its mellow stone-work, cloisters and clock tower was packed with people. Some, obviously lecturers, wearing gowns, strode up and down on the wide, crazy pavement which split the lawn into four. This sacred stretch of green grass is untouched by human foot, be it graduate or undergraduate. Among the other population in the morning sunlight were those who gazed around, tourist fashion, and stamped themselves as freshers.

With my friends, Maurice Deck and Neville Babbage, I walked all over the university grounds. We looked into the Medical School, territory only to be gained when the first year with its basic sciences was conquered.

Beyond it I looked wistfully at the School of Tropical Medicine and I dreamed a small dream. Beyond it was the major teaching hospital, Royal Prince Alfred. A year seems a long time when it's ahead and such a small space of time when it's behind. On arrival that morning at what some called "the Uni" and others "the Varsity" we had visited the Students' Union building and seen a considerable number of posters and placards inviting us to join this or that society or club. Neville, who was an excellent shot, decided to put down his name for the Rifle Club. Maurice's choice was more aquatic. I moved towards the oval. One of my ambitions was to gain a "Blue" in middle-distance running. An hour later we tasted together the statutory luncheon of steak pie – an imposing name for a layer of mince between two squares of tough pastry – garnished with a scoop of unskilfully mashed potato and a modest spoonful of green peas.

"Well," said Neville, as we stood up after this somewhat ordinary meal, "tomorrow we really start."

In our first year we tasted a little botany, discovered about the cell and learnt some new, very long words. We had a touch of zoology including the inexpert dissection of a sting-ray, the mouth parts of a cockroach, the legs and lungs of crayfish and other bits and pieces regarding creatures great and small. Added to this was a little chemistry and physics. The approach to studies was radically different from school both from the authorities' point of view and the students'.

The chemistry lecture theatre was a vast room with the seats arranged steeply and rising at least thirty feet above the lecturer's head. He was a tall, earnest man whose voice reached us with a monotone of chemical knowledge. He took so little notice of his listeners that one day a poker-faced student from far up the back rolled a sixteen pound shot down the stairs. It landed at each level of seats with an appalling crash. There were nine such performances. When all was still the tall professor, without changing his tone in any way said, "Lead, ladies and gentlemen, is an element with a high atomic weight and a number of special uses. But before we discuss these would the individuals in the eighth row leave the lecture theatre."

When his request was duly carried out he continued with his flow of wisdom. Discipline was very relaxed. Some students attended lectures and stamped vigorously if the lecturer made a joke or split an infinitive. Others preferred to play billiards. No one bothered if you studied or didn't. The thing I found hard to understand was how some, although never known to work, did handsomely in examinations, while I, punctual, regular and putting in hours of solid work could feel the quivering of the boundary line beneath my large feet at the time of the annual ordeal. The reason was painfully obvious. I was considerably more like a tortoise than a hare.

My time was split into three parts: university study, Christian activity and sport.

Maurice and I found one group who discussed many phases of life. God came into it too, while the Bible was regarded in much the same way as was a corpse in the dissecting room or a sting-ray in the Zoology school. We found ourselves out of harmony with these students. We both believed the Bible to be the word of God: they preferred to regard it as merely containing His words.

The Free Thought Society was aggressive, atheistic and vocal in its propaganda. We went to a talk, "Jesus Christ, God, Man or Myth." On my feet during question-time I was hissed down and later attacked by two stocky, tough men in our year nicknamed Larynx and Pharynx. Maurice was a quiet person, but muscular, and aggression was neutralised.

Undergraduates had, years before, started what was called the Tower Prayer Meeting. When the tower had been used to house the new carillon, this group, who called themselves the Sydney University Bible League moved across the quadrangle and met in the architecture room. We joined them. Audible prayer disappeared the moment the carillon gave tongue. I had no doubt that the Almighty was able to hear above that high level of sound but certainly no one else could. We changed our venue again. Occasionally there was a talk given by a visiting speaker. We were heartened to hear a variety of people:

University

theological scholars, churchmen, lawyers, teachers, business men and even a detective inspector who came and spoke to us about God. It was disturbing to find no one from the medical profession and no university lecturer who was prepared to speak to this conservative group. There was a drabness and lack of drive about these folk that irked me. However, I found that from amongst their numbers had come missionaries, clergy, and men who were making their mark in everyday professions.

From the sporting angle I became an established member of the Athletic Club. Running, while not a team game in the fullest sense, is a very useful sport for a student with little time. At school I had found both status and physique through running middle distance but at University no glad news had gone before me. This made me particularly happy to succeed rather resoundingly. In my first term as a fresher I created a two mile record – created is the exact word. It was an astonishingly simple thing to do for I was the only one to finish on the first occasion the race was held!

A week later and still proudly wearing my Sydney Grammar School singlet, I managed to win the mile from the very senior medical student who had held the title for three years. Any signs of swelled head were radically and rapidly dealt with by a most solid defeat in the Australian Intervarsity Sports. All my bright hopes of a "Blue" evaporated and stayed in that state for two years.

It was a full and interesting year suitably capped by my name appearing among those who had passed first year medicine. Telephones started ringing and we informed one another that we were one sixth doctors and found it most comforting.

Holidays were now called vacation. Again I spent these summer weeks first at a Beach Mission on the New South Wales coast and later staying with the Decks in the Blue Mountains as before. Katoomba is the showplace of the mountains. It was here that we met a young Irish doctor, Howard Guinness, who came via Canada and New Zealand to speak to university students about committing their lives to God without reservation. I was intrigued to hear that students in England had sold their sporting equipment to pay his fare. He was about the age of the apostles when they started following Jesus. He was full of enthusiasm and zeal and he certainly set something going inside me. Some ten of us sat looking out over mounains and valleys in the shade of gum trees. He talked about practical things that made the difference between mere living and real Christian action. He discussed subjects I would then not have known how to raise and came up with the answers. It was exactly what I both wanted and needed.

He talked to us all individually. He had found out that I had won the university mile. "You must use your special abilities for God, Paul," he said. "Young people these days will listen to sportsmen. I'm talking at the local church on Sunday evening and you're coming with me. I'm going to ask you to give a testimony. That means to tell people what Jesus Christ means to you and is doing for you these days. You have four minutes. Use words everyone can understand and don't give a mere recital of your past history."

My heart sank. It would be much easier to sit in the back of the church and listen than to stand up in front of everybody and find myself tongue-tied and not saying what I wanted to. It *was* an ordeal. In the church were a number of my friends and some acquaintances. There was a lecturer from the Anatomy school. I felt physically sick and prayed desperately. When Howard Guinness called me to speak I stumbled out of the pew and up three steps and saw vaguely hundreds of faces. What was said I do not know but certainly God helped me. Afterwards people came and asked how they could become Christians. I was acutely aware of my weak grasp of the facts of the faith and my inability to express such as I had. Both praying and reading the Bible took on a new importance.

One thing that Howard Guinness urged upon us was that everyone should ask God to help them to introduce at least one person to Jesus Christ each year. He told us forcibly that when people did decide to go God's way this wasn't the end of our responsibility to them, it was merely the beginning. Maurice and I started praying together for our friend Neville Babbage.

It was about this time that I met Roy Gordon — robust and smiling. He spent his time talking to people in the open air about Jesus Christ. He invited two of us to go with him for a week into country towns and help him with this open-air job.

He had a van with all that was needed for camping, sleeping and cooking neatly tucked away. One side of the vehicle could be lowered to provide a most adequate platform with a place for the folding organ and the piano accordion which provided the music. He played both of these expertly and he had the skill in open-air talking that kept people on their feet listening for an hour on a cold night. His repartee was quick and his wit kindly. He knew exactly how to handle a drunk and could answer people's questions and explain to them about God. I felt dumb and useless and unable to play a proper part. My student friend, Neville Langford-Smith, later to be a Bishop in East Africa, was infinitely more capable. That night as I lay on a camp stretcher and heard the wind blowing through the branches of the gum tree above me I told God what a failure I felt and yet again came the stimulus of the verse, "I can do all things through Christ who strengthens me."

The Australian bush is a good place in which to think. I realised that God expected hard work from me. I needed to keep my nose very close to the grindstone, not only to gain a medical degree but to be of use for God. My voice was hoarse and I had used it only for five minutes that evening. Roy Gordon had spoken for over an hour without straining his larynx. I determined to find out how he did it.

Next day I tore my trousers rather seriously and I had only the one pair with me. My capable friend laughed, "I'll fix them for you. I used to be a tailor. Sit up here on the front seat and no one going by will realise that you have a gap between the tail of your shirt and the top of your sox."

As he made expert repairs I asked a host of questions including, "How is it you can talk so long and loudly and your voice be as strong at the end as at the beginning?"

He bit the cotton with his teeth. "That's a tip I picked up by watching a communist open-air expert. He could go on for hours. I saw he produced his voice with real know-how. He articulated his words at his teeth, not at the level of his tonsils."

I learnt more about people and how to deal with them in that week than ever before in my life.

Back home from the bush I renewed my perennial battle with the lawn and the hedge.

Medicine II – Whiff of Formalin

Then came Med. 2, a new and exciting year which took us into the Medical School where we felt we were really on the main road to our objective. This led into the dissecting rooms. We entered a little apprehensively. Even now, a whiff of formalin takes me back to those large, pungent rooms where we were to discover the magnificence of the structure of the human frame.

Physiology made me aware of a vast, complicated, beautifully balanced mechanism inside my skin and how it worked. Biochemistry I regarded as a subject on the run. Research advanced far faster than our course of lectures. To me it seemed utterly frustrating to learn complicated material which would be obsolete before the examination could be set. The vitamins were beginning to come out of obscurity. We shared with Captain Cook the knowledge that there was something in citrus fruit which controlled scurvy. My brand new physiology book stated that vitamin B had been isolated and research into vitamin C was well advanced. These days there is more information on the sides of cereal packets regarding vitamins than there was in the standard text-books of 1932!

Early in Med. 2 I felt acutely the need for love and companionship. The obvious thing to do was to pray and ask God to show me the girl whom He had chosen to be my partner in life. Again and again I had prayed and expected answers by return mail. This is seldom God's way of doing things. However in this instance the answer came quickly and the situation became complicated; so complicated that my concentration on work was badly interfered with. Term followed term. The examinations came closer and I saw failure starkly in front of me. It was a turbulent year. A medical student in love could be fatally distracted. Again came the day when the results were to be in the newspaper. With great thankfulness I saw my name in its usual place near the bottom of the list, the only consolation being that the list was obviously alphabetical.

Medicine III – Fifty percent!

Third year was the high hurdle of the course. At the annual

university students' celebrations, the Commemoration, they used to sing,

> The senate has issued a firm decree,
> That fifty percent shall fail.

The loud laughter of first term would turn into harsh reality at the end of the third year, for figures showed that fifty percent did fail.

"We're going to work this year," said Maurice, "harder than we've ever worked before."

We did. Life was full. I needed seven hours sleep and so rose at 6.30. I spent half an hour reading and praying. I could shave, shower and dress smartly. There was time to talk with mother and do some of those odd jobs that always crop up in a house. With the advent of electric trains I could catch the 8.03 instead of the 7.58 and still arrive at the university via ferry and tram in time for a lecture at 9.05. In this year we looked forward keenly to the opening of the Sydney Harbour Bridge. Ten minutes would be cut off the journey, and it would be possible to travel over the harbour and beneath the city in the new underground railway.

There was little let-up between nine and five except for lunch time. The previous year Howard Guinness had encouraged us to form the Sydney University Evangelical Union in place of the Bible League. In this way we would link up with similar groups in the United Kingdom, Canada and the United States. I had been elected secretary and it seemed that the only way to fit in this additional activity was to drop the midday meal out of my routine.

There is something about the word "evangelical" that some people regard as a sort of ecclesiastical swear word. It merely means "concerned for the gospel." When joining the E.U. you affirmed your faith in Jesus Christ as your Saviour, your Lord and your God. To become an office-bearer you signed a statement of faith in line with the creeds and indicating that you believed the Bible to be the supreme authority in all matters of faith and conduct. I had the responsibility of writing letters to speakers – inviting them and thanking them. There were phone-calls to clergy arranging services at which E.U. members would tell of their faith. Early on I realised the complete importance of delegating phases of the work and at the same time making sure that it was done.

One event that stands out explosively in my memory is an occasion when we asked a forthright businessman to speak on the subject of hell. We booked the biggest available hall, the Students' Union Hall, and advertised the talk both by poster and by leaflet. I thought the project a great idea. Some other E.U. members weren't so sure. This was too good an opportunity for many students to miss. Well before the time when the meeting was due to commence, students had packed in and were singing specially composed songs and parodies, a figure with horns and a spiked tail flitted across the stage and then returned waving a trident and shouting, "To hell with the E.U."

This was greeted with cheers and shouts. The E.U. Student President walked to the front where he tried to introduce the speaker. There was pandemonium. That was the signal for the fire crackers. They exploded above and among the audience for several hectic minutes. The Chairman raised his hand and shouted for silence. He was standing on a long mat which reached from the stage to the back of the hall and covered the central passage way. A score of hands jerked it backwards. The unfortunate chairman landed on his back. The hall was full of pungent smoke, students burst paper bags and pricked red balloons. The reporters for the student paper, *Honi Soit*, scribbled delightedly. Then the noise faded. It looked as though we would be starting but I saw a kerosene tin being quietly pushed into the very middle of the platform. The speaker was on his feet but hadn't uttered a word when there was a shattering explosion followed by a cloud of smoke. A home made bomb blew the side out of the kerosene tin. An attendant rushed in with a fire extinguisher, foam sprayed round the place, and the meeting which had never started was all over. Covered with confusion we tried to explain to the speaker that we'd no idea that this would happen. We expected controversy, but not a conflagration. He smiled, "Did you ever realise that God can use a show like that to make somebody think?"

He was right. A second-year medical student tackled an E.U. member in his year and said that it was incredibly stupid to put up a subject like that. It was playing with dynamite and anyway hell was all a myth. Instead of dissecting they talked in the shade and the direct result was that the man who had been upset committed his life into the hands of the Son of God that same afternoon.

On the home front the company whose shares we had regarded as useless paid another dividend. This time, two hundred pounds. Mother was finding walking rather heavy going. She came up with the idea that we might buy a small car. Those were the days of the Austin Seven and we were able to buy one of these mighty midgets and register and insure it for that two hundred pounds.

A doctor from a nearby suburb who had recently gained his Fellowship of the College of Surgeons had the knack of being able to pass on his knowledge of anatomy. "Come to my surgery on Wednesday nights," he said, "and I'll help you revise your anatomy and neurology." Two hours with him gave us more light on the subject than we had obtained from a month at lectures. Without the small Austin, travelling across country to his surgery would have been impossible.

In that little car the most momentous thing of the year occurred. One Tuesday Neville Babbage had come with us to an E.U. meeting. The speaker, Canon S. E. Langford-Smith, had been simple, direct and challenging. When it was over Neville was silent. But the next day when we drove home, he said, "Eh, how do I fix it up?"

I explained. He listened, nodded, and went into his bedroom where he invited Jesus Christ to forgive his sins and to take control of his life. Maurice and I had been praying for over a year that this would happen. Now with the three of us facing in the same direction we shared true Christian fellowship.

This year athletics reached a high point and I found myself captain of the Sydney University team to run in Hobart. It was an eventful trip.

As a student group we started in a blaze of publicity. On the slopes of Mt. Wellington was a paddock; upon it were inscribed in large white stones the words KEENS CURRY. In the stilly night a number of sweating figures laboured and the dawn provided the Tasmanian capital with a surprise. The great stones now spelled HELLS CURSE. The papers made a story of it and extra precautions were taken which, however, did not prevent the Post Office clock from acquiring a wistful face with raised academic eyebrows. Security was again tightened.

In the sports, I ran second in the half-mile narrowly ahead of the erstwhile record holder. In what was termed the medley relay — four runners, the first covering half a mile, the second a quarter, the last two each a furlong — I again ran the longer distance and was again beaten, this time by a slim young man from Melbourne, Wellesley Hannah.

In the changing-room later, my New Testament fell from my pocket into the middle of the floor. A voice came, "Here endeth the lesson." Another very deep, sad and sepulchral replied, "Hallelujah, brother." Blushing all over I picked up my book. As I went outside I felt a touch on my shoulder and the young man who had beaten me a short while before smiled at me, pushing up a Testament in his pocket, "I'm one of 'em too." That contact with Wellesley Hannah changed both our lives. It is very clear that God's way of guiding those of his family is of spider-web texture on occasions.

As we left Hobart there were a surprising number of uniformed railway personnel at the station. They no doubt sighed with relief when the train pulled out. Half way to Launceston, there is a station, Parattah. Here cups of tea and pies were obtainable at a price. One solemn-looking student protested loudly on the platform that he had found a mouse's tail in his pie. There was a great performance during which one of the Sydney team (and I was captain!) annexed the station master's large bell. This he rather unwisely rang violently as the train moved out. The result was that at the next station helmeted police descended and our colleague was left in the hands of the law. He was taken before the local mayor — fortunately a graduate and not inexperienced in student activity — who fined him half a crown, paid it and put the delinquent on the next train.

This year I was awarded my "Blue." Being in track and field events certainly was useful. The people I met were interesting and my contacts were widened. There were open doors which otherwise could not have been approached. Being a University Blue cut some ice with both schoolboys and masters but there was the uncomfortable fact that things could and did get out of focus. One day my photograph appeared in the paper.

Practice on Sydney University oval, and (*below*) the Inter-Varsity Athletics team, 1930. Paul White is fourth from left, and Neville Babbage in the centre of the back row

Graduation Day: the new "Doctor" White looks down on the buildings of the Medical School

Underneath the photo were two words that set my head swelling, "Scholar, Athlete."

I glowed. Then came the sudden awareness that for one whose aim was to seek first God's Kingdom, I was behaving rather shabbily. In the train going home I quietly told God that it was obvious to me that now was the time to give up athletics. It was edging its way into the front of my living instead of being a useful springboard for passing on the Good News.

A few days later in the train a schoolboy sat next to me and started to talk athletics. He had seen a certain race and discussed it fully and knowledgeably. Then he asked me for help. He planned to run the mile for his school. I invited him to a Crusader meeting that Saturday night. There he realised his need of becoming a member of God's family. This started a long friendship. Ernest Harding not only won his mile but is now the Rector of a large parish.

I felt this was my answer. I had seen the amber light and was prepared to give up athletics if this had been what God wished. I kept on. On Sydney University Oval I helped two men to know God. One was killed in an accident a few years later. The other, David Britten, has been a close friend ever since. We together wrote four schoolboy stories full of events we had both lived. These are the Ranford Books. There has been keen satisfaction in seeing them come out in Finnish as well as English.

Then the exams came. We stood expectantly outside the solid black doors of the Great Hall. The clock said ten minutes to nine. Neville and Maurice and I walked a small distance from the crowd packed around the door. Neville paused, "We've worked," he said, "and we know it pretty well." We stood under a small tree and asked for God's help to understand the questions fully and to answer them clearly. The clock chimed. The doors swung open and we hurried to our seats. There was an awful hush as the hundred men and women in our year read the examination paper. It was beyond words. From all over the place came involuntary sounds of sinking morale. "Silence please," came the sharp voice of the Clerk of Examinations. This was greeted by a prolonged and universal groan.

But worse was to come: the other papers, that grim week, followed the same pattern. We were a silent, unsmiling group that moved away from the Great Hall each morning after the examination. In due course a notice appeared informing us that the following persons were to present themselves for a *viva voce* examination. The kind-hearted old attendant who had seen two generations of students come and go, pass and fail, chuckled. He was the only one who did. "Cheer up, boys. You're either going to collect the gold medal or creep through the gateway by the skin of your teeth." But as we pointed out to him, he did not have to undergo the inquisition.

Of the three of us only my name appeared. Maurice summed it up. "You two have Exhibitions, I haven't. Nev is in the credits bunch, Paul is cliff-hanging, and I'm down the drain."

I attended the *viva voce* examination, was asked about the functions of the spleen and answered fast and enthusiastically. "Stop," said the Professor, "you know that." The corners of his mouth twitched. He said, "It's far better technique to hesitate a little, then you can answer the question fully and perhaps use half of the ten minutes available." He asked another question. I knew the answer but not nearly so well. I endeavoured to sound enthusiastic but he smiled, "Not quite so at home there, are you?" But generally I could answer all he put up to me. When I'd finished he looked through my papers. With a twinkle in his eye he said, "I must congratulate you, White, on your judgment."

I hurried back home and found my Aunt Margaret was visiting us. I quoted the Professor's last utterance and Aunty was so pleased that she there and then presented me with five pounds. I spent one of them in finding out from the kind-hearted attendant just what that Professor had meant. He came back laughing loudly, "My dear fellow, don't tell your Aunt, but in the three subjects you scored fifty, fifty and fifty-one and as you know the pass mark is fifty and above."

Actually fifty-four percent of the year failed. Maurice was one of them and had to sit for a deferred examination, or as we called it a "post." The day that the fourth year started came the news that he was amongst the relatively few who had succeeded in jumping the third-year hurdle at the second attempt. Again we took time out to walk along the path in front of the Med. School and thank God.

There were quite a number who regarded certain professors

University

with a very jaundiced eye. They were excellent research-workers and scientists but as teachers they left very much to be desired. One particular gentleman had a Bugatti sports car. He was an Australian who had acquired an Oxford accent at that particular university. He also wore a continental-type beret when driving his red machine. On that day his popularity had reached an all-time low. He strode down the stairs, aloof, past a silent, hostile group of students. They watched with poker-faces as he made long and unsuccessful attempts to start the sports car. When the battery gave signs of failing he marched back muttering and ignoring as well as he could the cold looks of those whom he had treated so harshly, both as lecturer and examiner.

In due course a mechanic arrived. As the students walked past one angelic-faced individual with an Irish name said hoarsely, "She'd go better, mate, if you removed the spud from the exhaust pipe." He received a knowing wink and I have no doubt the professor received a substantial bill. It could have proved an expensive potato. Two hours later the great man descended loftily and drove indignantly away. There was a certain amount of balm distilled from this vegetarian incident.

Medicine IV – Stethoscope, more than a guessing tube

Med. IV, the first of the clinical years, was like coming out of a tunnel into the light. At last we were at grips with the enemy.

Bacteriology introduced us to some of the criminals and their techniques of violence and wholesale slaughter. We warmed to the counter-measures of immunology. Smallpox, yellow fever, typhoid, diphtheria, tetanus and gas gangrene all had an answer. There was still the challenge, as yet unmet, of poliomyelitis, tuberculosis, leprosy and many others.

There was the constant search for weapons to combat the great killers: pneumonia, septicaemia, meningitis, and the epidemics of infectious disease. With meningitis I had the feeling of a personal feud, since it had caused my father's death. It was disturbing to find no real answer to so many diseases.

Our pathology lectures were well taught and full of interest. In front of us in specimen jars we could see the actual damage done to organs by neoplasms – this word always sounded so much less harsh to me than cancer.

There was now the opportunity to see and examine people suffering from the diseases about which we learnt in the lecture room. We were a self-conscious group dressed in new white coats and bravely clutching new stethoscopes. These latter were a symbol of advance rather than an instrument useful in diagnosis. We were shepherded round the wards by Honorary Physicians and Surgeons and shown people with a wide variety of illnesses which we were able to correlate with what we saw in the specimen jars and under the microscope.

We met the sick people and heard what they had to say and saw and felt what they had to show. Some resented us as students, others were only too pleased to talk. It was not an easy situation and called for a sensitive approach. In these early days of Med. IV I found that I could get on with people. Certainly this was helped by not placing cold hands on warm bodies; also my hands told me more when they were warm and gently applied. Patients were less resentful and more co-operative when I said "please" and did all I could not to embarrass the one being examined. It took a little longer but it was most worthwhile to listen interestedly to what poeple had to say. When it was my time to talk it was helpful to use a language that could be understood and not to flash some of the large and learned words that I had only picked up in the last few months. A little kindness and encouragement often made it possible to talk quite naturally about the Lord Jesus.

This was a year of more firsts. Not only were the wards open to us but also the operating theatre and the post-mortem room. The first operation we witnessed was an unfortunate affair. There was a lot of blood and most uncomfortable-looking needles were inserted into the patient's spine. We stood well out of the line of battle – capped, gowned and masked. I was thankful that the mask obscured all but my eyes and that no one could see my clammy hands, but I feared that my heart-beat was more than audible. Later Maurice and Neville said they had experienced the same sensations. We noted that a post-mortem was scheduled for that afternoon and decided it was better to have two shocks in one day than to have the experience on two separate ones.

In the Sydney Hospital Casualty Department and various clinics we had many eye-openers. Ambulances arrived with motor accident cases, assault victims, individuals who fought with knives or fell from a height. There were broken bones and those who drank methylated spirits flavoured with boot-polish, those who took poison or overdoses of sedatives. It was important to face shattering situations without being visibly surprised by anything seen or heard.

1932 was a good year. As president of the Evangelical Union I saw much action. As far as possible I tried to come alongside every member of the Union and talk to them about the outreach of their life for God and to motivate them to follow through Jesus' instruction, "You will be witnesses to me," in their home, their suburb, their city, their country and to the widest limits.

Nearly every Sunday night groups of us would go to churches of various denominations. The talks were straight and direct, challenging people to ask Jesus to take charge of their lives. We would explain what salvation and forgiveness meant and tell how Jesus had become real to us and how He could be trusted. To me it was tremendous to meet people who said, "I've wanted to do this for years but didn't know how."

I contrived to take at least two members of the E.U. with me to each of these services. There are few better places to talk to people about God than in a car when you're on the move. The small Austin Seven was a God-send. Petrol cost two and sixpence a gallon at that stage. I was now receiving an allowance of a pound a week. Half of this went in nourishment for the car, the other supplied fares and lunches. At times things became a trifle frugal.

Athletics was a useful sport, for I could save threepence in fares by running from the University to Sydney Hospital. It was a little over a mile and helped to keep my muscles in trim. Again there was a degree of success in the running and again the award of a "Blue." Exams came and went smoothly. To that stage in the medical course my name had appeared neither in the distinctions nor credits. I was more than satisfied to see it amongst those who merely passed. Long vacations had shrunk to three weeks and at Christmas the fifth year started.

Medicine V – Success without a prize

There was a delightful, relaxed feeling about fifth year medicine.

The tall mountain of the finals loomed in the far distance. It would have to be climbed in due course but for the moment the pressure was off. We studied for the fun of it and absorbed a great deal of information. Life was full of new things and new experiences. Lectures in Public Health were splendidly given and to me full of interest. I could see their practical application out in Africa. It was obvious that a week's study of Medical Jurisprudence and Ethics was all that would be needed to pass that examination. Psychiatry was an entirely different matter. It was starkly clear what mental imbalance did to people and their relations. At that stage so pitiably little could be done to help. This was not my area of medicine. It grated on my nervous system. I realised that to cope with a sick mind was going to be very hard going for me.

Sandwiched into this year was a three-month visit to the Children's Hospital and four weeks' residence at the Women's Hospital. I was to realise that the first day of an individual's life was his most dangerous one. The same could be said of his first month or his first year. If children were so vulnerable and so greatly in need of help here, how much more so in Africa. The African scene seemed to frame and accentuate disease after disease that we saw. There was so much to be learned and this was my biggest opportunity to learn about children's diseases. The responsibility loomed of standing alone, inadequately armed and supplied, to fight a flood of disability and death.

Physically I was fit and relaxed. I was able to run better than ever before and did so. It was easier to learn facts and to correlate them with what was to be seen in the clinics and wards. The months really raced. Then came the exams. I enjoyed them. Our predecessors informed us that nobody failed in fifth year. Out came the results and it was true. Then to my utter amazement I was rung up by a fellow-student whose father worked in a newspaper. "Paul," he laughed, "you've topped the year!"

Frankly, I didn't believe him. But I had a secret ambition to achieve this distinction though I hardly dared to admit it to myself. The laughing voice said, "You're a strange character, Paul White. This is the way you do things. You top the year on the one occasion when it doesn't matter and do it in the one year when there is no prize."

Professor Harvey Sutton of the school of Public Health and Preventive Medicine was the best lecturer in the whole of the course. He was a most genial gentleman whose habit it was to invite to tea the student who came first in the examination for his subject. He was the president of the Athletic Club and when the Intervarsity sports had been held in Sydney he had given a notably witty after-dinner speech. As I was his guest and we drank tea and ate hot buttered cinnamon toast, he said, "You know, White, actually you did not score higher marks than the students to whom I gave second and third places." He smiled, "Examiners are only human. One man wrote forty-eight pages and he was appallingly untidy. The second recorded the facts in an almost unreadable handwriting and with rather poor expression. Your sixteen pages were clearly readable, you put in headings and summaries, and you had a sense of humour."

The Women's Hospital was an utterly new experience. Birth is a tremendous drama and a Caesarian Section is the one operation that produces a product you are not anxious to throw away. Again came the thought of Africa and the knowledge that I would be on my own. No consultants, anaesthetists, pathologists or X-rays. Each of us was given the opportunity of bringing ten infants into the world and seeing a hundred or more births. With skilled staff and modern equipment this took a lot of manpower and material and time.

Rather unwisely I took the baby Austin to hospital and parked it in a small corner. One evening it disappeared and almost simultaneously came a curt message from the matron, "Would Mr. White remove his car from the Labour Ward."

It had been squeezed into the main doorway. A diagnosis sheet stuck on to the windscreen read, "Impacted shoulders." It had been carried up four flights of stairs and I had the far from simple task of driving it down. Again my friends were a very real help. Stair by stair we descended doing out utmost not to produce bumps and thumps. At last, back in its proper spot, I found that a nappy had been attached most professionally to the spare wheel!

One of the pranksters was a socialite. He staggered into the hospital at 3 a.m. after a convivial night. So far gone was he that he didn't realise he was being bedded down in the food lift, white tie, tails and all. Early in the morning the kitchen staff pushed the button. The food lift obediently appeared and shrill screams greeted the arrival of "the body." The only people not vastly amused were the student victim, the matron and the cook.

Medicine VI – Last lap

When the glow of examination results had passed, and it did so very smartly, the final year loomed ominously. The pressure was on. I hung up my running shoes. I passed on the responsibility for my Sunday School Class. Saturday nights were still spent at schoolboy Crusader meetings and most Sundays there was the opportunity to speak to young people's fellowships and afterwards at the church service.

Time was hard to come by. Sleep was cut down, as was exercise. After years of merely smouldering, asthma produced a hearty blaze. Life became more and more earnest. We were invited to attend clinical evenings at the hospitals and some postgraduate lectures. These produced shock after shock. Here were conditions that we had never even heard of and varieties of treatment that we did not know existed. We had acquired a mass of medical knowledge. Now there was the actual need to put system into it. There were lectures, ward rounds, clinics and seminars. We attended the lot and hour after hour concentrated on intensive study. The calendar seemed to gallop.

One particular day was memorable. Following Professor Harvey Sutton's advice I filled in a long document of application for the Rhodes Scholarship:

What was my objective in life?
What part had I played in student life?
What was my academic record?
What was my fondness for and success in sport?

There were many other things. I discussed it all with Professor Harvey Sutton and said, "Sir, I don't think I have much chance. I'm rather ordinary material."

"Not at all," said the genial Prof. "I can feel that Cecil Rhodes would like a man who thinks as you do to have something to do with Africa in the days ahead."

Encouraged but not convinced I wrote briefly and honestly with all the windows into my life open. And then a monogrammed envelope arrived. I opened it carefully. It was a Royal Command to present myself at Government House. With a number of other students I was asked all manner of penetrating questions by a group of notables under the chairmanship of the Governor, Sir Philip Game.

They asked about my thoughts for the future. They wanted to know of my faith and what I had in view regarding Africa. After the interview I stood in the grounds of Government House and saw Sydney from a different angle: Macquarie Street, the street of the medical specialists, the Harbour Bridge, sturdy Fort Denison, the Botanical Gardens, the battleships, the Zoo and the ferries. My memory of travelling as a small boy in one of those sleek Manly Ferries was very clear.

Before I returned home from Government House I had the opportunity of congratulating Keith Bradfield, son of the Chief Engineer of Sydney Harbour Bridge, on being that year's Rhodes Scholar.

In August came a blow which threatened to put me out of the battle.

Chapter Eight:

Love

DURING MED. II, I FELL UNDRAMATICALLY IN LOVE WITH MARY Bellingham, who was a lovely girl with a touch of Cinderella about her.

Mary's mother died within days of her birth. She left school unusually early and did not follow the pattern of the older members of her family who were more than successful in their studies and careers. She stayed at home and helped her stepmother. They lived in a quiet street in Gordon. At the far end of their long garden was a tennis court. It was here I came to see Mary as she was. Tête-à-tête conversations were not easily achieved but there were ways and means of arranging mixed doubles so that she and I could talk between sets. Mary would forget her quietness and tell good stories about people and events and funny happenings. She had abilities but little opportunity to express and expand them. As a Christian her activities were limited to services and selected meetings in the church at the end of their street and very occasional Scripture Union house-parties.

Those days every time I saw a yellow robin I thought of Mary - quiet, gentle-eyed, busy and useful. She made no attempt to be a peacock or a parrot. She was shyly able to meet people in high places and to smile her way into the confidence of children.

There were so many things that greatly attracted me to Mary. One Saturday afternoon I realised what had happened to me and at once came face to face with a quandary. There were at least five years before I could even think of marriage. A medical degree was uncomfortably distant and even more uncomfortably problematic. Long engagements did not seem to be the answer. I had heard Mrs. Bellingham speak tersely and forcibly in this matter when Mary's elder sister became engaged. I saw eye to eye with her. If I was to pass examinations and obtain that desired degree, hard work and concentration were necessary. I had found this out at school and it certainly was not easier at the university. I knew only too well the time my heart would demand would be too great a charge on my head. The inevitable result would be landing far short of my target.

I took another close look at the path which I firmly believed God was pointing out for my life. All that I had heard or read made it clear that medical work in East Africa at that stage was rugged, pioneering and life-time in extent. Every bit of medical know-how needed to be tucked away in my mind. More important still, if I was going effectively to pass on the Good News to African people in a language not my own, there was the need first of all to be able to do this capably in Australia in my home tongue.

I soon saw that Mary had realised that I was not just one of the boys who came to play tennis. We talked together about my aims in life. She listened and understood. Quietly, but with tension in her voice she said, "You'll need to work very hard."

Enthusiastically but with a lack of sensitiveness I nodded and talked fast about the Beach Sunday School that Maurice and Roger Deck and I ran. On and on, about talking in the open air, about articulating words at the level of the front teeth, about audio-visual devices and holding children's attention. On and on. Mary smiled and nodded. I was off again. This time about the young people's services we and a group of other undergraduates went to on Sundays. A troubled look came into her eyes as she listened to the way we had passed on how Jesus had come to be real in our lives.

She said, "You must be nervous before you speak."

"It's not easy. My mouth goes dry and there are always butterflies in my stomach but Maurice is often so nervous that he goes outside and is sick before he speaks."

Again came her quiet voice, "I would too."

I was so insensitive and inexperienced that this slid by me at the time but later came back, bold and arresting as black headlines. In my brashness I crossed swords several times with Mrs. Bellingham. I did the same at home. Young people in the spring of life do not find it easy to travel smoothly with those in its autumn. When I tried to ring Mary, Mrs. Bellingham would most often answer. Mary was busy. No, she wouldn't be able to come with me on Saturday to the athletics carnival. Would she be able to come to a youth service we were holding in a church in the district? Next Sunday? No, I'm afraid not.

Should I be fortunate enought to hear Mary's voice at the other end of the line inevitably she would say, "I must ask Motherie" – as she called Mrs. Bellingham.

The negative replies were frustrating as were the decreasing invitations to tennis. At no time did Mary ever share with me the exciting things that came my way in those undergraduate years. How greatly I wanted her to understand the thrill of fast running, the flavours of winning and losing, the stimulus and the fatigue of battle as you passed on the Good News and faced people your own age with God's challenge.

"Lord," I prayed, "what can a fellow do?"

Action! I wanted action! At home I'd go outside and look north-west and pray for patience and a quite mind. Mary was only three miles away geographically but we might well have been separated by the width of the world.

Some nights I would close my anatomy or physiology books, jump on my bike and pedal those three miles past a dark house. I could see her window shaded by a jasmine vine. It was dark. To make things worse kindly folk started giving me advice. "Paul, its time you started thinking about a life partner. Look for a graduate, someone mentally your equal."

I told them in a quiet voice that for a long time I had been asking God to guide me to someone who was a member of His family. I had no desire to make the primary mistake of being unequally yoked. Then mother took a hand in things and started inviting some girls to dinner, one at a time. I felt like Samuel inspecting the sons of Jesse!

At about this time I had my exciting adventure with the athletic team in Tasmania. Somewhat diffidently I purchased a carved bird that would fit in an envelope. With it I sent a poem to Mary – a piece of non-distinguished verse which gave plenty of scope to read between its rhyming lines. Bubbling with excitement I went to see Mary the Sunday afternoon following our return and spent the majority of it singing Moody and Sankey hymns to an inaccurate accompaniment by my hostess.

The only joy in the whole situation, and it was a considerable one, was the opportunity of holding Mary's hand behind the pianist's back. To my deep satisfaction it was an exercise that seemed to be appreciated.

Then I suffered a sharp reverse. My emotions overflowed my ability to study. Concentration suffered and my old enemy, asthma, appeared out of its allergic limbo and became aggressive. Some balanced, objective, Christian advice would have been of tremendous value just then. Examinations were two months away. I realised starkly that to continue as I was going meant failure.

In desperation I went to see Mary, requested the opportunity to talk to her in private and was given it. Miserably I blurted out my story. Everything depended on gaining that medical degree. The whole of my later effectiveness would hinge on my ability to pass. Mary was tense. She sat in a tall, hard-backed chair and her voice came jerkily, "I think you're right."

I started to sweat. "Mary, I can't go on this way. I must put everything I have into my studies and my witnessing till I'm through the finals and then, may I come and see you again? That will be in three-and-a-half years."

There was silence and an awful pause. At last she nodded and stood up. I said a shaky good-bye at the front gate and we shook hands. It was all like a page from Jane Austen.

I received occasional short "your sincere friend" letters, greetings, Christmas cards and congratulations. I wrote sending some information about a children's mission that I was to run with a university friend in a country town. Mary actually followed up the young people who took an interest. She wrote to a number of them for years afterwards. For me those next years flew. For Mary they travelled very slowly.

In the holidays before my final examination as I prayed one morning a sense of huge elation came over me. I realised the time had come to see her and to ask her to marry me. My work was better. I found the clinical years of medicine a delight. I liked people. With patients, my memory for things I could see and hear and feel was infinitely better than the one I used for memorising words.

For three days I prayed and tried to argue that all this was premature. I had waited so long that I could well wait another two months; but still there was peace in my mind and a vast joy. I had found a valuable pointer in knowing which way God wanted me to go. It was by letting His peace be the umpire in my heart.

I talked to mother. A little sadly she agreed. This looked like the last page of a chapter of her life which had meant a tremendous amount to her and to me. Then I went and formally put my case before Mrs. Bellingham. She agreed to my asking Mary to marry me.

She smiled at me. "You've been very wise, dear, but you shouldn't have a long engagement. Remember that."

The next day we set out for the lower slopes of the Blue Mountains in our second-hand Austin Ten, Mary in front with me, mother and Mrs. Bellingham in the back. We lunched and then Mary and I wandered off into the bush.

A yellow robin perched only an arm's length away. We sat watching him and I thought how for years he and his kind had reminded me of the girl whom I loved and whom I was going to tell all about it. But that day words did not come easily. At length I said untidily all that mattered, and Mary answered, "Oh, yes, yes." Not quite knowing what to do I put out my hand to her. She lifted it gently, put it over her shoulder and putting her arms round me she kissed me. It wasn't till an hour later that we noticed the robin again.

It was a golden day. We talked and planned and I told her how in the next two months I would sit for my final examinations and share every event and happening with her. We prayed together about many things. Then it was decided that she would come to our church on Sunday to a fellowship tea and meet my friends and start to find her way into my life.

The next few days continued to have their golden glow. But when it came to Sunday, Mary had been disturbed by a memorial service at her church that morning. It seemed a mere cloud moving across the sky. But at 2 a.m. the next morning the telephone rang shatteringly. I stumbled out of bed to answer it and heard a voice I hardly recognised say, "Is that you Paul, Mary here ..." Then there was a click as the receiver was put down.

Later came Mrs. Bellingham's anxious voice, "Mary is very strange, she is screaming and threatening to take her life."

Well before dawn, I travelled to Gordon faster than I ever had before and found a wild-eyed, frenzied girl who pushed me away from her and filled the house with a torrent of words that swirled from one theme to another. This was horrifying. I had seen the condition in hospital but never at close quarters. I never even remotely imagined that I could be involved with this sort of sickness. But here it was striking deep into the new life that the day before had seemed so full of promise – so blissful.

There were two schools of thought in the early 1930's about the treatment for this psychosis. The use of sedation, or "letting the process work itself out." Unfortunately the doctor chosen by Mrs. Bellingham, near neighbour and a well known physician, belonged to the latter school. Week followed agonising week. Mary raved day and night and lost weight. Her skin became infected and I was convinced that death was not far out of the picture.

Years before, on my way to school I had watched the swirling water as the ferry from Milson's Point pulled into Circular Quay. At that time I formulated a principle: if I make a promise when convinced of the rightness of the matter, I keep it. In spite of the apparent foolhardiness of the situation from a medical point of view, I really loved Mary and believed God had brought us together. I have never wavered in this belief.

And then came the time for my final examinations: four written papers and twenty-four *viva voce* examinations. Over those bitter days the peace of God that is beyond all human reason, kept my heart, my emotions and my mind in the knowledge and love of God. This was real, positive, almost tangible support. Maurice and Neville stayed very close to me and helped me in the details of final revision and the technique of examinations both written and spoken. They and many others gave me the greatest help that any one can give any one else: regular understanding prayer. The examinations were far kinder than I had dared to hope. I was calm and able to put on to paper and into spoken words most of the things that I was asked. The ordeal trailed on for over a month. Fatigue had brought a lull to Mary's turbulence. She was confused but no longer violent.

At my end of things the problem was to concentrate. Each afternoon at two o'clock our year of some hundred students would be ushered into the lecture room. Two by two in alphabetical order we would be called to give samples of our knowledge to sedate and solemn examiners. There are distinct disadvantages in being at the end of the alphabet. The afternoons seem endless. It was futile to try to study. We lost interest in playing chess.

In the last *viva voce* on obstetrics, Professor Windeyer, who had taught us well and thoroughly, invited me into his room. I went in last. He smiled at me, "White, being a W has its disadvantages in this sort of exam, hasn't it? Oh, yes, I have travelled this same road, but there are some saving graces." He clutched a teapot. "Here is my first question and I'm sure you'll be able to answer it most adequately. Do you take milk and sugar in your tea ?"

"Both, thank you, sir."

"Very good. Full marks so far."

I identified and explained the uses of various obstetrical instruments, described how I would deal with a baby arriving feet first and was having a happy time answering his question regarding umbilical cords and their tangles and complications. He nodded as I made point after point. "Talking of umbilical cords, a student once asked me if its separation was uncomfortable for the baby." He shook his grey head. "I told him, 'Frankly, I don't know, I don't remember'." He chuckled away to himself and started turning over the pages in a folder. His finger moved along a line. His eyes twinkled and he smiled whimsically. "We've had a busy day you and I haven't we, *doctor?*"

I gulped, "Sir, you mean. ..." He nodded, slowly. I walked unsteadily out of the room. "Er, thank you, sir."

Two days later the papers confirmed his prophecy. That night our front garden was littered with bones and in huge writing, both on the road and the footpath – DOCTOR WHITE. The telephone rang time and time again. The most welcome of all the phone calls told me that Mary had improved a little and had had an hour or two when her mind was clear. She had heard about the exam results and seemed to grasp what it meant.

A week later Mary could talk briefly on the telephone. Another week and she was almost herself again. Christmas was more than a happy one and three days later a radiant, normal girl helped me purchase a diamond ring.

Graduation

We stood outside the Great Hall of the university. It was my graduation day. There were scores of students and hundreds of their friends and relations. Mother looked round. "How few have hoods," she said.

I laughed and picked up Mary's left hand and looked at the third finger. "Money's hard to come by these days. It's cheaper to hire hoods than to buy them. When you can hire them and share them that's cheaper still. A lot of the boys have been doing it. You watch those hoods as they are passed quietly back from row to row. Everybody will wear one when they go up to collect their degree. Ten of us are sharing in the one that I'll wear."

My mother was talking to Maurice's mother. I took Mary quietly down the stone steps on to the lawn in front of the university buildings. "It was under this tree that we always prayed before we went in." She looked up. "And it was in the tower up there that Eric used to go to pray in the lunch hour." Her brother Eric, then the headmaster of a school in India, had been one of the members of the Bible League earlier on. The carillon started to play. We moved into the hall. I found my women folk good seats and then hurried to take my place with the group who were no longer final year students but graduands.

This was a beautiful hall. The sun splashed colour from the stained glass on to elegant stone work. High above were shapely beams. Sitting there waiting I started to day-dream. Often over the last six years when I had sat there thinking before putting pen to paper I had looked at all the oil paintings of past chancellors, vice-chancellors, professors, benefactors and notable scholars. In those days of trial they had seemed to frown upon me but today there was a twinkle in the eyes and a smile upon every academic face.

The door opened and the procession passed through. In front the Yeoman Biddell followed by the Chancellor and vice-Chancellor, the Dean of the Faculty and lecturers, all suitably capped, hooded and gowned in striking colours. They proceeded to the dais and sat solemnly down. Speeches were made, good speeches, and then they presented the important documents with our names inscribed on them in copperplate writing which indicated that we had become Bachelors of Medicine and Bachelors of Surgery. I thought, that is the only variety of bachelor that I'm going to remain for long. Neville was amongst the first to receive his degree; then I saw the hood make its way back to Maurice.

That day I saw with a new clarity a facet of my Christian belief. There I was – plain Paul White sitting in the back row, fourth from the end. In due course the hood was passed back to me. I put it carefully over my shoulders and walked quietly to the platform, up the steps and there was the vice-Chancellor, in his left hand the rolled-up documents, his right hand stretched out to shake mine. When my hand gripped his and I accepted those degree certificates I had officially become a doctor. As I walked down the far side of the platform and up the left hand isle back to my seat – the seat still warm – I was Doctor Paul White. That small ceremony had been the crossing of the boundary. The odd thing was that I felt not the slightest bit different, but I knew that would come later on with the responsibilities, problems, stresses, opportunities and routine of medical life.

Chapter Nine:

Junior Doctor

I WANTED THE WIDEST EXPERIENCE IN THE SHORTEST TIME. Royal North Shore Hospital had a lot of things to be said for it. There was the opportunity of doing a term of Obstetrics and another in Infectious Diseases. There were also clinics for diabetes and tuberculosis.

The assistant medical superintendent had been at Sydney Grammar School and was a hockey "Blue." "Come to North Shore, Paul, if you want experience. And you'll be in the money – eleven and threepence a week while you're a junior and thirty-five bob when you become a senior, if you ever do." He grinned. "You'll have one weekend off in three and only work every third night. If you don't like work, don't come."

And so the "three musketeers" split up. Maurice went to Sydney Hospital. Neville and I went to North Shore.

One great advantage was that it was only five miles to my home and eight to Mary's.

The starting date was January 7th at 9 a.m. I had been officially appointed as Junior Resident Medical Officer at the Royal North Shore Hospital, St. Leonards, New South Wales. I caught the ordinary train from the ordinary station. All very routine and commonplace – the same sort of thing that I had done for years. But today it was different. A new ambition had been compassed. I was starting work at my profession. I was no longer an undergraduate. I was wearing carefully shined black shoes and a conservative grey suit, specially dry-cleaned for the occasion.

One of my friends moved down the carriage. He sat down next to me and said loudly, with a chuckle in his voice, "Good morning, doctor."

The train was drawing into St. Leonards station – I grinned

and said in a voice that only he could hear, "I'm a new boy again. In half an hour I'll be a junior doctor at the hospital over there."

"Punctual Paul," he laughed. "Blessings on you."

I walked quietly along a stretch of the Pacific Highway, through the hospital gate and along a path shaded by willows and flowering shrubs. "Lord," I prayed, "help me to be useful for you here. Help me to pick up the experience that I'll need in the days ahead."

I walked rather tentatively into the entrance hall. Already on the indicator board of resident doctors was the name Dr. P. White. Neville Babbage had already arrived. He stood beside me and said, "There are only three new juniors."

The telephonist turned from her switchboard. "Are you Dr. Babbage and Dr. White?"

We admitted it. "The Medical Superintendent will see you now in his office. The second door on the right down the passage."

We were briefed and given our room numbers and I was told that for three months I would work for a surgeon and a physician. The Medical Superintendent finished up with, "This afternoon I will see what you know about anaesthetics. This morning my assistant will take you round the hospital. Here is a copy of the hospital pharmacopoeia. Use the medications in it. It's just off the press and right up to date." That was 1935. In 1976 there is not one of those prescriptions listed now in use.

We certainly worked. The mornings started early in the operating theatre where I assisted the surgeon or gave anaesthetics. These were open ether. The technique was the so called "rag-and-bottle" method. Pouring the anaesthetic on to a mask of gauze the object was to coax the patient into unconsciousness and then continue to pour in such a legato fashion that he reached the suitable depth of unconsciousness for the surgeon to work.

I was responsible for patients admitted under the care of my surgeon and physician. I would write the details of their history and physical examination, prescribing routine medications and having the necessary X-rays and pathology tests performed. I visited these patients several times a day. Twice weekly rounds were done with the honorary doctor.

Surprisingly quickly the routine was absorbed. Minor surgical procedures with tubes, needles, syringes, forceps, scissors and other devices were picked up. From early morning to late afternoon we were busy. Sometimes all night long. It is an experience to walk wearily up to your bedroom after a night spent in the operating theatre or the labour ward and see the sun rise. Then to undress, shower, shave, dress again and brace yourself for a new day's work. This called heavily on the reserves. Fatigue would become considerable by sunset.

Neville and I talked and planned how best to seek first the kingdom of God in hospital. An extra bit of care and concern for our patients gave us the chance to talk to them about God and lend them some books. People used to come round the wards on Sunday evenings singing the old hymns and doing it very well. One day their organist was ill. I offered to deputise and Neville and I both said briefly that we loved the Lord and that doing our bit for Him was the most important thing in our lives. The news of these activities spread widely and fast. We were branded.

I acquired the ability to use the portable X-ray. This gave me quite a lot of work, both when on duty and off. Confidence grew and Ted Collins, the acting superintendent, was always ready to give hints and to pass on ideas. I practised surgical knots and stitching on an ancient pair of trousers, and acquired quite a deal of dexterity with both knife and needle and other instruments by working on old inner tubes and pieces of hose pipe. Bicycle inner-tube was a reasonable substitute for intestine. My earliest exploits in eye surgery were done on pigs' eyes mounted in plasticine.

There was a considerable amount to do. Each evening I spent on the telephone talking to Mary and to mother. Again and again a voice would interrupt, "Doctor White, you are wanted in the obstetric unit, [or] casualty...."

On some of my nights off, fatigue was so vast that I stumbled into bed and slept ten hours. I took every chance I could to see Mary. There was the great desire to belong to each other and not to have a fence around us. Her home and mine limited our time together and our freedom of talking. Occasionally we went bush walking. Entertainments didn't really come into my head. To me it was a delight to read a book or to walk through the bush, identifying birds and their song, searching for their nests, or to watch a cricket or football match. I had learnt to amuse myself for so many years that I did it automatically. Greater understanding would have done much for Mary. She needed it and I didn't have the sensitivity to realise it.

Mother had centred her life round mine and immediately ahead was inevitable separation. I was an only child, but mother had been one of eight, six of whom had passed from the scene, and loneliness loomed ahead for her. She always had wanted me to be a missionary and always rejoiced in the thought of my marriage, yet when these things came closer and the reality of them touched her, their appeal became much less.

Each day added its quota of new experiences and new things learnt and also of laughter. My friend, the assistant superintendent, was an extrovert. There was a quarter of an hour between the time I finished in the operating theatre and the midday meal. I hurried up to my room, opened up my box of oddments and did three tracheotomies on a piece of garden hose. If this operation had to be done it had to be done fast. I knew how to do it really fast on that hose.

The lunch-bell rang. I saw an enormous meat pie, big enought to feed twenty of us, go past my door. My nose quivered at a strange aroma. Surely, I thought, that cannot be coming from a meat pie. Ted Collins walked into the dining room looked inquiringly at the pie, seized a knife and stuck it in deeply, chanting as he did so, "Make a *firm* incision." In surgical fashion he hacked out a slice. The strange aroma became suddenly stronger. He tied a serviette round his face, probed inquiringly in the depths of the dish with a fork and made a loud diagnosis: "Gangrene!"

Picking up the dish he moved solemnly to the upstairs window and hurled it high into the air. It seemed to hover then plunged to land upside down with a strange squelching sound. The contents sprayed in all directions over a neat lawn in front of some astonished visitors.

There was something unique about hospital food.

A few nights later, at 2 a.m. the night sister was shaking my shoulder, "Doctor White, a child has been admitted with laryngeal diphtheria. He needs urgent tracheotomy. Everything is ready. I'll call Doctor Collins." I heard her talking on the phone as I dashed down the stairs.

The villain of the piece is the diphtheria bacillus, which produces a lining to the throat looking something like chamois leather. If this comes across the vocal chords, breathing is impossible and another opening must be made lower down. As I ran I went over the steps that needed to be done and felt thankful that I had practised so thoroughly on the piece of hose pipe. A small boy lay there, blue in the face, deadly ill. I went through the routine – one, two, three. The new opening was made into the trachea and a special tube slipped in place. The small patient was breathing again.

I was washing my hands when heavy footsteps came running down the passage, "Where's young White? He ought to know how to do this by now." Ted Collins was in the room examining the patient and checking the tube. A smile came over his face, "Good boy!" He came close to me. "What's it feel like to have saved a child's life?"

"You taught me," I smiled, "and inspired me with the way you operated on that pie."

Half an hour later the child was comfortable and breathing well.

"Time we celebrated," said Ted. "The nurse in the men's ward makes good coffee; let's go."

We went. Two other R.M.O.s were already there. We listened to the news of the action in that great, quiet building which covered a hive of activity. As we came out of the ward we had to avoid a big rubber-tyred trolley with a handle in front. Ted picked this up, "Did you know you can steer with this thing? You didn't, eh? Well, just watch."

The pathway was asphalt. It sloped to a road which ran in front of a new ward block across whose entrance was a pair of wide, plate-glass doors. To one side of these, lined up like sentinels, were three unusual hydrangeas in large wooden tubs. These were the pride and joy of a sister whom no one dared to irritate.

Ted leapt on the trolley. "Watch me go down there like a rocket and make that corner on two wheels. Here we go!"

And away he went. I looked at those plate-glass windows, at those tubs of blue and pink flowers and watched the ungainly contrivance with its charioteer wildly gripping his clumsy steering device. He was gathering speed – too much speed. He had the choice of careering through the glass or annihilating those solid green tubs. There was an echoing thud. The second-in-command of the hospital medical staff shot into the air and landed in a garden of poppies, closely followed by a wrecked tub containing the largest of the hydrangeas. The trolley, with its front wheels squinting horribly, lay on its side. And all this at three in the morning!

The night sister appeared on the scene. We were helpless with laughter. "What ... Who ...?" she spluttered.

With commendable calm for one so liberally decorated with flowers and loam, Dr. Collins' voice came commandingly, "We are re-enacting an accident, sister, and fear that the milk truck may have disturbed Sister June's floral triumphs."

On May 24th the Hospital Ball was held. Realising that neither Neville nor I was particularly partial to this variety of entertainment we were asked to do duty that evening. We wondered about this, for we were both juniors. The answer came when the superintendent said, "You two fellows have worked very well and I am promoting you to senior positions as from midday on May 24th.

That evening the hospital was full of gaiety, long frocks and black ties. Midway through dinner a motor cyclist arrived with a broken leg. It was 8.30 when he had been dealt with. Then came an ambulance bringing an old man in his late eighties with a surgical emergency. His life was at considerable risk, but the honorary surgeon worked fast and dexterously. He gave concise instructions for post-operative care. At 11.30 another diphtheria case requiring operation arrived. Neville did it. Just after midnight a figure in evening dress stood by my shoulder, "How are you going, Paul?" I gave a brief report. Neville joined us and added his particular news. Again that infectious grin. "No better way of celebrating your seniority. Nothing else will happen tonight." But he was wrong. Before we went to bed at dawn, there had been two more emergencies.

Wages were paid every two weeks at the Royal North Shore Hospital. We queued up to receive our pay. My first envelope contained twenty-two shillings and six pence. I decided that I'd apply the principle of "first fruits" and gave my first week's pay to God and with the second I bought small presents for both Mary and mother. After I became a senior the pay packet became a heavier one. Again I applied the principle of "first fruits" and gave God the difference between what my pay was and what it had become, and after that I set aside regularly ten per cent — a tenth, a tithe or whatever you care to call it — as a routine from all my net income.

It was a full, happy and valuable year. I had gained experience in tuberculosis, diabetes, infectious diseases, casualty work, general surgery and medicine as well as gynaecology and obstetrics. There was also the opportunity to see and be able to deal with both routine and emergency in eye, ear, nose and throat.

Ted Collins took me aside one day. "What about next year? You're doing well. In, say, three years you could probably step into my shoes and study for a higher degree. That would help you to get on the staff here and you'd be on the way up. It's wide open to you. Think about it."

I did more than think about it. I prayed and asked for guidance. It seemed that back here in Australia the door was open to a useful career in medicine. But I had no peace in my mind about the matter. Circumstances are one thing; the advice of wise men must always be listened to, but my final line of guidance has always been to let the peace of God be the umpire in my heart.

A month before I had gone through the routine of applying for mission service to the Church Missionary Society. This is quite a performance. There are forms to fill in; questions on your faith, your motives, your desire to evangelise, your relations with other people. They wished to know all manner of personal details: Were you married, single, engaged, in love, were your parents living, what was their health, and many other things. Mary too had filled in these complicated forms. We posted them in and soon found that we needed to be interviewed by a committee and a variety of clergy, ex-missionaries and doctors.

Let me state clearly that now as a doctor, who has examined missionary candidates for years, I would have turned down Mary, as having suffered from a severe nervous disorder, and myself as an asthmatic.

As it was, the physician accepted me on the ground of

athletic success and queried my twisted right arm as a practical hindrance, while the second doctor, an orthopaedic surgeon, passed my arm but strongly queried my acceptability since I was an asthmatic! I went to see them both and laughed my way out of the dilemma. The "nervous disorder" specialist, with no first hand knowledge of Africa, gave Mary the "all clear."

In hindsight I realised that God's plan for our lives required our years in Africa, and He swept away ordinary routine. This, in my experience, is the exception and seldom the rule.

It was sad to say good-bye to Royal North Shore Hospital. Leaving it with no job to go to seemed folly and I was told so by many. My bank balance was only in double figures but I had found that Proverbs chapter 3 verses 5 and 6 were trustworthy in the matter of knowing what to do. You trusted with all your heart – your emotions: you did not rely on your own understanding; in all your ways – your decisions, your activity, you acknowledged Him: these three things, and the promise is, *He will direct your path.* He did.

I talked to Mary about it all. We prayed about it together, "It's all so vague," she said. "There's no track ahead of us, no way to go, that we can see."

"Faith's like that," I told her. "We're in His hands. It's His timetable."

She understood, and it was a tremedous thing to feel that we could walk together into the unknown trusting with our hearts and our minds. This I believe is what the Christian life is about.

I went home and spent the next morning mowing that lawn and cutting that hedge. There was no further indication of what to do so I followed through my routine and went into Sydney to do some shopping. On my way back to the station I looked across the street and saw a surgical supply shop where I had bought my stethoscope. Its window was decorated with a bleak skeleton, sterilisers and a variety of shining surgical instruments. I felt the urge to cross the road and go into that shop. I stopped in my tracks. This was absurd. I didn't want to buy anything. I was not particularly impressed by the voluble gentlemen who were the proprietors, but none of this even jolted the conviction that I should go in.

"Lord," I prayed, "I don't know what to say, but if this is what you want me to do I'm going in." One step over the threshold and I was greeted with an outstretched hand.

"Doctor, what a pleasant surprise! You're just the man I wanted to see. What about doing a locum job in the back blocks of Queensland?"

Ideas flooded my mind as he told me of a one-doctor town, thirty miles from the nearest medico and sixty from the closest railway. "Pay will be at the rate of ten guineas a week, first class travel to and from — a splendid opportunity. The doctor wants someone who will stay for six weeks." He flipped over some papers. "They have a twenty-bed hospital there, good operating facilities, a portable X-ray and facilities for everyday pathology."

This could test my initiative, I thought. It could give me an indication of how the last year had fitted me for "outback" medicine. This town, St. George, in the west of Queensland was certainly outback. I'd be on my own. I could see how a bush hospital was run, and would pick up much in the way of ideas. I had done some twenty surgical operations, and could use portable X-rays. My experience spread to giving a reasonable anaesthetic and coping with routine pathology. Expenses would be nothing and with my income I would be on the road as far as marriage was concerned.

"When do you want me to go?" I asked.

"As soon as possible," he said. "I'll send a wire now."

He took a railway timetable from the shelf. "There's a train that leaves at ten in the morning."

"I'll go the day after tomorrow."

"Splendid. Give me your phone number. I'll ring you this time tomorrow with details. Thank you, doctor. It was providential your coming in."

I gripped his hand and said quietly, "It was, you know."

He stared at me, but I was already on my way to tell Mary about it. We talked for hours on all manner of things. "I shall write you a letter every day," I promised.

She laughed, "Of course you must! But you'll only get one a week from me. So little happens in my life."

"So little has happened to date," I smiled. "It won't stay that way for long."

There was a railway junction a few miles north of home. Mary came to see me off. I had two suitcases: the larger full of such things as I might be required to wear, the second much smaller but much the same weight, full of books. There was my Bible, medical and surgical handbooks, a book on emergency surgery, and my latest acquisition – one on tropical medicine. There were two large volumes about East Africa. We had half an hour to wait for the train.

It's surprising how much can be said by two excited people as they stroll along a railway station. We talked about what we had been reading in the Bible that morning and what could so easily happen in the next six weeks. The train was due in two minutes. "Mary, my belovèd," I said, "I'm praying specially that we'll find it possible to be married soon."

The engine was coming into sight. I climbed aboard the train and waved till she was out of sight. Turning to my Bible I found the verses that I suggested Mary should read, and cash in on, during those days when we would be apart. King David wrote them in the thirty-seventh Psalm: "Delight yourself also in the Lord and He will give you the desires of your heart. Commit your way to the Lord; trust also in Him and He shall bring it to pass."

I sat quietly in my first-class, reserved compartment. I had never travelled first-class before. I let my mind wander into the back blocks of Queensland and I thought of my preparation for a job like this. If the worst came to the worst an ambulance could take a patient to Brisbane. There were doctors within an hour's drive if it didn't rain. It hadn't rained for thirteen months so why should it now? That year at Royal North Shore had been worth having, particularly in surgery. I had had the advantage of working with Louis Loewenthal, a small man with gentle, competent hands. He was big in kindliness and helpfulness. Under his careful supervision I learned essential points of technique.

I had spent a lot of time mentally operating, going through emergency operations step by step. As I sat there I did a Caesarean section. From my pocket I took some artery forceps, catgut and a tangle of rubber tubing. The night before I had gone over all the stitches required in the sort of abdominal surgery that I could meet. Now I imagined those various tubes as arteries and veins and tied them off, going for a rapid firm tie. From surgery my mind went to obstetrics. I was still mentally coping with complications when the train moved into the suburbs of Newcastle.

I had never before been on an expense account so I dined moderately on a meat pie, mashed potatoes, green peas and an ice cream in a cone washed down by a cup of tepid coffee – all for two shillings. I made a careful note of this outgoing.

That afternoon I read Albert Schweitzer's book *On the Edge of the Primaeval Forest*, and marked this particular quotation:

> It is my experience and that of all Colonial doctors that a single doctor in Africa with the most modest equipment means very much for very many. The good which he can accomplish surpasses a hundredfold what he gives of his own life and the cost of material support which he must have. With appropriate drugs and sufficient skill and apparatus for the most necessary operations he can in a single year free from the power of suffering and death hundreds of men who must otherwise have succumbed to their fate in despair.

From my bag of books came a collection of much-read letters from Africa. Several were from Neville Langford-Smith, describing his everyday activities. These were the details I wanted to know. Another letter, this time from a Tasmanian nurse, Miss May Dobson, made the problems of water supply and lighting very plain.

At dawn I was looking out over miles of plains – dry, brown and dusty. The sheep looked scrawny, the gum trees were red with dust. There had been a considerable drought. It was over a year since worthwhile rain had fallen. The train rattled over a bridge. There barely seemed to be a wrinkle in the landscape. The incredible thing was that after heavy rains this could be a river a mile wide. I saw a flight of white cockatoos and the grey and pink feathers of another cockatoo, the galah. The countryside spread on and on, then we arrived at the end of the line, Mungindi.

The mailman was there to pick me up for the long drive to St. George. I had bought a panama hat, seeing that the temperature often was above 105°F in this part of the world. That hat did little for my public image. The mailman looked me up and down and said, "Strike a light! You're going to be up against it, doc. They'll think you're a schoolboy. Get some tucker into you, and let's go. I've got the feeling its going to rain."

So it appeared had Dr. McDonnell, for whom I was to work. He was waiting patiently for me to arrive, but his car was packed ready to go. He handed me a list of things I should know then said, "What are you like at obstetrics?"

"I've just finished a term of it at Royal North Shore."

"Mmh!" he said, "I'm glad of that. My wife is expecting a baby within a month. Well, I'll be pushing off in a few minutes. The locals think its going to rain, and if it rains you're isolated. This is black soil country. If you're bogged in that, you stay bogged. Don't make any calls into the bush, the ambulance boys will bring them in to you if necessary. If it floods, you're on an island. Well, so long." He said good-bye to his family. I watched his car disappear. I was on my own. Two hours later it rained.

The air was full of the delightful smell of moist earth. Dust turned to mud. The leaves of the gum trees sparkled. The sullen grey earth, looking like a giant jig-saw puzzle, was drinking up water. Cracks that would swallow a tennis ball drank deeply and started to disappear. All night long, heavy rain drummed on the tin roof. By morning the black soil plains, magnificently fertile, were a vast sea of sticky, glue-like mud. The telephone exchange rang me up. "Thought you'd like to know the roads are all up, doc. The river will be flooded by midday. Put the chains on the car and don't get bogged in the main street."

I thought this was a joke but turning off the main street to go to the hospital I side-skidded to a stop, the wheels spinning. The mailman, my friend of the day before, driving in the middle of the road, stopped. "Watch it, doc. You'll dig yourself in that way. Drive out like a crab and I'll slip the chains on for you."

I learnt a manoeuvre then which saved me hours of delay in the black soil plains of East Africa. Wet and muddy, I walked up the steps of the hospital. A spade had been placed conveniently to scrape the mud off shoes. I introduced myself to the matron and was suddenly acutely aware of my youthful appearance. "Doctor," she said, "I am afraid I have a very real problem for you."

She took me to see an extremely small woman in her early twenties whose baby had been due three weeks before. For the last twenty-four hours she had become uncomfortably aware that that baby wanted to come into a wider world. It was clear that there was no possibility of the child being born naturally. The girl's pelvis was so small she would have had considerable trouble to give birth to a canary.

"Matron," I said, as we left the room, "the alternatives are, a Caesarian section or a dead girl and a dead baby."

"Or," added the Matron, "sending her off as fast as we can to Brisbane in an ambulance."

"The telephone exchange says that the roads are up. They would be bogged before they'd gone any distance."

She nodded. "Should we call the doctor from ...?" She mentioned the nearest town.

He said very firmly that the road was completely impassable, and flooding was imminent. We had no choice but to operate. While the patient was being prepared I prayed and turned over to my daily Bible reading. A verse stared up at me: "The Lord shall be thy confidence" (Proverbs 3, verse 26). I marked it: "18.1.36 – first Caesarian section." Then carefully I went over the operation step by step. A very short time later, after having anaesthetised the woman and handed over the ether bottle to the matron, I scrubbed up and was carrying through those steps one by one. It took me an hour but at the conclusion we had a living mother and a living baby.

Two days later when both were doing well, another emergency arrived on the doorstep, "She's an ectopic pregnancy, matron. Will you prepare the theatre just as smartly as you can? She's bleeding internally."

The matron nodded, gave instructions and said quietly to me, "Would you like time to go and read up the operation?"

I thanked her. "This is one of the emergencies I specially prepared for."

While starting the anaesthetic I wondered about the other two pieces of surgery that I had done mentally in the train coming up. Again the operation was done, planned action by planned action. It was dramatic. The moment the haemorrhage was controlled we could see the patient begin to recover.

Twice more that week in that small theatre I came up against critical situations. There was nothing straightforward or predictable about them. I drew diagrams and had the surgery books open at the appropriate pages on a conveniently placed table. As the floods went down travel again became possible. I was very busy, all the time picking up ideas which could fit into the African scene.

And then came a letter adorned with stamps picturing lions and giraffes and Mount Kilimanjaro. It was from the Bishop of Central Tanganyika and said, "Come. We need you. Remember you're going to start from scratch. You will have no equipment, no instruments, no supplies. We have the beginnings of hospitals in seven places. It's a thousand miles from the nearest to the furthest. We have no money to build them up. Bring the supplies with you. Bring the equipment. Bring enough money for new buildings."

I sat looking at this letter for a long time and then told God all about it. The path ahead was beginning to come out of the haze.

There was a knock on the door. An elderly woman stood there. "Doctor, I think you ought to go to the Presbyterian Church. The minister is ill."

I went. At the back of a wooden building with a corrugated iron roof was a small room, furnished with a camp bed, a primus stove, a chair and a bucket of water. In the bed lay a sick, anxious-looking man. I was able to assure him that his cough was bronchitis and not yet pneumonia but to avoid this he needed reasonable food and reasonable accomodation. The temperature outside was 104°F and considerably more inside. The cause of his worry was that there was no one to take the services on the coming Sunday if he was in hospital.

"I'll do it," I said.

He blinked at me, "But, er..."

I smiled, "I've done it before and I'll be doing it again and again in the future." I pulled my African letter from my pocket and said, "Listen, I've received a letter today which could be the first step in my becoming a medical missionary." We talked together and prayed together and as I packed his things and wrapped him in a blanket before taking him off to hospital, he said, "I believe God has sent you up here."

I nodded. "Of course!"

On the Sunday I was to discover that he had crept out of hospital, found his way to his camp bed, and lying in it had

Medical hazard? The top picture shows the road bridge over the Balonne River at St. George, Queensland, and the lower one, shewing the same river in flood, explains why a newly-qualified Dr. White learned to cope with many medical and surgical emergencies which would otherwise not have come his way! The river rose a further five feet after the lower picture was taken

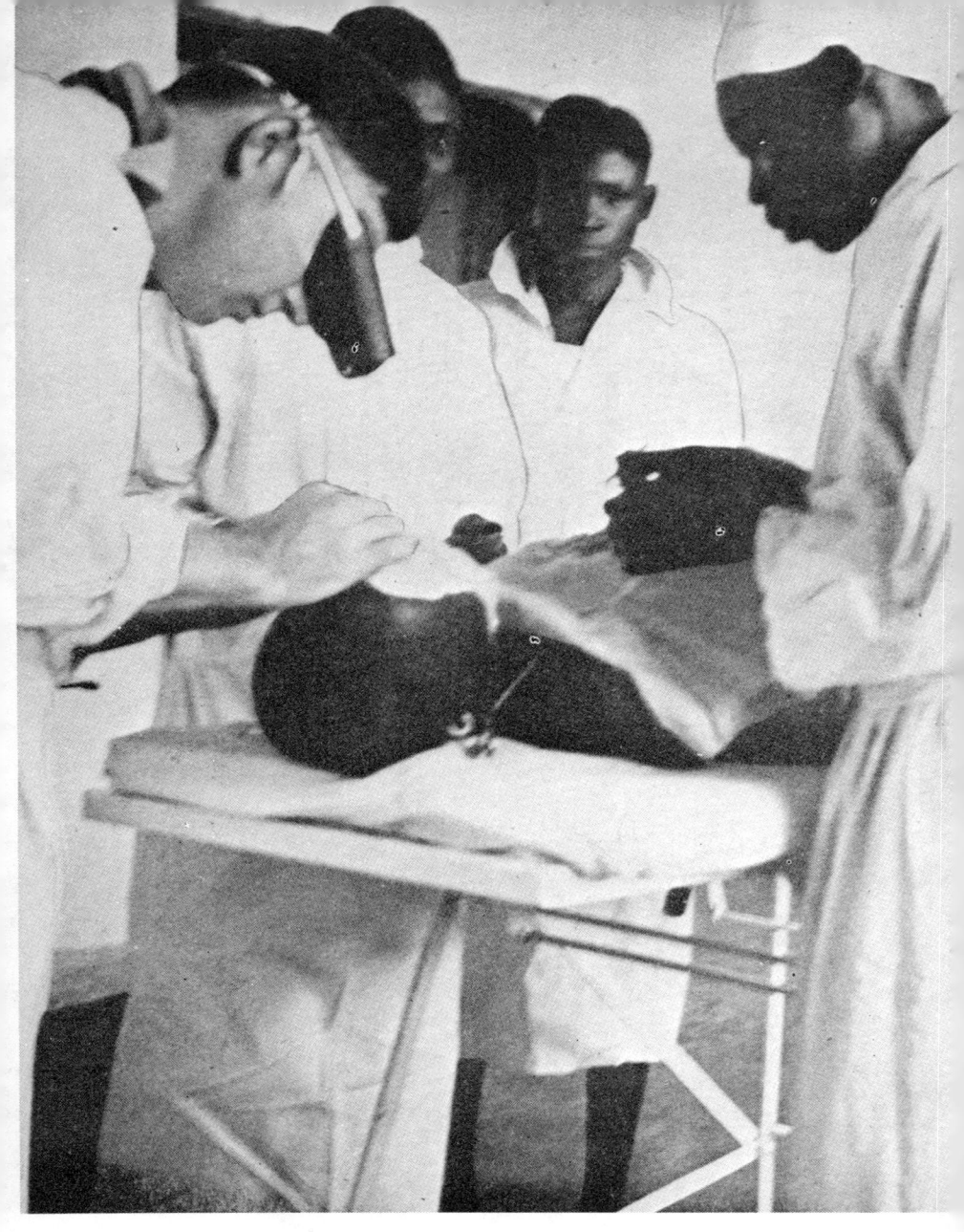

Jungle surgery: operation for cataract in progress, Daudi assisting. "The first Monday afternoon of the month was set aside, obstetrics permitting, for making up my monthly report. 'Two thousand four hundred and sixty-two out-patients seen; thirty cataracts done; twenty eight of them had gone home under their own steam, full of the praises of the hospital. They could see again after years of blindness'."

listened to the service. I spoke in that church most of the Sundays I was in St. George.

There were other adventures in this town including mending the casualties of a beer-bottle fight held in the local pub by three thoroughly inebriated characters. The technique of this sort of warfare is to knock the bottom out of the bottle then grasping it or them by the neck, viciously jabbing the opposition, preferably in the face. Repairs involved a certain amount of complicated needle-work.

There was also an amusing sidelight to a local sports meeting. Some of the young men of the district who went to the local pub for reasons other than surgery were amazed to find that the doctor who preached in church on Sundays was able to show a clean pair of heels to the local athletes in both the half- and quarter-miles. Into my suitcase went a sugar basin and a fruit dish (an artistic horror) which were the first contribution to the glassware of our china cupboard.

My six weeks in Queensland were nearly over. A letter was back from the Tropical Medicine School accepting my application for the six-month course it offered. I was uneasy about it. I had hurried in my application without much thought and with little prayer. It seemed the obvious thing to do. The commonsense thing – a definite step towards Africa. Now it loomed ahead of me. In five days time I would be back at Sydney University.

The doctor returned to St. George in the middle of a heat wave, and some four hours before his wife presented him with a son. I knew he was back because Elsie, the middle-aged lady on the telephone switchboard, rang me up. "He's back, doc. He's up at the hospital checking up on you," she laughed. "What a shock he'll get when he hears about Mr. J's hernia, Mrs.K's ectopic and Marj's Caesarian."

"How do you know all about that?"

"I'm not on the switchboard for nothing. And don't you start carrying on. I've always got you through to the hospital quick and smart whenever they needed you and that's more than an automatic telephone could do. And when you talked to Doctor Scott in French, that didn't bluff me. I've been to high school too. Anyhow, everybody knows everything out here."

Doctor McDonnell arrived as I put down the receiver. He

was delighted to find the cases of beer he'd left under the house undrunk, the car intact, and the books written up. I gave him a list of the thirty operations I had done and outlines of medical treatments given. He presented me with a bonus of ten pounds and I set out for home with seventy pounds in my wallet – more than enough money for a honeymoon.

In the train there was time to think long and carefully. In my loose-leaf notebook was written:

> Ways of keeping corrugated iron roofs cool.
> Address of the firm making a white paint containing asbestos.
> Termites – how to be a step ahead of.
> Primus stoves, Hurricane lanterns and Pressure lamps.

There followed half a page on how to service and repair them.

There were details of primus-heated sterilisers and a list of instruments that I had needed for the operations in the St. George Hospital. There was a note of how two tablespoons could be bent suitably to take the place of expensive retractors.

I made a note of the hints the mailman had given me of how to drive through mud and sand. "Fix yourself up one of these, doc," he had said, opening a stout wooden box which contained a roll of fencing wire. "Great stuff to get you home if you break a spring." There was also a hacked-about cake of soap. "It will plug up a hole in your radiator or your petrol tank – save you a lot of strife." With pride he had produced a gallon tin with a rubber tube running from it. "Fill it up with juice, doc, and strap it on to the roof. Use it as a gravity feed if the fuel lines get blocked or the pump plays up. If you blow a fuse some silver paper wrapped round the old one will get you home." Then there was the usefulness of an old felt hat to filter water out of petrol – an idea which saved me hours of delay.

The train rolled on. Through the window innumerable gum trees were visible in the starlight. There were occasional houses and scattered lights of an outback town. The visit to St. George had been worthwhile. I had picked up a lot of useful information and no little experience but it was clear that I was far from ready to deal with what Africa would require.

Uncertainty thumped at my mind like the bogie beneath me, and I prayed, "If I'm being pig-headed, Lord, please show me very clearly what you want me to do." As I drifted into uncomfortable sleep I realised that all my plans needed to have Mary in them now.

The Tropical Medicine Course started uninspiringly. Tapeworms, round worms, guinea worms – all sorts of worms and their dreary but sinister life-cycles. Sheer memory-work. The corners of my mind and mouth drooped. At the end of a week Mary asked me if I was sick and mother was concerned because I wasn't interested in the choicest culinary morsels that she produced.

I went to see Maurice and told him the whole story. He said, "Tropical medicine is important but this course is specially geared for our near north. The thing that really matters is that you are short of peace of mind."

"Well, I have asked God to put on the brakes, if I'm following what I think, rather than His way."

Maurice was silent for awhile then said, "Jonah landed properly in trouble when he took his own choice of direction."

Two weeks after the course began I went on Sunday afternoon to talk at Barker College, a boys' school some twenty miles north of Sydney. Among those who listened was Norman Powys, later to be one of our Jungle Doctor team. In the middle of the talk I developed a sharp abdominal pain and diagnosed it through my right trouser pocket. Acute appendicitis. By sunset I had lost a hostile appendix and this closed the door, for the moment, to tropical medicine.

Maurice came to see me in hospital. "With Jonah it was a great fish, with you it was more of a worm." He laughed, "I told you it's risky to ask the Lord to thump you if you're going off His path. But listen to this; my uncle, who is a homoeopathic physician, wants to go away for ten days. He wants someone with a degree to be on the spot. There are a few patients who need injections but there is really nothing to it. You'd be paid to convalesce."

And so it proved. I sat in a comfortable home, saw three patients a week and read all manner of books and articles. The ninth day arrived and I had no plans ahead of me. I prayed and turned the pages of the Sydney Morning Herald to "Positions Vacant."

The Ryde District Soldiers' Memorial Hospital required a

senior resident medical officer at a salary of seven guineas a week. "Lord," I prayed, "is *this* the next step?"

Almost at once I was aware that the peace was there. I rang up. They wanted to interview me. "Can you come this afternoon at three?"

At that hour I presented myself. The secretary's name on his door was S. A. D. Storey. I have learnt never to make jokes about people's names or initials. It has always been done painfully often before. The hospital secretary looked at me. In his hand was a scribbling block with my name on the top and a lot of shorthand beneath it. "Are you the Paul White who ran for the university?"

"Yes."

"Do you drink?"

"No."

"When could you start?"

"Monday. I have references."

"Don't worry, I have checked already. I want you to interview the secretary of the Medical Board. He wants to see you at four o'clock. He's very punctual."

At two minutes to four I stood outside a door with a brass plate reading, Doctor W. Kirkwood. I was shown into his drawing room. From a photograph I gathered he was also Colonel Kirkwood. He came into the room and looked every inch a Colonel. "Sit down, White, I'm glad you're on time. What's your experience?"

"A year at Royal North Shore, and six weeks in the back blocks of Queensland."

"Mmh, do you drink?"

"No, sir."

"Do you smoke?"

"No, sir."

"Well what the devil *do* you do?"

I grinned. "I'm planning to go to Africa to do a medical missionary's job, sir."

There was more than a hint of Scotch in his accent, "Dr. Livingstone I presume." And then he laughed and slapped me on the shoulder. "I think you'll be all right. You couldn't be worse than the last two we've had. You realise that you'll be on your own. Wednesday afternoons off and alternate weekends

from midday Saturday to midnight Sunday."
"Yes, sir."
"And I start operating on Monday morning at 7.30 a.m."
"Yes, sir."
And then he relaxed. "I'll be looking forward to working with you, laddie."

On the Sunday I took Mary to church and we talked for a long, long time. She had given me a letter from her brother who was a doctor with a practice in Belmore, one of Sydney's western suburbs. We read it together. He and his wife were planning to go overseas. Would I be his locum for ten months? There was scope for surgery and a considerable amount of obstetrics and general medicine. I turned to Mary, "You realise what this means?"

She nodded, "A wedding in August, a house and a job."

Ryde hospital was six months of worthwhile work. There were happy relations with doctors, nurses, secretaries and patients. There were Bible studies with the nursing staff. Some patients listened to what I had to say about the Lord Jesus Christ and became members of His family. Sunday after Sunday I spoke in churches. I found out about the work of other Australians in Tanganyika and talked about the possibilities that lay ahead. For talks I used the title, "Medical man or medicine man?" Always I made the point that this was a double-barrelled work: to tell men and women about Jesus and what He could do to spiritual disease, while you attacked their physical weaknesses. Mary often came with me. We grew closer together. It was a splendid and productive half-year.

Then came the big day. We were married. A week later, with little in our pockets but big targets in our sights, we started at Belmore. For the first time I was a General Practitioner with a house in the suburbs as the centre of my activity.

"A house to ourselves," laughed Mary, "and only a thousand patients to share it with."

She cooked and answered the door and the phone — a considerable task. I was busy but not nearly as busy as in hospital. At last we had time to be together, to think, to talk, to pray. There was a gap between morning surgery and the calls on patients. We would drink tea and eat our favourite biscuits.

We decided that for a few weeks we would buy some of the

things we had always fancied and never been able to afford, like prawns, asparagus and steak. It was a delightful experience, but before I could suggest that we continue for some time longer Mary said, "We're not going to have this sort of thing in Africa. Let's save all we can here and now. There is one thing I want to discuss with you." We talked long and happily and the conclusion was unanimous that we commence a family as soon as was possible.

More and more news kept coming in from Africa. We talked and laughed and shared. We drew up lists of things we would need to take to Africa. A patient made me two large camphor-wood boxes. We bought a second-hand piano for ten pounds, and carefully perused the "For Sale" columns in the newspaper. We took particular note of auctions.

A letter came from Sister Dobson, one of the courageous women who were running bush hospitals. I copied out one part of the letter word for word. Here it is:

> Having no doctor at Mvumi, all I can do for surgical cases is to try and send them to the Government Hospital at the coast, 480 miles away. They never consent. They'd rather die than have to go so far away.
> It is heart-breaking for one.
> Everything is very primitive at Mvumi Hospital.
> We are away in the bush and have no operating theatre, no electric light, no water laid on. Hurricane lanterns are our only means of lighting at the hospital. Our water is brought in kerosene tins from wells three-quarters of a mile away. Our only instruments are some antiquated forceps and some needles, while all we have to sterilise things in is a fish-kettle.

One morning I came back from rounds and found Mary sitting at my desk carefully consulting a calendar. "It'll be the first week in July and if he's a boy we'll call him David. And if he isn't we'll call her Helen."

Chapter Ten:

The Adventure Begins

AFRICA WAS COMING CLOSER AND CLEARER. THERE WERE A number of letters with Tanganyikan stamps on them. A stout envelope housed a growing collection of snapshots. An overall picture of Mvumi, near Dodoma, Central Tanganyika was being built up. Many of the gaps were most capably filled in by Neville Langford-Smith, who had gone to East Africa directly after graduation. He was my age – a clear-thinking, very observant person with the mind of an administrator. He was back on leave and full of concern for a growing country with a population equal to Australia's.

Neville had produced a well-written pamphlet called "A day in the life of a missionary teacher." I read it with interest. This was the stuff – clear, detailed, telling about people, problems, opportunities. When he came to see us, I fired questions at him about hospitals, water supply, rainfall, food, roads, sanitation and availability of supplies. His answers were immediate and clear but far from reassuring. "You start from the very bottom," he told me. "If you don't take it with you, you won't have it there."

"That means instruments and equipment ?"

He nodded. "That means blankets, hospital hardware, all your medical equipment and most of your drugs. It's important that you think up ideas for lighting an operating theatre." He let this sink in. "Kerosene is the source of power and lighting. Hurricane lanterns, pressure lanterns, primus stoves – big ones, little ones – you can buy them all over there but you need to have the money with you."

Mary and I talked on in bed until the telephone rang calling me to an obstetric case. As I dressed Mary laughed, "I wonder how many times this is going to happen in Africa."

I found it difficult not to yawn the next day. It was hard also to listen to what people had to say about their medical troubles. My mind was busy with information and figures that needed to be put down on paper. That evening we started and drew up the small pamphlet which we called, "Medical Man or Medicine Man?"

After a while I started to walk up and down the room. "Do you remember on the Milson's Point wharf there was an advertising firm's display? They had a little rhyme that stuck in my memory." Mary was knitting. She smiled up at me, "Go on."

"The codfish lays a million eggs,
    The helpful hen lays one.
The codfish never cackles
    To tell what she has done,
And so we scorn the codfish,
    But the helpful hen we prize.
And the moral of this little tale?
    IT PAYS TO ADVERTISE."

Mary put down her knitting, "You're not going to advertise?"

"Oh, yes, I am. I'm going to tell people about this job in a way that they will be able to see and understand. Hen eggs you can see. You know about them. You know what happens when you crack the shell. I'll put a shell round each of one of our needs. See, Neville has given me figures which work out that a bed in the hospital could be supported for a year for six pounds ten. We have thirty beds that we know of for sure."

I wrote, "You may have your own cot or hospital bed in Tanganyika for one year for six pounds ten."

My wife gave me a skein of wool to hold and as she wound it into a ball said, "That sounds good, but didn't Neville say that there were five hundred babies born each year in that hospital?"

"He did. And he said that in the villages, three out of every four babies die before they reach their first birthday."

"Put that in," said Mary. "And what does it cost for a baby to be born in the hospital?"

"Two shillings, and twins half-a-crown."

"Put that in. And what about nappies and baby-clothes and cotton wool. You'll need lots and lots."

The Adventure Begins

I grunted and wrote fast. "And I'll put in the bit about keeping a nurse for a month for a pound. And I reckon it will cost ten shillings to bring back eyesight with a cataract operation."

"Put that down," said Mary.

A few days later the draft was ready for the printer and by the end of the week I had ten thousand of these pamphlets ready to give away. Mary looked at the bill. "I suppose this is like buying a packet of seeds; but it's going to eat a big hole into the housekeeping."

It was two in the morning. We were both sound asleep. The front doorbell rang and rang again. I struggled into a dressing gown, switched on a light and opened the door. There was a weary looking man, "Doc," he said, "what's your charge for a night call to Moorefields Road?" This was a new street in a new part of the suburb, a couple of miles away.

"Twenty-five shillings, at this hour of the night. Is it urgent?"

"I'd say it's very important."

A few minutes later I backed the car out and we drove through silent streets. The weary-looking man was counting out money. He pointed ahead. "That's the place."

I pulled up at the front gate.

"Did you say twenty-five bob?" he asked.

"Yes," I answered, reaching for my medical bag.

He pushed the money into my hand. "Thanks doc. Very decent of you to come out here at this hour. I couldn't find a taxi anywhere." He disappeared into the shadows.

For a moment I was furious. Then I started to laugh. Back at home I crept into bed and a sleepy voice said, "You were quick."

I told her the story. It tickled Mary's sense of humour and just as I was going to sleep again she said, "We'll put that money towards the 'Medical Man or Medicine Man' pamphlets."

These certainly were well received. People's interest was captured as I went to church after church telling about the work and afterwards handing them out. They were put in letters. Some were sent to the hospitals where I had worked. The bulk of the gifts were for ten shillings.

One Sunday the organist at the church, Mr. Livingstone

Mote, pressed a ten pound note into my hand. "I want you to know that I'm behind everything that you plan to do. I only wish I could go with you. Use this to buy instruments."

Following up an advertisement I went to an auction sale and saw a cardboard box full of surgical instruments. I looked through them with eyes that shone, lifting one out and then another. They were exactly what was wanted. My hands started to tremble. A man in a shapeless grey suit came quietly up to me, "Don't show you're interested in 'em mate. They'll cost you more if you do."

"I'm afraid I'm not used to auction sales."

"Offer a quid for 'em."

"But there are hundreds of pounds worth there."

"They're second-hand though. How much have you?"

"Ten pounds."

"Leave this to me, mate, and I'll buy 'em for you."

At last they came up. "Lot two hundred-and-one," said the jocular auctioneer. "Now ladies and gentlemen, here is your opportunity to do your own operations. You'll find everything that you want, except the anaesthetic."

There was a ripple of laughter. My new friend spoke up.

"A quid."

Someone else bid, "Thirty shillings."

The little man shrugged his shoulders, then laughed, "My appendix is worth two quid."

"Any advance on two pounds?" he paused. No one spoke. The hammer fell.

"It's all yours, mate," he smiled. We went together and paid up. He handed me the receipt. I watched the box being wrapped up in brown paper and felt a warm glow spread round the bottom of my ribs.

The telephone rang. "Dr. White, I've read your "Medical Man or Medicine Man" pamphlet. My husband was a doctor. I have a lot of instruments and equipment. Would you care to come and see them. You could have the lot for a nominal sum. We have to put something down as their value."

In an hour I was looking at two sterilisers and a metal box. These contained well-used but entirely efficient surgical instruments which would cover most situations.

"Tell me what you're going to do," said the doctor's widow.

I explained to her. She sighed, "I would have loved to have had a hand in that sort of thing, but it's too late now."

She was quiet for quite a time. I tied up this magnificent collection. "Oh, and there's a foldable operating table in the shed. It's rather dusty but you can have everything for five pounds."

I rang up the organist that evening. "Mr. Mote, we have over six hundred pounds worth of instruments and a portable operating table and I still have three pounds to spend."

There was deep pleasure in his voice. "And I have been asking God to help you and I'll continue to do so."

But we didn't always meet sympathy nor were we always given help. At one of Sydney's so-called high class suburbs I had been asked to speak to a group of people invited to the home of some friends of the Bishop of Central Tanganyika. I told the story of what was being attempted and explained the crudity of conditions and the considerable need. When I had finished a large man with a resonant voice confronted me. "And what are *you* giving to this project?" he asked.

"From the money angle I haven't much but there's my life and all the medicine I know."

He spoke loudly. "How much is your salary?"

"Frankly I don't know. I haven't asked."

He didn't believe me (I later found it was a hundred and fifty pounds a year) and turned on his heel saying over his shoulder, "The truth of the matter is you're only going over there to practise on the Africans." Rarely did anything like this happen but when it did it was hard to take. Literally I saw red but was very thankful to my Lord that He kept my mouth shut.

So much happened that was tremendously encouraging. The news of our African plans spread in Belmore. People dropped in to talk about it. One of them was Fred Murray, a patient who lived only a few doors away. "Doc," he said, "I've some knowhow and there are a lot of people at work who are interested in this sort of thing. Tell me, how do you bring water to your hospital?"

"Kerosene tins, Fred. The nurses carry one on their heads from the wells a mile or so away. That's their first job of the day. Then some water-carriers make twelve journeys a day with two kerosene tins, one on each end of a pole."

He thought about this. "And what about lighting?"

"Kerosene lamps."

"Watch that," he warned, "you don't want to mix an open flame with ether or you'll go through the roof of your operating theatre, patient and all."

"I thought of using a pressure lamp hung on a nail outside the window and an ordinary electric torch adapted to fit on my head like a miner's lamp."

He sniffed, "Rotten light for surgical work."

A month later he was back at my door with a mysterious smile on his face. "Come down to my place, doc."

"Who's sick, Fred?"

"Nobody, I just wanted to show you something."

Firmly mounted on a light, moveable platform was a bicycle frame. "Hop on to her," said Fred Murray, "and pedal. See, you charge this accumulator. A bloke at the shunting yard gave me the frame and the fellow at the garage had this generator amongst his junk. We dug up four head-light reflectors and fitted 'em with these forty watt bulbs. They fit into this frame and would be mounted above your operating table. Pedal steadily and there's your light. The boys would like you to take delivery of her on Saturday night. Will you and your wife come down?"

Mary and I felt considerably warmed and encouraged by their enthusiasm. We met and thanked his friends. I noticed one of them writing industriously. Fred Murray had ideas and he'd invited the local paper to send a reporter. They published the story, which brought unexpected results.

First I received a phone-call from a battery firm. "I read about your jacked-up-bike battery charger," said the voice, "and I was very interested. I'm the manager of Erg Batteries — the unit of power, you know," he chuckled. "What sort of battery are you planning to use?"

"I hadn't thought of that as yet. The one we're using at present is borrowed."

"We'd like to have a hand in your project, doctor. We're going to send you out six heavy-duty Erg batteries," said the brisk voice. "You'll have them by midday. Before you go to Africa, come in to see us. We'd like to keep in touch with you."

The batteries opportunely arrived some half an hour before a reporter and a photographer from one of the evening papers. The next day a two-column article appeared with a large picture headed, "BICYCLE POWER TO LIGHT DARKEST AFRICA HOSPITAL." This was in big, black letters and underneath it, "TRUSTING GOD, SYDNEY DOCTOR TO LEAVE WITH UNIQUE EQUIPMENT." The article went on in normal type,

> A young Sydney surgeon, Dr. Paul White, is giving up his career to work in East Africa. He is taking with him a most ingenious portable lighting plant which is carried like a stretcher. This was built by a railway shunter, Mr. F. J. Murray of Belmore, and consists of an ordinary bicycle without wheels. The bicycle will be ridden to drive a generator which will charge batteries. The operating theatre and any other part of the hospital may have light brought to it by a six volt system of four lights. The cost of running the whole equipment will be about ten shillings a year. Half an hour's pedalling produces ten hours supply. The electrical equipment has been termed, "The Light of Tanganyika."

The morning papers followed this up with an even larger picture. Fox Movietone News was the next to contact us. The whole thing was duly filmed with me demonstrating how it worked. The story went all over Australia and soon letters started coming in. Would I care to pick up another portable operating table?" Gifts came in, ranging from five shillings to fifty pounds.

One morning the telephone rang and a woman's voice said, "We have my father's eye-instruments. They have been valued at three hundred and fifty pounds but we've had no offers. Would you care to make one?" Then in a conspiratorial whisper, "We suggest three pounds ten."

I chuckled, "Madam, may I offer you three pounds ten for your father's eye-instruments? They will be well used."

"Splendid," said the voice. "Will you come and collect them this morning?" I did.

A firm which made stainless steel dishes, bowls, basins, bedpans and other hospital gear, rang me up. "We'd be happy to supply you with whatever you want at cost price. Our products will stand up to phenomenal wear and tear."

I was invited to speak on a Sydney commercial radio station, 2GB. "Why are you going to Africa, doctor?"

"Here in Australia," I answered, "there is one doctor to every thousand people. Over in Tanganyka I will be the only doctor for a quarter of a million people. They have no hospital, no drug supply, no way out except the medicine man and I don't think you'd care to have him treat you."

He smiled, "Isn't East Africa full of risks?"

I grinned, "Well, my wife and I have been immunised against yellow fever and typhoid. We take quinine pills regularly to help us to be one step ahead of malaria. Sleeping sickness is not much of a risk where we'll be working."

He interrupted, "I'd say you're a mug to go over there."

"You're right. I would be if I wasn't working for God. This makes all the difference." I told him about the lighting equipment and the instruments.

"Mmm," he nodded, "and what else?"

"Today I was offered at cost price utensils which will be invaluable in the hospital. I need two hundred pounds' worth."

"Where are you going to find the money?" he asked.

"Well, you see, trusting in God means you ask Him to supply your needs. My wife and I prayed that God would do this and here are you asking me questions and people are listening to us over the air."

The next day he rang me up, "There are a dozen letters in here for you, doc."

I opened them. There were two hundred and eight pounds in those envelopes. He was amazed, "I didn't think this sort of thing happened." He paused. "You're going to have a lot to tell people when you come back from Africa. Now listen. Go down to stations 2GZ and 2KA. They cover the plains beyond the Blue Mountains and the Mountains themselves. The manager says they'd like to interview you."

I went and was immediately put on the women's sessions. "How many babies did you say are born each year in that African hospital?"

"At the moment five hundred, and there is one nurse, no doctor."

"And when you arrive there more people will come?"

"I think so. I certainly hope so."

"And how much does it cost?"

"Two shillings for a baby to be safely born into the world

The Adventure Begins

and looked after for the first week. Then, of course, we have the chance to follow up both mother and infant."

"Where does the money come from?"

"I have the job of interesting people here in Australia so that they will help. The African bush people have practically nothing in the way of money. They find it hard to raise a shilling for a woman's confinement. As I see things I shall be able to give people back their eyesight at a cost of ten shilling a time. And a hospital bed can be supported for a year for six pounds ten."

"And how can we help you, doctor?"

"It would be wonderful if any listener felt like putting in some of the necessary to help us to start the hospital and keep it going."

When we were off the air the announcer laughed, "You're not very good at asking for money. I'm much better at it, I'm going to see what I can do."

Over three hundred pounds came in from those two stations and I had made a contact of the first importance.

The nurses from Ryde hospital prepared bottles and bottles of catgut for surgical use. One nurse invited a number of her friends to help. They prepared dozens of theatre-gowns, caps, masks, and piles of gauze swabs.

There was a man whom I greatly respected in our church, one Ossie Harding. He was an international football referee and an expert at packing. He planned the whole operation. There was not a wasted inch nor any breakable that was not firmly wrapped in blankets, sheets or surgical dressings. He made a drive for old linen. I did not realise till later on how valuable this was going to be.

Mary was very happy. Her knitting needles seemed busy whenever her hands were not doing something else. She was convinced that our child would be a boy and laughingly told people that she felt full of life. Our days in Australia were running short. There were many invitations to speak and it was surprising how many folk came and told me they had asked Jesus to come into their lives when I had spoken at a church, camp, or at the university.

"Why didn't you tell me then?" I asked.

"We never thought of it," came the reply. "But now you're

going overseas we thought you'd like to know."

It was tremendous encouragement. I asked people to pray for us and I knew that many people said they would, but that their memories would let them down. To overcome this I suggested that they should pray for us when they were cleaning their shoes or at least when they were putting them on. I still find that there are many people who remember this and still do it regularly.

One chilly afternoon Mary said, "I think David's up to some new trick."

A few minutes later the suitcase was in the back of the car and we were on our way to hospital. At eleven o'clock that night Ted Collins' voice came through the phone, "You're a father, buster. Mary's all right and the youngster is a tough-looking character like yourself. Go over and see her after breakfast."

I had a very early breakfast.

In three months I spoke a hundred times and then the great day came. I went to see our local minister, The Rev. W. J. Roberts, who was a grand old man. We prayed together. Then we were on the familiar road to Sydney.

At Circular Quay wharf was the P. & O. steamship, Cathay. I looked at her from the height of the bridge. A quarter of an hour later I was looking at the bridge from the deck of the Cathay. Dozens of people had come to see us off. Mary had David in her arms. Mother was travelling with us as far as Hobart. There were handshakes, and farewells, a few tears and an acute touch of sadness. However we knew that behind us was a team who would support us.

A bell rang. Reluctantly our friends went ashore. One by one the ties with home were going. The gangways went down; then there were the scores of multi-coloured streamers. In the background were the sturdy old trams that would travel past my old school, past the university and the hospitals. Over the bridge went the trains to the home where I would never live again. The streamers in our hand broke one by one. As the last snapped the faces on the wharf were hard to see but hands still waved. Then we were out of sight.

This was the first step of our eight-thousand-mile journey to East Africa and a new life. Past us swept gracefully my

The Adventure Begins

favourite Manly Ferry, the Barrenjoey. The P. & O. liner steamed sedately up Sydney Harbour. There was Government House and the battleships, the Zoo and Maurice's home on the foreshores of the harbour. Then the Heads, and Sydney and New South Wales faded into a blue haze as the Cathay nosed the swell of the Pacific. In the hold somewhere beneath us were our piano and the wherewithal to fight the medical battle which lay ahead.

David was asleep. Mary and I prayed that God would hold up our going in His path. We both knew the way would be uphill but we both had our trust very securely in our Lord.

We tasted the joys of the Great Australian Bight — a very rough passage. Our last stopping-place in Australia was in Perth where Wellesley Hannah was a Resident Medical Officer. He and I spent some hours together while I shared with him all that had been done and planned. He had a special interest in the work to which we were going.

Again there were farewells, but not so many streamers this time. We stood by the rail at the stern of the ship, thinking a lot but saying very little. I took from my pocket a list of Swahili verbs and made an attempt to learn one small corner of the common language of East Africa. Little headway was made; the coast had become that familiar blue line which all too soon would slip under the horizon. Mary said quietly to the baby in her arms, "David, that is the last you will see of Australia for at least four years."

Weeks later we sighted in the dawning a faint line, a little more solid than the horizon. It came up rapidly. We were soon looking at palm-fringed beaches, and there was the narrow opening to the bottle-shaped harbour of Dar-es-Salaam, "the haven of peace" if you translate it from the Arabic. We anchored well out from the shore. Barges were coming from the customs-shed.

A young Indian with his hand full of documents came up to me, "Doctor White, I have been instructed to look after you in all matters of your landing, baggage and nineteen crates. Will you please fill in these forms and I shall return. I represent Smith, McKenzie and Company, Shipping Agents."

When at last we left the ship I was aware of a horrid empty feeling. Our last link with home was gone. The heat was oppressive and inside the custom-shed was an indescribable babble of language, the strong odour of sweating humanity, with a faint tang of cloves, the main export of Zanzibar. From outside came the rattle of winches loading and unloading ships, the musical chime of the clock on the red-tiled Lutheran church and the never-ceasing tooting of horns and the ringing of bicycle bells.

My Indian helper was beside me again with his staccato instructions, "I have arranged for Mrs. White and the child to rest in the Supreme Hotel, where you may obtain food. You would be wise to supervise the loading of your goods on to the train. The handling can be somewhat rough and perhaps cause breakages. Railway tickets are in envelope. Train leaves in two days' time at 4 p.m., lorry will arrive at railway station in approximately one hour's time. It is in a direction west, half a mile from here. Hotel is to the east, a similar distance, journey may be made in taxi, fare two shillings. Tip is not more than sixpence."

We drove down Acacia Avenue. The Supreme Hotel was a two-storey, white-washed building that belied its name. I went upstairs with Mary and settled her in a room which had a large, single-bladed fan which turned lazily, stirring the hot humid air. It was obvious that David did not approve of Dar-es-Salaam.

"From the moment you set foot on Africa," the ship's chief engineer had warned me, "do not drink a drop of water which has not been boiled."

I had obtained a supply from the ship to tide us over our railway journey. Mary unpacked what was required and I set out for the railway station. The tree-lined streets were crowded with a medley of people from Asia, Europe and, of course, Africa. In Dar-es-Salaam you sweat. I was no exception. I stopped and looked in shop windows. Certainly a variety of goods were available. I was perhaps a little slow in my journeying and arrived at the station in time to see one of my precious crates dropped to the ground. The two men who had done so roared with laughter and one of them picked up a stone and drove in some nails which had been displaced. I arrived on the scene fast and said, *"Pole, Pole.* Gently, gently."

They replied, *"Ndio, Bwana mkubwa.* Yes, great one," and

The Adventure Begins

proceeded to manhandle the box across some railway lines to a steel railway truck. Everything was marked in English HANDLE WITH CARE. It was about as intelligible to the loading gang as the words of their work-song were to me. Then they picked up the most delicate of the lot, the steriliser. My heart went into my mouth as I saw this box placed on the head of a small but exceedingly cheerful man. I fired my second Swahili barrel, *"Angaliya!* Oh, be careful!"

"Ndio, Bwana mkubwa." They laughed cheerfully, realising that I had come to the end of my vocabulary.

The sun beat down. I dripped perspiration. It took an hour for everything to be pushed safely into that truck of the Tanganyikan Government Railways.

Back at the hotel I found Mary sitting very straight on a wooden chair with David in her arms. "What's up?" I gasped. mopping my forehead.

There was no smile on her face, "Dudus. They told us Africa was the land of the dudu. I'm glad we'll be on our way soon. There are bugs in that bed." Then I told her there was no train for two days.

I went out and bought a bottle of insecticide and a spray. At last we were in the train for the long journey on the metre-gauge, iron-sleepered railway that largely followed Stanley's trail to the Great Lakes.

I sprayed every corner. "That's better," sighed Mary. "It certainly seems that our number one enemy will be insects."

There was a knock at the door. An attendant put wire screens over the windows and said, "Tsetse flies." Then very thoroughly he sprayed the compartment. He smiled, "Mosquitoes, very nasty." Deftly he tucked mosquito-nets round our bunks.

In the late afternoon we climbed the foothills and passed extensive sisal plantations. The granite-studded Uluguru Mountains were deep blue against a brilliant sunset and then, rather suddenly, came darkness. We were only three hundred miles south of the equator.

We stopped at a station. I bought two pineapples for ten East African cents each (the equivalent of one cent each Australian). As I climbed aboard again mosquitoes buzzed around my ears and I thought of Stanley's words regarding the Ugogo plains where our main hospitals were situated.

You will keep in mind it is a remarkable spot for earwigs, and plagues of locusts. Fleas and lice sink into utter insignificance compared with this damnable collection of earwigs.

As far as I knew earwigs carried no disease, but then I thought of the other insects like flies, carrying typhoid, dysentry, gastro-enteritis and polio. Fleas spread plague, lice, typhus and ticks, relapsing fever. The greatest killers of the lot, mosquitoes, had the ability to give malaria, yellow fever, dengue as well as the crippling and deforming elephantiasis.

We finished our pineapples. Mary was tired out and went to sleep quickly. I tucked in the mosquito nets with special care and hunted inside mine with a torch. Then I lay awake listening to the noise of drums and of logs being loaded on the tender of the wood-fuelled locomotive. We moved on again into the darkness. Lulled by the rattle of wheels, I drifted into sleep.

Early next morning I was up to see the plains of Ugogo. I looked at the thorn-bush, the tangled undergrowth, the baobab trees, and was tempted to wake Mary when I saw monkeys scampering through the tree-tops. Then a knock came at the door as the conductor called, "Dodoma in thirty minutes, doctor, thirty minutes."

Hurriedly we dressed. Here we were midway between the Indian Ocean and The Great Lakes. Not far from this spot we would be working, and I would have a chance to use my training of the last nine years.

Chapter Eleven:

Doctor Meets Jungle

"IT'S RUGGED OUT HERE," SAID THE DRIVER OF THE ANCIENT CAR that was taking us out to Mvumi, the centre from which we would work.

We shuddered over corrugations and bounced in and out of potholes on what was then called the Cape to Cairo Road. The driver swung off between two granite boulders, changed into low gear and said, "Dodoma is twenty miles behind us, ten miles to go, and twelve rivers. You bog unless...." He went into details and I thought of the mailman at St. George and what he had taught me.

We clung on. ... "If it rains, stay at home, this is black soil, worse than glue, sink to your axles...." He went on and on.

Mary and I took in the country — the tangle of undergrowth and thorn-bush. Guinea fowl scuttled across a clearing. A small antelope bounded in front of us. Vultures circled high in the air. We passed a village and looked at the gardens of ripening maize and millet, the mud-and-wattle houses with pumpkins on the roof, the humpbacked cattle, and the skinny sheep and goats. The driver's voice broke in, "Over there, up the hill, see? That's your hospital.

From a distance the hospital looked gleaming and white. On the spot it was rather different. The two nurses, May Dobson from Tasmania and Betty Banks from Manchester, took me through a grove of baobab trees to the hospital. At the gate we met Sechelela, the African head nurse and Dan Mbogoni (Daudi of the books), who was to become my chief assistant. The old African woman pointed with her chin and May Dobson translated. "This mud brick building was the place where the maternity work started." Sechelela was laughing and indicating one of the corners. "She's remembering how in 1920, while twins were being born in here, a cobra came out of a hole that used to be there."

We crossed a dusty courtyard and walked underneath an umbrella-shaped thorn bush to the men's ward. There were six beds in this mud-and-wattle building, the lighting coming from small windows. The beds were made from rough-cut timber and the mattresses criss-crossed raw-hide. Beside each bed was an ingenious locker built from an old petrol box. The only luxury in the whole place was the concrete floor. Nearby another mud-brick building with a sloping corrugated iron roof served as the out-patients' department. People came, sometimes walking twenty miles to be examined and given medicine. Bottles were in such short supply that if you wanted medicine you brought your own bottle. There were crowds of people that morning. In careful, slow English Dan said, "They have come to greet you, doctor. We have said 'greetings today, medicine tomorrow.' I have written out for you here the greetings to be said in the morning, in the afternoon, and at sunset."

I thanked him and smiled. "Dan, I shall need your help greatly."

He smiled back. "Together we will work for the Bwana Yesu Cristo and you will help me to understand the ways of medicine." I still feel that Dan is one of my closest friends.

A number of pepper-trees had been planted. We walked along a path between them to the new wards – granite and concrete buildings – each housing twenty beds. Large windows covered with chicken wire and mosquito gauze let in considerable light and ventilation. The water supply was a forty-four gallon drum into which the water carriers poured their brimming kerosene tins. Two water carriers made twelve trips a day, a total of nearly two hundred gallons. This provided about two gallons each for both staff and patients daily.

We visited the food store, its thick mud-brick walls whitewashed inside and out, and the inside jammed tight with bags of millet seed. Two kerosene tins full twice a day and you had fed your hospital staff. I looked enquiringly at three large drums filled to the top with green powder and asked, "What's that?"

They led me to the kitchens – mud-roofed, mud-and-wattle buildings. The whole thing was completely African style. Outside, women pounded the millet in great wooden mortars with heavy wooden pestles. Others separated the husk from the grain by shaking it skilfully in round, flat-bottomed baskets. Flour was produced by grinding the millet between two stones, the larger one beneath, the smaller one above. The coarse flour that resulted was used to make *wugali*, porridge. It was cooked in great clay pots, stirred with a spoon, double-ended like a canoe paddle, and as long as your arm. The stove consisted of three stones with the fire between them. There was no chimney. To me, the smoke inside the hut was blinding. On smaller fires were smaller pots into which was put the green powder which I discovered was made from dried herbs and called *Ilende*. A score of voices urged me, "Taste it, taste it."

"Do what I do," whispered Dan.

The porridge, which was dry and looked like a steamed pudding, was heaped up on a plate. Dan took a lump of this the size of a walnut, squeezed it in his hand and pushed his thumb into the middle. I did likewise. He dipped in into the *Ilende*. I tried to do the same but the stuff came out in long strings like chewing gum. To their great diversion it went all over my face and hair. Such as reached my mouth tasted savoury, if a little gritty. There was strict silence until I laughed. Then everybody laughed. Sechelela smiled at them and said, "He will learn. Give him time."

I turned to the two nurses, "What are we going to do if urgent surgery is required?"

"The only place," answered May Dobson, "is the room where we see the outpatients."

We went to look. My heart sank. Again there was the tin roof and the concrete floor. There was a solid wooden table which did not give you much room for your knees. There were kerosene-box cupboards in each corner. Next door was a room where dressings were done. Sterilisation with primus stoves could be done in there without the risk of ether fumes coming in contact with open flame, but lighting would be a considerable problem. Betty Banks seemed to read my thoughts. "Three electric torches would give a certain amount of light. We could stand people on boxes."

I agreed, but hoped we wouldn't need to. May Dobson informed me, "There is a big room down at your house – we call it the ballroom — where we can put all the crates and unpack them as time permits. That place where you'll be living is quite historic. It was built when Tanganyika was German East Africa. It was a school then. We have fixed up one room for you and lent you some lanterns and things. It takes time to settle in."

I looked down from the hospital and could see three buildings in a line; the first a church, the second had children moving in and out, and from it came the sounds I associated with teaching. This must be the school. The third, it seemed, was to be our home. There was purple bougainvillia growing over one corner, and a venerable baobab tree, now losing its leaves in the early autumn, shaded another.

Later Mary and I went to investigate our new home. The whitewashing of the walls had in places been gouged out by driving rain. The red mud mortar had trickled down in long, sad streaks. The irregular corrugated iron of the roof was in places held down with large stones. In the heat of the early afternoon there were few people about. The windows were merely frames covered with mosquito gauze. We opened the door. It creaked complainingly. The floor was largely made from lime and sand mortar with some of the holes filled by cement. It was gloomy inside and my nose told of the recent extensive use of creosote. From above came the stale smell of bats — one flew through a gap in the white-ant-eaten ceiling.

Mary put her arms round me and her head on my shoulder. I could feel her sobbing. I stroked her hair for a while and said softly, "It's rugged, belovèd, but between us we'll make something of it." We walked into the room that had been prepared. Two locally made beds, rope mattressed, curtained with mosquito net, faced a wide window. Through it was a view of blue mountains, a great grove of baobab trees and a wide sweep of thorn-bush jungle. Directly outside was a clothes-line and a pawpaw-tree. A long line of people were coming single file up a path to the hospital. In front of us our suitcases were on petrol boxes and there was a cot ready to receive David.

We looked through the window silently for quite a time. Mary squeezed my arm. "Let's go and make an inventory." There were two chairs. "All those need are some cushions and then they'll be reasonably comfortable, and there are four

Doctor Meets Jungle

ordinary chairs beside that rather interesting-looking table. See, its legs match the door posts."

They did. They had been rough cut with an axe. "When I polish those they'll look quite something. Whoops! what's this?" Confronting us was a double bed complete with brass knobs. The wire mattress was gashed and gapped. In a quiet voice Mary said, "You'll be able to mend that with some of the wire that's round the packing cases."

I nodded, "They tell me that Elisha, the carpenter, can do useful things with packing cases. I've already thought that the piano case can become a dresser."

Mary stood back and looked at the windows. "I've lots of cretonne. They need a lift. Oh, we'll make it quite attractive."

At that moment an outsize in cockroaches scuttled across the floor.

That night, for me, sleep did not come easily. The thump of drums, the singing of people round their camp fires, the yelping of jackals, donkeys braying, and the sinister howling of hyaenas all produced a strange uncanny atmosphere. I thanked God for our collection of crates and what they contained. It was clear that there was nothing in them which could have been left behind.

Next morning I settled down to the biggest outpatient job of my limited career. There were well over a hundred women and children, all ages and sizes, some neatly dressed, some in utter rags; but all of them wanted to see me and, as they termed it, taste my medicine.

There was real interest as my stethoscope appeared. The pitch of their whispers heightened when they saw a battery lighted device for examining ears and eyes. All conversation had to be carried on by interpretation. The small amount of Swahili that I had learnt was of little value when most of the women and all the children spoke only the local language, Chigogo. Symptoms, whether important or not, were vividly described and dramatised.

There were numbers of deep, stinking ulcers, and skin irritations — sometimes just itchy, but many of the children were heavily infected. There were cuts and wounds and damage done by thorns. I found folk with leprosy. With some the disease was burnt out, with others it was obviously infectious.

One girl, a school teacher, had a disfiguring scar technically termed a keloid. "Doctor," she said in English, "please help me. This thing makes it impossible for me to marry. No one wants a woman for wife who has a *cilema*, a cause for refusal." What could be done so easily in the home countries where there was X-ray therapy and radium could not be dealt with then. Later it was removed and she married one of our male nurses.

There were paralysed children, children and adults with deformity. There were literally dozens of blind people, some mere babies. Dan told me, "It is the medicine of the medicine man." Elderly people with cataracts were led in by their relations. There were malaria cases huddled up in blankets, shivering in the hot sun. Others complained of pains in every area of the body. There were coughs, colds, burns, cuts, bruises and the inquisitive who merely felt they would like to look at me and see what my medicine tasted like.

By midday I felt completely overwhelmed. I had seen enough major surgery to keep me going all day, every day for a week. A considerable group had P.U.O. – pyrexia of unknown origin. I would need to sort out with my microscope which tropical fever was which. There was several hours' work needed to do this. Someone would need to be trained speedily. The lorry had not arrived with the crates so I could not give out medicine. Everybody, however, was remarkably philosophical. They laughed aloud and shook hands when I used the midday greetings.

That afternoon three babies were born. I was impressed with the skill of the girls who had been trained in midwifery. Sechelela came over to me, said a lot in Chigogo, smiled, shrugged her shoulders and then pointed towards the road. I saw a great cloud of dust and realised that our supplies and equipment had almost reached its destination. An enthusiastic group of strong men helped unload the lorry. Dan and Elisha superintended.

Into the large, dark store-room in the middle of my house were put box after box. When the piano in its case was lowered to the ground it became obvious that it would not fit through the door. After considerable talk Elisha brought his tools and took off the door frame. In went the musical instrument and back went the door after creosote had been carefully smeared over every bit of accessible timber.

"Dudus," said Dan. "Bad enemies, dudus."

"How do I say, 'Insects are bad' in Chigogo?"

"*Madudu gali mabi.*"

I said this a number of times. That afternoon we found scorpions and lizards and centipedes. There were thousands of flies and I knew at sundown there would be thousands of mosquitoes; but before the sun set we had every box under cover. With darkness, unloading stopped and lamps were lit. We bathed by pouring tepid water from a jug over us while standing in a zinc tub.

The evening meal was predictable – tough, bantam-size chicken, spinach, rice and sweet potato to be followed by pawpaw. I set to work with the insect spray and told Mary that *Madudu gali mabi.* We prayed together and sleep came, but not for long. The fifth hour of the night, or if you prefer it, 11 p.m. there was a noise outside our window. Dan's voice called, "Bwana, come to the hospital. A child with great sickness requires operation."

It was a horror accident. In the early morning a ten-year-old boy had fallen on a sharp stake. It has torn into him like an axe. For most of the day the medicine-man and others had made ungentle attempts to force the bowel back through the wound. It was now nearly midnight and every hour that passed made his chances of recovery slimmer. Infection and peritonitis were certain. Paralytic ilius (paralysis of the bowel) was almost as great a threat.

My heart sank. We could spare the little chap agonising pain but could do little more. There was no way of giving a blood transfusion and antibiotics had not as yet appeared on the scene.

With a sickening feeling of helplessness I prepared for operation. There was no time to unpack. The outpatients' room was set up. I collected emergency instruments, bent the handles of three tablespoons into retractors and sterilised everything in kerosene tins.

Using electric torches for lighting we set to work. The operation itself was simple and took only a short time. Dan said, "It's wonderful to see the child made better so quickly."

But I shook my head. "I'm afraid he'll die." I walked slowly along the path to our house feeling numb.

At dawn I was called again. A small girl with dysentery had suddenly collapsed and died. The boy on whom we had operated was profoundly shocked. Nothing helped him. He quietly slipped out of life. I listened to the wailing of his relations – an eerie, despairing sound.

Dan spoke quietly, "Bwana, do not have sadness, God will give us help. When they understand, those who now come only when it is hopeless, will come early."

That day it was obvious that many of the people of Mvumi village and those who came in from the countryside were looking at me suspiciously. Before the day was out a baby with convulsions, due to malaria, had also died. Again came the desperate wailing. My heart was heavy.

Mary had had a busy, useful day. The house was quietly becoming more of a home. She had much to show me and to tell me. David was happy. One of the crates had been turned into a temporary play-pen for him. The unpacking was going well. She brought me into the room which had been dark and the walls stained. Our new powerful kerosene pressure lamp hissed cheerfully. Books gave character to a dark wall and there was nothing crude in the appearance of the shelves which were wood from the crates balanced on shapely lumps of granite.

That night, although tired out, I found it hard to sleep. My mind kept drifting wistfully over those six thousand miles to home where it seemed routine to have skilled people with whom to talk over difficulties. Hospitals were expected to be fully equipped with facilities like pathology, X-rays and a dispensary. If a special drug should be required a phone call would see it rushed to the scene.

Here I was alone, painfully aware of my limitations, apprehensive of what lay ahead. No electricity – therefore no X-rays. Even if there had been, there was no money to buy film or developing chemicals. Pathology would be easier. I had brought the microscope that I used in my medical course. Self-pity and fear started gnawing at me. Out of the darkness beside me came Mary's voice softly, "I've just been thinking of those three mothers who lost their children. ..."

I blew my nose. "And I've been feeling lonely and incompetent and tongue-tied. ..."

She lifted the mosquito-net. Her hand touched mine. "We must trust and not be afraid," she said.

I nodded, but nodding in darkness is not much good. I decided that one of the jobs for the next day would be to mend the mattress of the archaic double bed. Drums and singing sounded through the night. The wind made the shutters creak and there was a grating noise from a piece of loose corrugated iron on the roof. "Mary, belovèd," I whispered "you're right. We must just carry on trusting Jesus." But she was already asleep.

Next morning we all met at the hospital and prayed together. Then we went to see the sick. The pathetically small supply of effective drugs made me thankful that I had brought far more than seemed necessary. The problem would be how to make them last.

Two hours later we all sat down round a pot of tea to solve the problem of an emergency operating theatre. The solution was to move the grain store to the far end of the kitchen. It took some time to shift the heavy bags of grain but no time was wasted while this was going on. Outside the windows were repaired with mosquito gauze and strips of canvas nailed in position as impromptu blinds to keep out the abundant red dust. Inside, brooms and scrubbing brushes were busy on the floor and walls, and finally Elisha and his helper patched up the floor with cement. "Tomorrow," I managed to say in stumbling Chigogo, "we will finish the unpacking."

It was a day full of excitement. Dan and his assistant Samson, suitably so named, carried off the steam steriliser in triumph. The collapsible theatre table went to the hospital carried on a nurse's head. My heart was in my mouth when I saw a glass jar of catgut following in a similar style. Boxes containing dressings and medicine were placed on their side and one upon the other in the "ballroom." By the end of the first week we were reasonably unpacked and ready.

I became acutely aware of the differences from home. There were many things I had taken for granted in Australia, like the morning paper, the radio, clocks, a butcher's shop, a bank, the postman and being able to talk to practically everyone I met. In Mvumi, the "Tanganyika Standard," with the news, arrived weekly. The mail-bag came twice a week, carried over paths that were also used by lion, rhino and other interesting creatures. When the mail-man came singing up the hill there was a high degree of excitement. Letters were important. The disappointment of a mail-bag without letters was acute. The joy a letter gave was a new experience, and how my eyes gleamed when enclosed were clippings from the newspaper: cricket news, and the everyday matters in which I was interested.

Time was told by the sun. The equator was a mere three hundred miles north so sunrise was 6 a.m. and sunset, 6 p.m. Seven in the morning was *saa moja*, the first hour of the day. Midday is the sixth hour. They did this, of course, in Bible times. I soon fell into the new way and adjusted my watch accordingly.

Money was different – shillings and cents. Cheques could be cashed at the Indians' shops but we were still three hundred miles from a bank. There was no butcher or baker although if a cow looked as though it might not survive there would be meat in the village. It was surprising how fast we adjusted to the new life.

Immediately ahead of us, weatherwise, were eight months of complete dryness. We worked busily to make the most of this, and sank twelve-foot-deep water tanks the size of a home swimming-pool ready to harvest every drop we could. An operating theatre of local granite, cement and corrugated iron was erected for a hundred and twenty pounds. Into it went the bicycle battery charger, "The Light of Tanganyika." It worked excellently. On a shelf was an anaesthetic machine, contrived from a pickle bottle, the foot pump of the car, a football bladder, the Y-shaped portion of a stethoscope, an eye-dropper glass and some yards of rubber tubing. It was a highly successful device.

Our medical care was proving acceptable. My working knowledge of the Gogo language was a great help. Among our patients were even some medicine-men who tried hard to be anonymous. One who had had hiccoughs persistently for two weeks was amazed to have them stoped in half an hour. Another who had what he called "an enemy" in his jaw, rolled his eyes with astonishment when the offending molar was removed with relatively small pain.

A woman had an umbilical hernia the size of a pumpkin. This she carried in a bag hung round her neck. She was delighted at its removal and informed me that I was one of the truly great for she had entered life with one navel but after my repair behold now she had two! Her approval would have been termed inexpert sewing by my surgical tutors. Another satisfied patient was a woman with a vast ovarian tumour. When it came to operation we found ourselves in need of a second operating table — one for the patient and one for the tumour.

Great praise came our way for removing a tick from the ear of a chief's son. A sophisticated pair of forceps did a very different job from a three-inch thorn favoured by the opposition. Our reputation for giving back sight through cataract operations spread far and wide.

There was wild and extraordinary obstetrics mixed in with a considerable number of satisfactory, ordinary births. The African women were strong and muscular. Anyone who can carry a kerosene tin full of water on their head for a mile or more has magnificent posture. The muscles used in pounding grain and grinding it fitted them exceptionally well for motherhood.

There were drawbacks, however, in our success. It was an amiable but somewhat alarming circle. The more sick people we helped, the more came in and the more medicines were swallowed and injected. This in turn brought a number of others clamouring for help and supplies grew visibly shorter.

In October great cotton-wool-like clouds appeared, with the rumble of thunder. The baobab trees came into leaf and looked like huge oaks. With November came more clouds and storms with torrential rain. In a matter of minutes a wide, sandy river-bed could become a red torrent. The brown and arid tangle of thornbush and undergrowth would suddenly become green. Grass would grow within forty-eight hours and morning-glory would climb exuberantly and blossom in pastel shades. The countryside was quilted with colour. I was exulting in the smell of moist earth, and the news that our new cement underground tanks were three parts full, when the countryside shuddered with an earthquake. Mvumi was within a hundred kilometres of the Great Rift Wall. There was no damage to life, but great cracks appeared in our two biggest tanks. We watched three months' water supply disappear in less than an hour.

In the isolation of the savanna country of East Africa the encouragements were easy to take but the reverses were particularly heavy.

The months of the dry season had been times for preparation – hard, hot, tiring days. Grinding away at the language; building – and I was no expert – training the willing and the dull, the literate and the almost illiterate, planning for the next ten years, setting a routine, budgeting both money and medicines.

With the coming of the rains I hoped for better things. But in the wake of the earthquake came myriads of mosquitoes. People shivered with malaria, and we battled for the lives of the very young.

Frustrations were legion. Sick people were brought in desperately ill when both medicine-man and witch-doctor had been unable to help.

Hospital work and nursing were entirely foreign to many of our helpers. It was not part of their tribal thinking to look after anyone who was not a member of their family.

Time didn't really count. There was one oft-repeated word that to me was unspeakably irritating, "*bado*," which means, "not yet," and conveyed a feeling of complete non-urgency.

It was hard for some of the trainees and many of the patients and their relations to understand the way of hospital routine. It was equally hard for me to understand the African approach to many things. I could wound and damage and set back the task so easily without even realising I was doing it.

The wheelbarrow had for me a special usefulness. Asthma hit me hard and to carry on the routine I was transported from home to hospital and vice versa in this handy but uncomfortable vehicle.

Then there was the proper routine of missionary organisation, which I needed to understand and comply with, and the unpredictable matters that came mainly through the mailbag:

> Please supply a complete record of your building costs by the end of the month.

I was and am a ponderous and inaccurate book-balancer.

A Government form which read:

> Please supply in full detail the numbers of cases of the following diseases seen in your hospital during the month of. ... Differentiate between inpatients and outpatients.

There were four pages to be filled-in – foolscap pages in small print.

A small, typewritten note which said:
> Your first language examination must be completed before the end of June.

From the bishop:
> I would like to visit with you the hospitals of the Central and Eastern province during the week commencing....

Another official document reading:
> It is requested that you visit the Director of Medical Services in Dar-es-Salaam in two months' time.

Then an envelope with an Australian stamp:
> Please send me as soon as possible at least six stories of your work, not more than five hundred words (doubled spaced, one side of the paper only). Also good clear photographs.

Many of the most useful things we did could not go into stories. They involved gruesome obstetrics and often photographs were completely out of the question. One scorching day an unhappy old man with a scrotal swelling larger than a football arrived. He shyly exhibited his trouble. There was a wistfulness about his approach. The removal of some half a bucket of fluid was not a complex surgical job. In some twenty minutes under a local anaesthetic his distressing disability was relieved and cured. He seemed dazed but the next morning this changed to jubilation. He shook my hand. "A work of great wisdom, Bwana. There are many others with this thing."

Within a week twenty more such cases, some unbelievably large, presented themselves. Some travelled by night because of the difficulty and embarrassment of walking the paths through the thorn bush.

Many lives were saved through obstetric work. This was greatly rewarding but took considerable time and energy. Hours sliced out of nights could not be made up during the day. Fatigue welled up and shortened my temper. There was the constant need to pray the prayer, "Lord, please help me not to speak out of turn."

Mary and David were able to do much in gaining the friendship of the women and our ancient home had a warmth and cosiness about it which was wonderful when there was opportunity to take advantage of it. Then Mary informed me, "We must start thinking out a name for David's sister. She should arrive some time in the next dry season."

This piece of joy was partly overshadowed by a plague of cockroaches which crunched uncomfortably under foot. These whiskered nimble dudus found their way into the most unusual spots.

A small willy-willy, to use the Australian term for a whirlwind, was interesting because it would stagger like a snake balancing on its tail across the dry plains. The interest disappeared when they were big. One as big around as a circus tent made its crazy way up the hill past our home, hesitated then seemed to rush at the new buildings. A woman with a baby on her back was hurled to the ground. Stones, cornstalks, limbs from the baobab trees, kerosene tins, timber and the hospital washing swirled up into the air. Then, with a screech, iron was wrenched from buildings. Sheets of it soared upward like leaves. One sheet knifed deep into the ground perilously close to an unroofed ward. The damage was considerable but we succeeded in putting the roof back in place before the rains came again. The maize and millet gardens were a gentle green. The crops were excellent. Rain poured off our roofs and proved the soundness of the repairs to our water tanks.

A cheap and acceptable method of coping with malaria was devised, and some ideas to combat soil erosion worked out well. The rain ceased, green faded into brown, the sun beat down and the harvest was excellent. My grip of the Gogo language was improving. I read my New Testament and this verse stood out, "Do not lose heart nor grow weary in well doing for at the right time will come the harvest if you don't become dismayed and give up."

We did not give up. That dry season brought an epidemic of meningitis which we fought successfully with the new sulphonamides, the first of the antibiotics. Never had the hospital been so full. I could think in the Gogo language and at last could take opportunities of explaining God's way to the people I treated.

At home Mary's pregnancy moved on quietly, but in my mind was the lurking consciousness that mental unbalance could show up at any time. Month by month went by, the village women and the hospital staff were delighted. Small gifts of eggs and fruit and skinny chickens were brought. Mary could speak Gogo well and David chatted with childish fluency with the women who visited and congratulated Mary on the "excellent dinner she had eaten."

To my great relief nothing untoward occurred. The mission authorities insisted that the confinement be in Dodoma, some twenty miles away as the crows fly and that the Government Medical Officer be involved. At the last moment he was unavailable and Rosemary Helen arrived at 2 a.m. The expectant and delighted father was also obstetrician. In the cool of the afternoon we looked at our new daughter. "She is beautiful," I breathed.

Mary took my hand. "We asked God for her and that all might be well." The window was shaded by a spreading mango tree. Beyond it was a small hill, grey with granite boulders and ornamented here and there with tall cactus plants. The sun was setting and the sky golden. We were sharing a joy around which it was more than difficult to weave words. Quietly we talked to God together about the baby and our own lives and future. We both realised that our great wish was to be available to God, when, where and how He wished. The clouds behind the hills were deep red. The baby started to whimper. I put down the mosquito nets and placed Rosemary into Mary's arms. Her well-loved voice said happily, "She knows exactly what to do and doesn't hesitate to do it." Life seemed very wonderful.

A voice came from outside. It was the Bishop of Central Tanganyika. "Paul, I think you ought to know that the news has just come through on the radio that Britain is at war."

Chapter Twelve:

Doctor with Pen

A BROKEN FINGER AND AN UNCOMFORTABLY-PLACED BOIL WERE important bridgeheads in the sequence of events that started me writing books.

As far as the broken finger was concerned it belonged to Geoff Young, who is a Flying Doctor and an expert pilot and driver. However, an English country lane was too much for his skill when he had only two wheels under him and no wings to lift him up. His motor-cycle was forced off the road and he landed heavily in a ditch. Geoffrey picked himself up, inspected the damage and found the last joint of his little finger was wrecked. The insurance company paid up and he sent one hundred pounds to me in Africa.

It arrived strategically, within a week of Mary's coming back from the very gates of death.

"Let's make a safari and really see something of Tanganyika," I suggested.

A month later, and three months before we left East Africa for home, we set out for Lake Tanganyika and Lake Victoria Nyanza.

The story of our safari is in *Doctor of Tanganyika*; but that book and the others that followed would probably never have come into being but for Geoff's accident and generous gift.

The Tanganyika express which hurtled along at some sixteen miles an hour gave me time to write and describe what I saw, felt, smelt and heard. There was even more to record as we moved through the west of Tanganyika in ramshackle buses and lorries and while relaxing on the comfortable lake steamer. There was a chance to think and talk. People listened to stories of how a medical missionary's life works out. They laughed at the funny bits and from time to time there was that hush which tells that listeners are gripped by the story.

At night as Mary slept I wrote down the happenings of the day. There was the smell of the pounded earth floor and the kerosene pungency of the hurricane lamp. Sounds came through the mosquito-wire-covered windows: the howls of hyaenas, drums, rhythmical African singing. It was so easy to capture atmosphere when you wrote it at the time. Once when we were bogged I sat in the mud on a stone with a mosquito obbligato in the background and wrote pages by the miserable glimmer of the tail-light. There was no idea in my mind then of any such thing as a book or a broadcast script but I felt impelled to put pen to paper.

When you ask God to take charge of your life you often do things like this without spending hours in prayer or seeking for motives or targets. There is no weighing up of talents or bemoaning the lack of them. You just push on with the job. I wrote and wrote, sometimes in my notebook, sometimes jotting things down on odd bits of paper. I read some of these outpourings to Mary. She laughed and encouraged me.

One night we were sleeping in the odd little tower-room of the church in Bukoba, very close to the bank of Lake Victoria. Apart from being the source of the Nile, this lake is also larger than the island of Tasmania. Mosquitoes were having choir practice, and hippos stomped round the place making loud cow-like noises. The lesser woodwinds were represented by frogs and crickets. I wrote pages by moonlight that night.

The considerable jottings of that safari filled two notebooks and a big envelope full of scribblings in pencil. This joined other big envelopes filled with stories, descriptions, ideas and word-pictures.

That was the "broken finger" phase of my book writing.

And now for the boil.

This made its uncomfortable presence felt in Ceylon. It was wartime. Mary, the children and I had covered the first leg of the journey home. We sailed from Mombasa across the Indian Ocean. It had been a safari without incident but we were prepared for any wartime emergency. It was good to sight land and find oursleves in Colombo. We were met with the news that our stay in that hot, humid spot could be considerable. There was no available information as to when the next ship for Australia would arrive. We stayed in a guest-house close to the beach with its fringe of palm trees. Between us and them was the main road, the happy hunting-ground of an amazing variety of vehicles, each enthusiastic with its horn – electrical or mechanical, modern or antique. It was true cacophony.

Here the boil was quick to assert itself from its lair immediately beneath my hip pocket. I limped to the market, bought a cheap and elderly chair, sawed a hole in it and seated myself with considerable care. On the table of our rather small room was a plump writing pad, while all over the bed were my envelopes full of notes, now joined by a box filled with mediocre photos which were excellent food for the memory. I was brimming over with human interest stories – stories different from the ordinary run. Many were frankly unusual, some almost unbelievable but fortunately backed up by photographs. I sat carefully poised and wrote with my mind throbbing with words at one end of me and the boil throbbing at the other. Before that boil had healed I had finished a pile of manuscript – thousands upon thousands of words.

Six weeks had gone by. It was late at night. Mary was asleep. For hours, book bubbled out of me and then abruptly I had run dry. Stiffly I stood up, tip-toed on to the verandah and crossed the road to stand looking out over the dark sea. The air was tropically soft and warm and heavy with the scent of frangipanni. I sat down carefully on the sand.

It was a night like this nearly a year before that Mary had started to talk and act strangely. It was painfully obvious to me that she was again acutely mentally ill. The bottom seemed to fall out of life. I felt numb. This was the end of our work in Africa. The small corner of the great continent where we lived and worked had become very important to us. We were getting to know the people and could chatter away happily and crack jokes in the Gogo language. We had learned both to eat, and how to eat, African food and sing African songs. There were scores of people who were our friends. Hundreds had been helped. Some could see after years of blindness. Tumours had been removed, epidemics successfully fought and smallpox prevented by wide-scale vaccination. Some people, grotesque with leprosy, were able to live normally again. Tropical diseases had been hurled back while pneumonia and meningitis had lost their teeth with the arrival of the antibiotics. Would God allow things to happen this way and then let the job grind to a stop?

Then I thought of the children. If Mary's illness progressed in the way the book said it would, a great hole would be torn in our home. David was four and Rosemary a two-year-old.

Sitting there in the darkness on that tropical beach the crushing hopelessness of that hour became starkly real. I watched the vague pallor of the breaking waves.

There had been the successive hopes and despairs as treatment after treatment had been tried and proved useless. As days dragged by, the wife I loved lost her grip of sanity and life itself. Many people had much to say. Some came with advice, others to shake their heads sadly and mumble platitutdes. One most sincere soul advised me to confess my sins and God would heal Mary.

"Have you asked God to make her better?" asked another. I nodded. I had asked Him again and again to do so in His own way and in His own timing; but it was all bitterly hard to talk about.

The medical job had not let up. "Bwana, a woman has just come in. She has been in labour for two days. Can you come at once?"

"Bwana, the old man who has been blind for ten harvests is ready to have his eyes operated upon. Will you come in half an hour?"

All day long and half the night there were voices at the door.

Pictures and conversations flashed through my mind. A small boy touching me on the arm, "Daddy, I'm hungry." His needs are met. He sits on my knee and asks, "Will Mummy be better soon?" My daughter, still a toddler, smiles at me, trips and tumbles. She needs to be comforted, very specially comforted.

An epidemic threatens. The African staff cannot cope. The English nurse has malaria. Our annual drug supply is torpedoed. There is the deep stress of war news, of insufficient supplies, of uncertainty. Time drags on.

There is a consultation with a Senior Government Doctor who says quietly, "You can't look after your wife properly here. I strongly urge you to put her into hospital." I knew that hospital, with its bolted doors and its barred windows. There was the necessity for a certification of insanity. Making an effort to control my voice, I asked, "What is the prognosis?"

In what I knew to be his best bedside manner he replied, "Who knows?" And seeing me look up at my shelf full of medical books he said rather hastily, "Don't look at those psychiatric text books. They won't help you. But cheer up, old man, something may turn up."

When I saw his safari-model car drive away through the thorn-bush I knelt down beside my bed. There were no words to shape my prayer, but through my mind came what Jesus had once said to Peter when He had washed his feet, "What I do you do not know now but you will later on."

A wave moved further up the beach, breaking close. I scrambled to my feet. There was a movement behind the palm trees. Through a small break in the leaden clouds was the vague outline of a large ship, completely blacked out, moving up the harbour. I strolled along the wet sand trying to catch a further glimpse of what was going on, but could see nothing.

Walking slowly back I thought about the stretch of Indian Ocean that lay between me and Africa. In those waters less than a year before a raider had sunk two of three merchant ships of the same shipping line. In the third was my friend, Dr. Wellesley Hannah. If he had been lost at sea how utterly different the present picture would have been. His arrival in Tanganyika had made all the difference.

Mary had been desperately ill for eight months and been given only weeks to live. Then Wellesley had arrived with information regarding Insulin Shock Therapy for Manic Depressive Psychosis. With only a medical journal article to guide us we had given this radical treatment. It had seemed a pious hope that it would produce improvement, but after an agonising morning Mary had amazingly improved only to slip back after twelve hours of clarity of mind. Further treatment, which required courage even to attempt, worked dramatically and now complete normality was back. We knew that we faced a recurring problem and that the door on Africa was closed as far as we were concerned.

I climbed up from the beach, dodged the palm trees, crossed

Doctor with Pen

the road and before I slipped into bed set the alarm clock for dawn.

At sunrise next morning we were intrigued to see the four-funnelled trans-Atlantic liner, Aquitania, at anchor. That evening after sunset she slipped out of harbour again, but with us on board.

Again I put my head down and, submarines or no submarines, I went on writing, and when at long last Sydney Heads came into sight I had written fifty-thousand words and finished the draft of *Doctor of Tanganyika*.

There is a great gulf fixed between the publisher and the author, hopefully clutching his manuscript (which must always be double-spaced, one side of paper only and wide margin, please!).

An Australian bookman looked at me, glanced over my hand-written bundle and said patiently, "I'm sure it is very interesting, doctor, but it's wartime you know. We're very busy. There are all kinds of shortages...." He shrugged and opened the door.

I had interviewed my first publisher.

I walked out rather sadly into one of Sydney's busy streets and came face to face with Archdeacon R. B. S. Hammond, one of the great men of our country and generation. He stopped me, "Why don't you publish your story, Paul? I read your letters from Africa and they were fascinating."

I grinned and held up the manuscript, "Here it is, but so far no one is interested, not even a little."

"Ring B 3875 and ask for Captain Dash." He smiled, gripped my hand and was gone.

B 3875 proved to be the phone number of the Red Cross. George McDonald Dash took the manuscript home and read it in one night. Next day he asked me to go and see him.

He had two telephones on his desk and was talking into one of them when I arrived. He put down the receiver and shook my hand, but before he could speak the other phone rang. A voice crackled distantly. George lifted one eyebrow and said, "It's the printer." His answers were short and crisp and finished off with, "We'll go ahead, thank you very much." He rang off, leant across the desk and said, "We'll publish this book, you and I. It's wartime. Paper is more than hard to obtain, but

I want to see *Doctor of Tanganyika* in print fast. Have you any money to help me float it?"

"I've a hundred-and-ten pounds in the bank, Captain. When I left Tanganyika I was receiving a hundred-and-sixty-five pounds a year. It was enough to live on – just – but it wasn't easy to save much."

He thought for a minute. "Will you put in a hundred pounds?"

I did, and two months later, after all the excitement of galley proofs, paste-ups, page proofs and dummies, out came a modest paper-covered book on newsprint, price two shillings. There was a giraffe on the cover and some of my more dramatic photos printed on art paper were bound in.

There were two thousand of that first edition. Archdeacon Hammond wrote the foreword, a famous ex-Prime-Minister, Billy Hughes, wrote fulsomely, and the *Sydney Sun* was more than kind in its review. Amongst the people in my immediate circle there were those that liked it and said so. I was given the creeps by those who said, "It was quite nice." There were those that sniffed. One gentleman asked, "Couldn't you do better than newsprint?"

I thought of my hundred pounds and smiled, "Would you care to help me with the next edition?"

He did not – nor did anyone else.

To pay the printer looked like a real problem. However this was solved before it ever existed, for that second imprint was sold out and largely paid for in two weeks. George Dash was delighted.

By now I was getting feed-back. More detail was required, more instances of how the Christian message was brought home to people. I set to work, and twenty-five thousand more words were added. The seventh edition, enlarged and cloth bound, came out within two years of my sawing that hole in that chair in Colombo.

Amongst those who read *Doctor of Tanganyika* was a country broadcasting executive. His reading and subsequent talks led to an Australia-wide broadcast which meant considerable and continuous writing of radio scripts.

It has been my custom never to waste anything. I am a prize hoarder! The scripts were put in a heap on my table. One day

Doctor with Pen

on the bus I was writing notes on the back of one of these when the thought hit me that here was material for another book.

The thirteen-minute broadcast had to be written so that, "Another thrilling episode will be heard from this same station the same time next week." When I was not writing radio scripts, every spare minute during the next two months went into rewriting, polishing and shaping those stories into the everyday activity of a jungle doctor. I tried to give the reader a full opportunity of looking over my shoulder into our East African hospital.

One evening in a small Greek cafe which George Dash patronised we had a chop and some chips and I produced my manuscript. George was delighted and said, "I'm not a bit surprised, you know. I've been waiting for this to happen for quite a time. You'll finish up by writing a dozen at least and I like the title, 'Jungle Doctor.' Those two words have grip."

I chuckled. "I thought of them under the shower. There's that chap who writes the 'Diary of the Doctor who Tells.' So, I thought, why shouldn't we have the 'Diary of the Jungle Doctor who Tells?' That became the 'Diary of the Jungle Doctor' and then, 'Jungle Doctor'."

George nodded. "We want action. I'll have the manuscript back in your hands tomorrow." It was – this time with two pages of suggestions.

In due course out came *Jungle Doctor* and it was well received.

A new bunch of scripts was put into a folder and I worked on *Jungle Doctor on Safari*. Each week I found myself writing four thousand words and talking at least ten times.

George had found me a second-hand dictaphone and a suitcase full of wax discs. I was able to dictate and listen to what would shortly find its way on to paper. This provided a chance to correct and revise.

When speaking from platforms or pulpits it was possible to see how people reacted. If a particularly good word or phrase came to light I wrote it down at the earliest possible moment. It's so easy to forget and so frustrating to do so.

Slowly I realised the musts for a writer in search of readers: hook 'em, hold 'em, hang on to 'em, humour 'em and hit 'em! This last is known as the punch-line. To make a scene come alive, the eyes, the ears, the nose and the skin all need to be involved and, where possible, the reactions recorded.

I felt impelled to write. Listening back to broadcasts and to the dictaphone made me realise that some of my work had rhythm to it, other parts were lumpy. This slowed me down and made me far more selective about words.

Jungle Doctor on Safari came out. *Jungle Doctor Operates* was corrected and re-corrected, and a file was filling with material and photographs for *Jungle Doctor Attacks Witchcraft*. Then I had ideas for *Jungle Doctor's Enemies* and *Jungle Doctor Meets a Lion*.

The broadcasts were going well on thirty-five radio stations from Perth to Sydney and from Townsville to Hobart. What people listen to they often like to see in print. This fact, coupled with the circumstances of wartime and a dearth of new books, meant that the series sold phenomenally. When I travelled interstate or into a country town where Jungle Doctor was on the air, crowds of people turned out to listen in churches and halls.

This sometimes had unusual results.

Melbourne Town Hall was packed with three thousand people. There were a number of notable people on the platform and myself, the speaker. The chairman turned to us, "We are now going to show a film. Would you care to sit in the reserved seats in the front row?"

The lights went out. We walked carefully down the stairs in the gloom. I was the last and looked easily the least imposing. A boy with open autograph book in his hand approached me and whispered, in good round Australian, "I say, mister, which one of 'em is the Jungle Doctor. Do you know?"

I drew in my stomach, smiled and said, "Well, as a matter of fact, I am."

He looked me up and he looked me down. Slowly he closed the autograph book, sighed, put it into his pocket, and as he moved off into the darkness of the Town Hall his voice came clearly, "Aw, gee!"

What he expected I do not quite know; but at the very least it must have been a tall, lithe figure in a leopard-skin.

Jungle Doctor Operates and *Jungle Doctor Attacks Witchcraft* had both sold like hot cakes. *Jungle Doctor's*

Doctor with Pen

Enemies was with the printer. The jacket, I thought, was a beauty, being a close-up picture of a very hostile witch-doctor. It was the real thing.

Elated with the way things were going I finished *Jungle Doctor Meets a Lion* and asked myself the question, "Why only produce Jungle Doctor books in Australia?"

George Dash was now the Australian Potato Controller. He was at his desk early and late and he never took a holiday. He did not ever seem to rest. Always busy, he was never too busy to help me. When I suggested that we should try to expand overseas he smiled and nodded, "See what you can do. You have the contacts."

I wrote at once to my friend, Ronald Inchley, of Inter-Varsity Press in London. He was the ideal person to put his finger on the pulse of the appropriate publisher. I sent him copies of the five books and the manuscript of *Jungle Doctor Meets a Lion*.

While I waited for his reply — those were sea-mail days — a reverse came my way. Bookshop after bookshop, person after person, criticised strongly the cover of the "Enemies" book. "A new jacket or we'll send them all back," threatened some. Others said quietly, "I could never give that book."

While another jacket was being drawn the letter I was waiting for arrived. Again there was the publisher problem. The first said, "No," but did so charmingly. The second, a very well-known firm, offered to buy the rights of all five books at fifty pounds each. Ronald Inchley's advice was strongly against doing so. I heartily agreed.

A third publisher wrote saying, "We're prepared to try one title." My heart sank, but I was too busy to follow it up.

Bread and butter was earned in those days by being Medical Officer to the Sydney County Council in the early morning. For the rest of the day I was Honorary General Secretary of the I.V.F., now known as the Fellowship of Evangelical Students, with time off for the weekly broadcasts. Saturdays were for home and family and on Sundays I travelled extensively, speaking three or four times and telling the Good News with an African flavour.

My fortieth birthday arrived in the middle of this down-turn in our fortunes. George gave me a desk with bookshelves on each side. Into these went a pile of *Jungle Doctor's Enemies* and, staring at me from a number of angles, was that witch-doctor picture. It was certainly eerie but utterly true-to-life. I still thought it was very good. George had doubts, and expressed them, but I had talked him into that unacceptable jacket. However, what book-buyers had to say settled the matter conclusively. The sinister face seemed to leer at me. At that moment a parcel was placed on my table. In it was a review copy of a book from The Paternoster Press in London. I picked up a copy of the "Enemies" book and wrote in it, "To The Paternoster Press. May I count you among Jungle Doctor's friends in the days that lie ahead?"

An airletter was sent as well saying that perhaps The Paternoster Press might be interested in publishing Jungle Doctor books for a world-wide market. Howard Mudditt, the proprietor, told me his end of the story. He had read my letter and put it aside until the book should arrive.

At about this time, Ronald Inchley sent him five Jungle Doctor books. In the train he settled back comfortably to read one. The story gripped him and he nearly overshot his station.

The full details came out one Sunday in Stockholm. He told them by interpretation to three thousand Swedish people in a vast church where both he and I spoke – Howard explained how he had been praying for a series to publish. He had asked God for *six* books. When told of this Ronald Inchley had smiled quietly and produced the manuscript of *Jungle Doctor Meets a Lion* from his drawer.

This was the sign for action. With George Dash's blessing large English editions of each book were produced and, what is more important, sold. Again Australian and New Zealand book-buyers came enthusiastically to the party. And the United Kingdom added a vast new market.

By this time the broadcasts were in their eighth year and the pile of scripts was growing high upon the shelf. Invitations came from Rotary Clubs, from luncheon groups, from university societies – all manner of invitations from all manner of places.

An enthusiastic letter came from Howard Mudditt, urging me to write six more books in the next three years. I set to work. Not even half of my diaries or photographs had been used, each of which had its own story built in.

Letters from Tanganyika told intimately about people and happenings. Wellesley Hannah wrote magnificently. He had a real gift for description of both people and situations. But letters were not enough. I felt the need to go back to the country of Ugogo to greet and to chat with my friends and patients of the Wagogo tribe. I felt it was important to talk at length, and if possible, to record or to write down what they had to tell me. I wanted to use my second language, Chigogo, and to bring out the full flavour of it, translated back into English.

There was a growing sense of homesickness for Africa. It came to a head in 1950 when armed with a portable tape recorder and a borrowed movie camera I made the safari as a slice of a round-the-world trip.

Writing books was fair enough. But I wanted them to be read by the people for whom they were planned. Talking, whether it was face to face or over the radio, gave me the chance to contact thousands of people, but I wanted more. Books went into places where I could never go. There's a permanency about a book which is lost in a talk. Already there were translations into Norwegian, German and French. But why stop there?

These were not merely African yarns for children although there were a considerable number of illustrations in them. I wanted children to read them, but the books were especially designed to give people an insight into African life as it was.

I found it hard not to grind my teeth when educated adults glibly came out with the uninformed cliché, "Leave them alone. They're happy enough as they are."

I hoped that medical students, doctors and nurses who found it difficult to talk to their patients about God might pick up a way of helping a sick soul by using the parable of the sick body. These things boiled in my head. I wanted to make people understand.

Then it was I received an exciting letter from the Readers' Digest offering me a fee of U.S. $1,000 for an option on the use of *Doctor of Tanganyika* as a condensed book. I visited them. They laid on a magnificent dinner and gave me V.I.P treatment. Unfortunately, however, they did not accept the book. Nevertheless that option-fee flew me from Australia to London via the United States where I met up with the American publisher and helped to launch the Amercian edition of the books on its long and happy voyage on the vast ocean of the American bookworld.

The safari was very successful both in Tanganyika and in a dozen corners of the world. New translations were made in Spanish, Portuguese, Swedish, Dutch, Urdu and Chinese. I returned with two thousand feet of unique colour film and twenty thousand feet of sound on tape that would not have been played, sung or spoken for one who was not regarded as a close friend of the village people. The six new books were on their way and I had splendid background sound for the broadcasts which were to spread right throughout Australia and beyond.

On this journey through East Africa I travelled an adventurous road which had the lovely warning sign, "Elephants have the right of way." There was also a neat notice which said briefly, "EQUATOR." Here I stopped and savoured the imaginary feeling of change when I stepped from the southern to the northern hemisphere.

I had much the same feeling when towards the middle of 1959 the millionth book was sold although The Paternoster Press could not pinpoint the particular language in which this precise sale was made!

It was obviously an occasion for celebration.

Many times I was being asked, "Daudi, Sechelela and the others that you talk about – are they real people?"

"Do these places and conditions really exist?"

"Are these true stories?"

"It's time we put a window into the Jungle Doctor books," said Ossie Emery, a most skilled photographer and my close friend. "Why don't we give those that read 'em a chance to *see* the people you talk about, the places where you worked and the problems that have to be overcome. Put in some of the animals too. Show 'em life as it's lived in Central Tanganyika."

"Let's do that, Ossie. There'll be nothing in it for either of us. But I'll cover expenses."

He nodded. "Fair enough, but it'll cost a lot of money. We'll need five hundred photographs for every ten we use." So we set out for Africa with thirteen cameras and Ossie took over ten thousand exposures in colour and black and white, including some pictures of a charging rhino! As he took shot after shot of the great two-ton beast pounding noisily a few feet behind our Land-Rover, he remarked dryly, "you have horribly bad breath, Rhinoceros."

Graham Wade did the layout and Paternoster worked hard and expertly. The quality of the book is an index of the skills put into it. To me it was more than satisfying to see photographs smile back at me from a beautifully planned, laid out and printed volume.

This was the most successful failure I have ever written. People were intrigued. They looked at *Jungle Doctor Panorama* for hours in book-stores and on book-stalls at conferences, conventions and missionary summer-schools, but only the very few bought one. The whole project meant digging very deeply financially. I nearly succumbed to the temptation to purchase a neatly framed little motto which said, "God bless our mortgaged home!"

Bishop Stanway, known affectionately in four continents as Alf, said enthusiastically, "In its field nothing has been produced like it. Tell people," he urged, "that *Jungle Doctor Panorama* is a custom-made tool for those who want to talk about the missionary task to their friends and those who visit their home. It is not made to rest on a bookshelf but to work from a lounge room table."

It was designed to contain a number of pictures which when appreciated by the owner, could start a conversation, help in the understanding of what missions are all about and, perhaps, introduce people to the Lord Jesus Christ Himself. Some saw the possibilities of this and used it – and are still using it.

"Don't let it sit on the shelves," urged Alfred Stanway. "Lend it, give it away. Put it into people's hands, into churches, schools, libraries, the lot." To me he said. "Give it away, God won't let you go broke."

The striking result was that slightly more than the six thousand pounds which it cost me was given to the work in Central Tanganyika by people from places all over the world. More important still, there were young people who looked, saw and perceived that there was a place for them in God's wider plans.

One night at Nairobi airport a young New Zealander came up to me and said, "You're Paul White?"

"Right, I am."

"Boy, am I glad to see you. I heard you speak in Auckland and listened regularly on the radio. I've read most of your Jungle Doctor books and then I saw that photographic book."

"What are you doing here in Kenya?"

"I'm working with ..." He named a missionary society.

In London, Copenhagen, Chicago, Bangkok, Hong Kong, Wellington, Capetown and in four Australian capital cities I have heard very much the same story from young men and women.

Putting pen to paper and helping in the production and publication of books has taken time, energy and sweat as well as much of the contents of my pocket. But it has been infinitely worthwhile.

One day in a radio interview a hard-eyed announcer remarked, "No doubt you've done rather well out of your writings about Africa, doctor. A little cream to put on your bread and jam."

I was happy to tell him that my aim had never been to make money out of the books I wrote. This has remained the case till I packed away my stethoscope to become a full-time writer. To be specific the royalties on all the books until 1973 went back into the job, be it the work in Central Tanganyika or an effort to help children to understand about Jesus.

The medical journal informed me that the average doctor died at the age of fifty-seven. I was determined to do certain things before that day dawned. This included a weekly Jungle Doctor broadcast without interruption for twenty-five years and the production of twenty books of various sorts.

Always I had been intrigued and gripped by filmstrips, flash-books and comic or cartoon books. I was determined to set a collection of these rolling before I graced the obituary columns. With a certain amount of satisfaction I woke on my fifty-eighth birthday and found that my target had been more than met. The weekly broadcasts were not only still on the air in Australia but had spread to New Zealand, Ecuador, Haiti, and parts of the U.S.A. Some had been translated into French. Twenty-five books were out and one or more of them translated into fifty-two languages.

In all, over two million copies had been sold. The fable books, a collection of African animal stories which helped to ex-

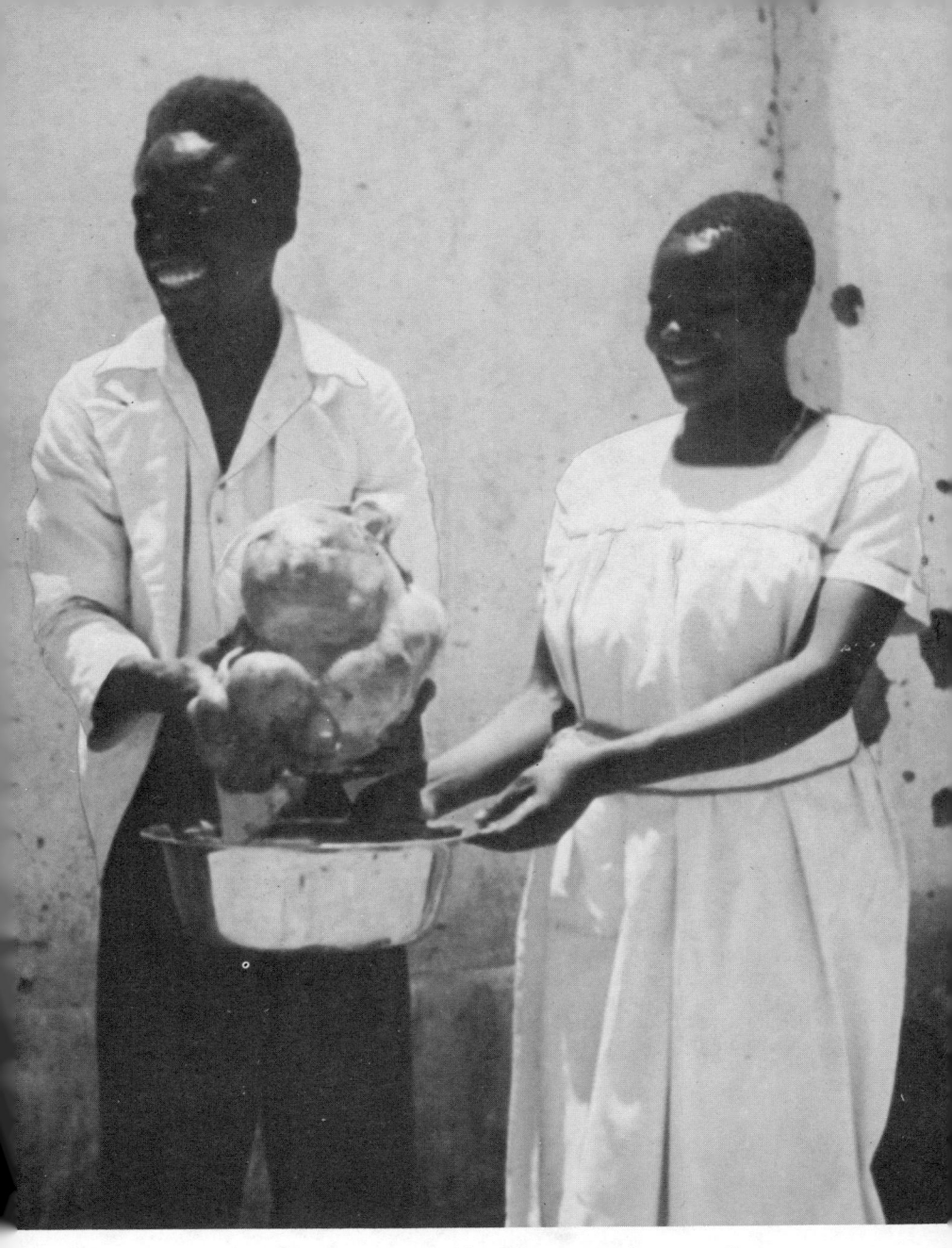

Daudi and his wife and a tumour weighing fifteen pounds removed from a woman patient. After two stormy post-operative days she passed twenty feet of tapeworm. She then made an uncomplicated, slow, complete recovery

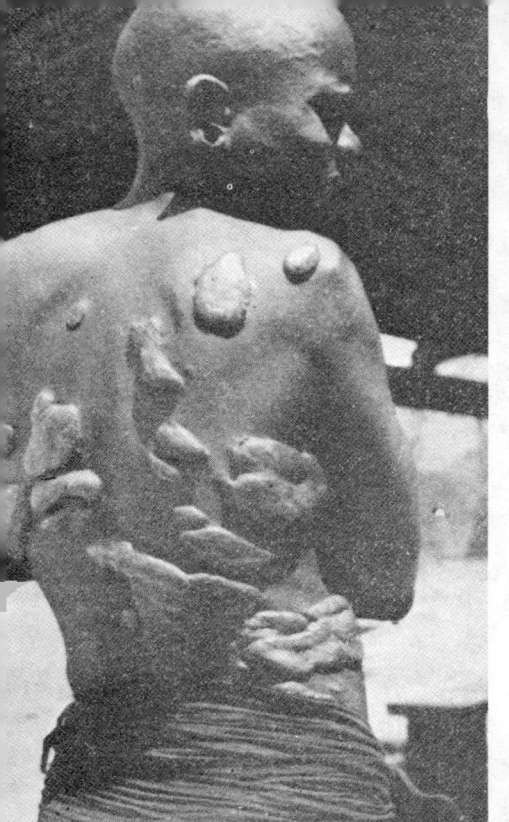

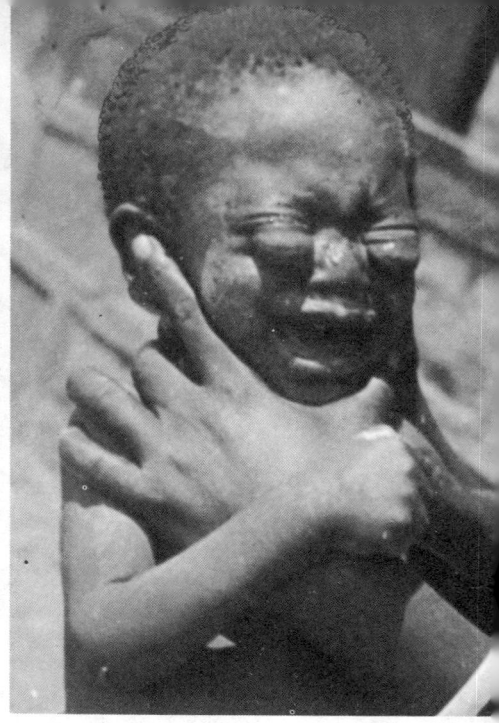

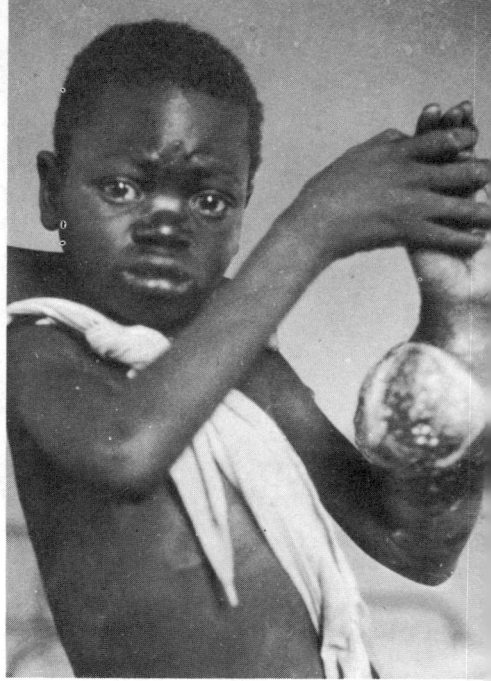

Witchdoctor's handiwork: The huge keloid scars on the man's back are the work of the witchdoctor, as are the blinded eyes of the child, who originally suffered from trachoma. The other child has cancer

plain abstract thoughts and long theological terms, had appeared – three of them – and had spread and blossomed into films, filmstrips, television material, flash-cards, flash-books, comic books and records. Quietly I thanked God for making it all possible and I asked Him to help me to use to the best advantage such time as He chose to give me in the days ahead.

Chapter Thirteen:

Doctor at Work

ON A CONSPICUOUS SHELF IN OUR HOME IS A SILVER TEAPOT inscribed:

> Presented to Allen Bradley Morgan, Esq.
> by his Wagga Wagga friends as a mark of
> their esteem and regard on the occasion of his
> departure for England
> Wagga Wagga, January 1869

Grandfather Morgan was a horse-and-buggy doctor in the days when there were bushrangers galore in Australia. His brother was an eye-surgeon in the early days of Sydney, while a Morgan uncle was a general practitioner in the centre of Tasmania. On the White side of the family, first, second and third cousins were and are gracefully represented in the medical profession.

By this time you will realise that medicine to me was a great deal more than a profession or a means of earning a livelihood. I had tasted hospital work, country general practice, industrial medicine and the sketchy life of a doctor who does locums in various places, gives the occasional anaesthetic and assists surgeons in the early hours of the morning.

Mine is the sort of nature that likes life as a mixed grill. Working among students, preaching on Sundays, broadcasting and book writing, and asthma, make settling into a routine practice difficult, since a doctor's life is unpredictable. Daily in my prayers I asked God to show me where He wanted me to be and what He wanted me to do.

For an uncomfortably long time there was not the slightest hint of an answer. One morning I opened my mail. A letter from the bank showed my balance was down to six shillings. Silently I put up an urgent prayer. Our family finances were perilously close to the bottom of the barrel. The telephone rang.

The student who wanted to talk to me was in trouble. I groped for a pad and my papers went all over the floor – a not unusual occurrence. Through the door came a special friend, Dr. Ian Holt. He picked up the papers and looked at one of them. The phone call finished. Ian is a very direct man and was a Rugby footballer of note. He said, "Is this all the cash you have?" His finger pointed to the bank statement. I nodded.

"What do they pay you in this Inter-Varsity Fellowship job?"

I grinned, "I'm *Hon*. Gen. Sec., Ian."

"Well, where does your cash come from?"

"Good question. I pick up a few quid by giving anaesthetics and doing the odd surgery for the local G.P."

He looked me squarely in the face. "I didn't come here to read your private papers or to pry into your private finances, but somebody must do something about this."

"What are you going to do?" I demanded

"The obvious thing," he answered. "A lot of us can afford to throw in a bit. You're doing a job we aren't able to do and we want to see it kept going. The Bible says very clearly not to muzzle the ox that grinds up the corn." Out he went – big, burly and purposeful.

He came back some hours later. "Paul, you now have an income of four hundred pounds a year. All of it comes from doctors who feel as I do. One man, Leslie Parr, says he will put in half of this if you work half a day a week for him."

"He's the rheumatism bloke?"

Ian nodded. "And a very good one."

Together we knelt down and I thanked God for supplying what had become an urgent need. When God says a thing and you're going His way and doing what He orders, then He supplies.

"On with the job," came Ian Holt's hearty voice as we got up from our knees.

When I was a medical student, a leading physician told a story during ward rounds. My imagination was fired:

"A doctor should always keep his eyes and ears open. Don't laugh off odd stories. By so doing you may miss your place in the hall of medical fame.

"In 1920, a pale man came to consult me. My clinical diagnosis was endorsed by blood examination. He was suffering from Pernicious Anaemia; there was then no known cure for this condition. I advised him to put his affairs in order. He enquired about therapy and I had to admit we had nothing to offer. He asked the inevitable question, 'How long?' I told him six months.

"A year later I was astonished to see him walking briskly through the city. His colour was good and his energy obviously considerable. He crossed the street and greeted me. 'Surprised to see me aren't you, doctor?' I mumbled something and he answered, 'A Chinese herbalist cured me with crow's liver.'

"My eyebrows went up and as I walked through the hospital gate, I smiled. 'Crow's liver, eh?'

"I could well have been the first medical observer to come up with the answer to Pernicious Anaemia if I had put the accent on *liver* and not turned up my nose at the *crows!*"

In Africa I was intrigued to find that only twice did I need to remove an appendix. The toxaemias of pregnancy were extremely rare. I saw one cerebal catastrophe and no coronary occlusions. Rheumatic disease was also a rarity. There had been no time to go into the reasons for all of this.

In Australia I was intrigued by a spinal disease which is a mere page in a thousand-page text book and termed variously Marie-Strumpell disease, Von Bechterew's disease, and Ankylosing Spondylitis. To me it was the latter; a disease of young people, especially athletes, that could rapidly become crippling. It could stop or go ahead without any particular rhyme or reason, was hereditary, and associated with the uncomfortable eye complaint, iritis. The book said it affected mainly males but my experience showed an equal number of females. "Diagnose it early," urged the authorities. When you did and there was no obvious crippling, there was the risk of professional noses turning up. If the diagnosis was left till it could be made with a telescope, the battle against pain and disability was made so much the harder. In that it was an hereditary disease I felt there was value in shaking the family tree. Doing this brought to light many unsuspected cases. So much so that one gentleman with vinegar in his vocabulary said in a seminar, "If you do not suffer from Ankylosing Spondylitis go and see Paul White and you soon will."

Twice I produced papers on this complaint and read them at

International Conferences overseas. Months went into their preparation but they produced very little impact. Latterly, since I have hung up my stethoscope, I have been happy to hear that a new blood test has been devised which assists considerably in early diagnosis. This has shown very many more females were sufferers than had before been believed. The proportion is closer to fifty-fifty than ten per cent as was previously thought. The closer the sufferer lives to the equator the less he suffers. The further north or south the patient lives the more uncomfortable his spine.

It is interesting to note that since the atomic age, less people have obviously suffered from Ankylosing Spondylitis. There has been some gain to a small portion of mankind from atomic fall out!

Working half a day a week with one of the country's keenest medical minds started me on a specialised career which fitted in with my nature, abilities and physical limitations. In hospital I had been intrigued by chronic disease. For six months I had worked in the tuberculosis clinic and also been considerably involved with diabetes. In Africa the problem of leprosy had been a challenge. Now I faced one of the dense jungles in medicine, rheumatism.

I found myself working as a junior physician in a Rheumatism Clinic and had the use of Dr. Parr's rooms and facilities on Thursday mornings as the first step to building up my own practice in Sydney's Macquarie Street. The street is decorated with doctors' name plates and is famous for its quality of work. My medical future was slowly taking shape. The income was sufficient not only to deal with everyday needs but to buy a serviceable, second-hand car. This did little for my public image, but at a squeeze it supplied travel of a sort for the family and the dog.

For four years I understudied at the clinic. My senior colleague was deaf, and one small service I could offer him was to carry spare batteries for his hearing aid. One day before I could produce one of these, he informed me and sixty or more patients in a loud voice, that he had decided to go overseas to a medical conference. He couldn't hear the reaction but I could:

"I hope he finds a cure."

"I don't think I'll bother coming till he comes back."

"Four months is a long time. You'd think he could do it quicker than that."

"Poor Dr. White is going to have to work very hard."

"He's only young but he does his best. Anyhow he's always kind to me."

Above it all Dr. Parr's voice boomed out, "I believe the Yanks have something up their sleeves."

They had. Cortisone was about to be launched.

When the new batteries were in place in the hearing aid, the clinic moved along in fine style. After it, rather hesitantly, I offered to try and keep the practice together for the four months that he would be away. He agreed and was most generous with financial arrangements. He suggested that all the new patients I saw would come on to my list if they were agreeable. His final word was, "This could build up your practice. We'd better arrange for you to work another half day a week at Macquarie Street."

Up to this stage of my life I had had the advantage of relative poverty. Now there was relative affluence in view. Money is a useful commodity but I recognised that the love of it is a trap. The Bible draws up some valuable prophylactic principles in this regard. First there was the giving of ten per cent of income; then there is the matter of first-fruits. The day Leslie Parr went overseas I re-read the appropriate passages in Proverbs 3 and promised to give God the first week's nett takings which I estimated at about thirty pounds. It turned out to be a hundred and fifty.

I was aware of the tempter's soft whisper in most logical English. "God wouldn't expect you to give all that. It's bigger than any week's income for years. Strike a happy, honourable average."

I listened only long enough to recognise the voice. Without delay I wrote a cheque and posted it to a missionary society. Undoubtedly God means what He says and when His conditions are obeyed, He pays. I've been struck by the fact that when He talks about money He generally talks about a bonus. It's clear, however, that if the motive in giving to God is to collect the bonus, that clause in the contract is struck out.

Those were four extremely busy months. The practice had gone exceptionally well. Old patients had, for the most part, been willing to trust themselves to my ministrations and new patients to keep on seeing me. I made sure that all the statistics and figures were set out clearly. They showed the income was right up to average. When Leslie read these on his return he slapped me on the shoulder. "Well done, Paul!" He then proceeded to write me a cheque for one hundred and fifty guineas. In modern currency, three hundred dollars had been given with no thought of anything coming back, but back came three hundred and fifteen. In his Sermon on the Mount, Jesus said, "Give and men will give to you, yes, good measure, pressed down, shaken together and running over, will they pour into your lap."

This was illustrated by that cheque and borne out by what happened in the practice. Three half-days instead of one were fully occupied. I started early and finished late. Soon I had a waiting list. Then and there I decided that this was the way my life would be split up, with not more than half my time being spent in medical matters.

Working in rheumatic diseases cleared the air as far as those who questioned my motive were concerned. This was one area of medicine where I had not been able to "practise on the natives." I had dealt with tropical diseases, a variety of surgical conditions, thousands of eyes and hundreds of chests but there was nothing particular from my African experience that in any way assisted me in the arthritic corner of medicine.

Before I had put up my plate on the sixth floor of the B.M.A. Building I contacted a member of the Ethics Committee of the British Medical Association. He had been one of the physicians for whom I had been resident medical officer. I wrote, "I am more convinced than ever that man's soul is far more important than his body. I want to talk to people face-to-face and on radio whenever and wherever the opportunity opens. I'll tell them about God and His good news to men and I'll illustrate it from what I saw and did in East Africa. I'll be talking medicine but saying nothing that would attract people to my practice. Would you give me your thoughts on the matter, for I certainly do not want to be a rebel. I would far rather give up medicine altogether."

The senior physician invited me to talk it over with him and asked pointed questions about my pay in Africa and about my activites since. Then he smiled. "I don't think there is much to worry about."

Arthritis is a jungle with few paths leading into it as far as the doctor is concerned. It is a spectre in the minds and imaginations of many patients and of those who know them. Wheelchairs and walking sticks, elderly folk with gnarled hands and crooked backs – these are the pictures that the word arthritis conjures up.

There was intense satisfaction in being able to assure most of the folk I saw that this would not be their lot. When they had come early and persevered with treatment the condition could be kept under control. Whenever wheelchairs were mentioned, in almost every case I could say with complete conviction, "It won't happen if you're consistent with your treatment. If I'm wrong and you do find yourself chair-borne, I will come and personally eat the wheels."

A tincture of laughter and a good measure of encouragement are both important in successful treatment. This includes pointing out the shadowy secrets of an X-ray and explaining the formidable words of blood-counts and biochemical reports. In this way both patient and doctor are united in the attack against the enemy. Co-operation can make all the difference. Sometimes to save face the patient can twist the truth to the confusion of the unfortunate physician. A rather mountainous lady whose knees were in considerable trouble, had been advised to lose weight. A careful diet was drawn up and explained minutely.

After a month she returned and in a dreary voice complained, "I'm no better. My feet, my legs, and the cramps – doctor, you wouldn't believe it, but the calves of my legs are fair cows!" I'm sure such language would never be heard outside Australia. I stood her on the scales. There was no loss in weight at all. "I can't understand it. I've done everything you told me. I've got the diet stuck on the kitchen wall. I just can't understand it."

Unfortunately for her that day was my wedding anniversary. I was taking my wife to dinner at a well-known Chinese restaurant. We were given a two-seated table placed between a brace of potted palms. We ordered, then I looked around. There was my patient of half an hour before, expertly consuming with chopsticks a considerable dish of prawns and rice. I extracted one of my cards and wrote on the back, "I am delighted to know that you have now decided to keep strictly to your diet." This was delivered by a smiling waiter. The potted palm suitably sheltered me from her gaze and I was happy to note that my card had ruined her appetite. She lost seven pounds in the next month! The various joints we use in walking take unkindly to the insults we heap upon them with knife, fork and spoon.

Treatment of arthritic disease calls for patience, understanding and regular review. Considerable advances have been made over the last twenty years. This happy state will continue.

Leslie Parr asked me to keep my eyes open for capable and compatible people for our medical team. My conviction is that when partners are selected a Christian should link up with a fellow-Christian — this applies to both marriage and medicine. News came to me of Philip Benjamin, who had been a Wing-Commander in the Air Force and had both an M.D. and M.R.A.C.P. While a G.P. at Albury, on the banks of the Murray River, he had been converted at a tent mission. The locals were intrigued to see the most senior medical man of the city walk quietly to the front of the tent and kneel there to show his willingness to become a Christian. I contacted him asking if he was interested in joining us. He came and talked at length. He visited both the clinic and Macquarie Street following which he joined the practice. We were delighted with the quality of his work and his dedication.

Leslie Parr, who had recently been elected to the State Parliament, was pleased, for this enabled him to press on with his objective which was to battle for rheumatic sufferers at government level and have a hospital especially for their treatment and care.

One Friday afternoon, Dr. Parr rang me. "I want you to carry on with the practice with Phil. On Monday I'm having ..." He mentioned an extensive operation for an aggressive new growth. "I'm finishing the paper on 'Chloroquine and Rheumatoid Arthritis.' Pick it up at the hospital and look it over then put it into the Medical Journal." He passed on suggestions about half a dozen other matters, and rang off.

He did not survive that operation.

He was fifty-nine years old and had put more working hours

into those years than most people do in seventy. Sadly, Phil and I carried on. We and the rheumatic cause had been heavily hit.

Wilbur Cathers, an experienced General Practitioner, who had worked for years in the clinic, joined us. He was a very good doctor and a most kind man.

The opportunity came to read a paper on my favourite subject at an International Rheumatology Conference in Rome. With my partners doing my work, I went overseas. In Switzerland came a phone call. It was Will Cathers. Philip Benjamin, a strong and capable swimmer, had been drowned while surfing. The tragedy of sudden death had come twice into our practice. Jean, Phil's wife, was very courageous. She was a doctor, experienced in rheumatology, and quietly took over Phil's work.

After ten most enjoyable years in the practice, Wilbur Cathers, who carried a much heavier medical work load than I did, was forced to move into a less energy-consuming sphere of medicine. Wilbur was more than a partner, he was a close personal friend and I missed him keenly.

I rang up some physicians who might be interested. Among them was John York, a young man, with very high qualifications. He immediately responded, "I would very much like to join you. Only days ago I was talking this over with my wife, Helen. We both felt it was time I moved into specialist practice."

"That's splendid, John."

He went on, "Do you realise that you helped me at an I.V.F. Conference before I even started medicine? You gave me some very practical advice about guidance and it worked out. From that conversation I learned to trust God and put what He says into practice." John was a splendid colleague.

I was convinced that the people who came for my help were a special responsibility. First of all I needed to practise medicine as well as I was able and really to care for my patients. As a yardstick for care I kept the fruits of the Spirit in clear view, especially longsuffering, gentleness and joy. I would not expect to speak about God to every person who came to me, or even a high percentage of them. Some would appreciate it, others would not. There were those who might even resent it. Sometimes the most unlikely people brought up the subject spontaneously.

Every day I prayed that I would have the opportunity to help people's minds and souls in a language they would understand The waiting-room seemed to me a strategic place to sow the seeds of a conversation. There were on the table always some pictorial New Testaments in modern translation or specially produced separate books of Scripture. Not only would these be taken home but frequently they were conversation-starters.

One day a lady walked in holding J. B. Phillips' translation of Paul's first letter to the Corinthians. "Did you write this?" she asked pointing to the last page where PAUL was printed. "Well, no. You see...."
"It's nothing to be ashamed of. It's a fine piece or writing. But I can't go along with this."

She put the 15th chapter about the resurrection in front of me. Here was an opportunity asking to be taken.

For a long time as a medical student and ever since I had noted down good ways of starting to talk about God. We had been carefully coached as to how to take medical histories and question patients about their symptoms and how to break bad news to them and their relations. How much more important to be efficient in the matter of the life and health of the soul.

In my drawer was a Bible ready for use and copies of the New Testament as well as a number of paperbacks covering a range of Christian subjects. Christian patients generally appreciate a thought on what God has been doing. I found that friendship, fellowship and encouragement lifted a person's morale. Encouragement, be it physical or spiritual, is the most powerful and useful tonic in any pharmacopoeia.

Chapter Fourteen:

Committees

BY DEFINITION COMMITTEES ARE A COLLECTION OF THE UNFIT, selected by the unwilling, to do the unnecessary. This, of course, isn't true. Or it shouldn't be. So much time could be saved if chairmen took the trouble to study their function and responsibilities. What a service if someone would run a course for chairmen and for committee personnel. Millions of useless words would be left unsaid. It must be obvious from the above that I have served on many committees. It's very difficult to know what to do when people who haven't bothered to read their minutes stand up in committee and think on their feet and, it sometimes seems to me, *with* their feet, and use bushels of words in so doing.

On one particular occasion I was first annoyed and then bored so I proceeded to do exercises to tighten up my stomach muscles. On the way home the offending committee member said, "It was splendid to see the way you concentrated on what I was saying."

My nimble-minded and amusing artist friend, Graham Wade, who has illustrated so many of my books, had a different way of occupying his time. I watched him look with interest round the committee room and set to work with a large pad of paper. On the train going home I asked him what he was making notes about. He smiled and produced the pad. On one sheet were drawn scores of ears – all those within his view were there in black and white. Before I could make a comment he turned the page and there was a collection of noses. He grinned at me, "Gotta do something constructive!"

Committees can become tense as well as boring. I have found an occasional wisecrack helps. It tends to soften the seat and will help to produce harmony again. There are occasions on

Committees 149

which individuals who are not amenable to a lighter touch can produce quite an ugly situation if opposed or in any way limited in their spate of words. One such gentleman of a learned profession stirred me to such a degree that I realised that something had to be done to keep my mouth shut. I prayed one of those short urgent prayers and then had an idea. I had been reading advertisements in the medical journal for a well-known antiseptic. This safe and useful substance had proved valuable in my African experience. Why not write some fifty-word advertisements for its use over there? On the back of my agenda I started to write in Swahili a number of advertisements using lion, giraffe, hippo and hyaena as those involved in jungle dramas where a useful antiseptic could make all the difference.

Writing these scripts took a deal of concentration. Doing them in Swahili made the need for concentration still greater. Time flew. I was surprised when I heard another voice speaking on another point.

This proved to be more than a gag to my all-too-ready mouth, for the manufacturer of the antiseptic graciously sent a number of gallons of their produce to our various hospitals in Tanganyika. And the "red rebel behind the white fence," as someone has aptly called the tongue, was effectively kept out of the field of destructive action.

Committees are excellent opportunities for the individual with ideas. There should be no seat available for the blockers or knockers; however this does not include the thoughtful conservative. Committees should certainly not be a haven for "yes" men, but a persistent "no" man greatly holds up the action. A vehicle may need a brake, but little progress is ever made if the handbrake is stubbornly held on. Harmony in committees is sweet music.

Anyone accepting a seat on a committee should realise the prime need to do the homework. This keeps the minutes to minutes. Time saved is valuable in quality as well as quantity. The later the hour the less effective is the thinking, in the majority of cases.

Harold Knight, at the moment Governor of the Reserve Bank, is one of the best committee-men I have met. He would listen to a long, rambling utterance by a fellow-member and then refer to his note-pad and say, "I will gladly second the motion if my friend is agreeable." He would then proceed, with commendable clarity and brevity, to frame the motion.

Few have not been riled by the statement, "I have been for twenty years on this committee and I have never heard. ..." Once when grinding my mental teeth at having to listen to this I told myself that if ever I spoke those words I would know it was time for me to resign. It happened one day. I found the words in my mouth. Fortunately they did not pass my lips. I went home, thought and prayed about what I should do and three months later I resigned. It is unwise to make up your mind on the spur of the moment. It is even more unwise to stay on a committee when you are merely a passenger. A useful job may be done by many with specialised knowledge or experience in the position of vice-president. They are not regularly on the committee but they may be called as consultants from time to time. They may be able to help and advise within the confidential limits of committee planning.

May I tell you the tale of two committees? The first when I was thirty-five, the second when I was in my sixties.

I was at a committee which was chaired by the then Archbishop of Sydney, the Most Rev. H. W. K. Mowll. A businessman stood to his feet and said what I considered to be sour, unkind, biased things about my friend and boss, Herbert Maxwell Arrowsmith, in his absence. I jumped to my feet and in a hatful of words said what I felt was the truth of the matter, with cold politeness but with hot anger inside me.

Suddenly I realised that my tongue, normally reasonably athletic was really set to break a record. There was shocked silence. The object of my tirade wrote rapidly on a piece of paper, and without a word, walked up, placed it in front of the Chairman and walked out.

I sat down feeling suddenly flat. The six-feet-four Archbishop conferred with Bishop Hilliard who sat near him and then said, "Shall we adjourn for ten minutes and, Dr. White, would you care to talk this matter over with Bishop Hilliard?"

"Yes, sir," I mumbled.

"Sit down, Paul," said Bishop Hilliard, whose background included a headmastership, first-grade cricket and the finest oratory.

He drew an armchair up and said, "You were correct in what you said and I agree with you." I gasped. "You didn't know he has been under severe stress or you wouldn't have hit him to leg like that."

"No, sir," I blushed. "Should I apologise?"

"It would be the Christian thing to do."

"But, Bishop, he was so wrong in what he said. I can apologise for being angry but I can't let him get away with that attack on Bert Arrowsmith."

"I was going to straighten things out in my own way," smiled the Bishop. "If you care to apologise, will you let me talk the matter over with him?"

"Thank you, sir. I'd gladly do that." He bowed his head and we prayed. I felt a very small potato indeed – even more so when I stammered out my apology.

A week later a letter arrived. "Dear Paul, I thought you'd like to know I had a most satisfactory luncheon with our mutual friend."

He was a well-known Christian leader and a shrewd man, with an accountancy diploma. We were at an Annual General Meeting. He shattered the smoothness of the meeting with questions that were quite in order but asked with a jagged edge that was, I felt, sub-Christian

I have a small aphorism: never write a letter, make a decision, or speak your mind if you're sick, angry or tired.

I went home from that meeting feeling bruised, waited three days and wrote a quiet letter saying directly and shortly what I felt.

A week later I received his reply.

"Thank you for your letter of 20th December. I have taken careful account of its contents as I appreciate greatly the prayerful efforts of sincere and experienced servants of God to help me to become a better Christian."

My heart leapt up.

Chapter Fifteen:

Houses

YOU HAVE LOOKED INTO OUR WEATHERBOARD HOUSES IN BOWRAL and seen our brick cottage with lawns and hedge in the Sydney suburb of Roseville. You have visited our temporary residence and surgery at Belmore where Mary and I lived before going to Africa. You have been welcomed into our jungle home at Mvumi in Tanzania, but at no time had I owned a home of my own.

When the Aquitania swung through the heads into Sydney Harbour we were unheralded. Those were war days and you had to be careful because the enemy listened. It was good to have our feet again on Australia, but where we were going to put the rest of us was a different matter. It was Saturday. I battled my way through customs, immigration and health – the usual routine – and at last found a telephone and rang mother's home number. A man's voice answered, "Mrs. White? No, she doesn't live here now. In hospital I believe – very ill. No I don't know where. Sorry I can't help. Good-bye." And he rang off.

As it was Saturday, my next three calls produced no reply. The bells rang on and on monotonously. A little bewildered, I emerged from the telephone box and found myself facing a tall, cheerful man. He beamed at me, "Welcome home, Bwana. I'm Arrowsmith, C.M.S secretary. All's under control. You're staying with Mr. Hordern. Your mother's very much better." He put his hand on my shoulder. "You and I have work to do for C.M.S."

We found ourselves in the home of Maurice Hordern, a director of one of Sydney's big department stores, and the man who had taught me in Sunday School. It was spring. After an African dry season with everything utterly brown and leafless my eyes opened wide to see the friendly, twinkling, green on the

Houses

gum trees and the dark red of the new foliage – the gum tips. Under these tall trees was the rich carpet of azaleas and multicoloured flowering peach, plum and apple trees. My nose delighted in the fragrance of jasmine, honeysuckle and violets. This is my own native land, said my heart. My head answered, there's a war on. Enlist as soon as you can.

Nothing was possible till Monday. On Sunday I went to church where the familiar sound of the bell greeted me instead of a drum. The service was in English instead of an African language. The hymns, to a pipe organ accompaniment, lifted me but as I knelt my mind went back to my African friends. I wondered what was going on in that outpatients' room. What the microscope was bringing to light, what problems they faced in labour ward and operating theatre. That handful of years in East Africa would always make it impossible to live the comfortable, insular life of the homeland.

Monday came and I went to the Army Barracks, filled in papers and was lined up for medical examination. I felt a hand on my shoulder and recognised a friend from the athletic club. "Paul," he said, "what's the use of going any further with this? You know, and I know that you're an asthmatic and an asthmatic doctor is not a help in a war. You are more likely to occupy a bed than to treat the patient in it." He filled in a rejection slip, handed it to me and said, "Give this to the sergeant."

My efforts to become a soldier began and ended that morning. In my wallet was a small slip of paper saying that I was unfit for military duty. This was scant comfort, however, when later on I was to receive anonymous letters containing white feathers! Of the doctors who enlisted that particular week the majority were located on the hospital ship "Centaur" which was torpedoed and lost with only one medical survivor.

Frequently I have been asked, "Why does God let you have asthma?" Others have said, "Why don't you ask God to take away this uncomfortable complaint?" I would have been a fool not to have done so but to date the answer has always been in the negative. God certainly knows what He is about, not only in the matter of health but also of housing.

Mary and I set to work early to find a place to live. Our hunting was considerable and unsuccessful. Not that there were not houses but my salary was thirty-three pounds a month and in most cases the rental was such that eating would become a forgotten habit if we had rented the house.

We found a flat at last which would just hold us and our few possessions but we all felt a trifle caged. After huge areas of country spreading out in all directions, being in Flat 4 with a garden the size of a tea-towel, and the availability of a clothes-line on Thursdays only was not a little restricting.

Before we had arrived and regularly afterwards we asked God, as a family, to guide us to the house where He wanted us to live and grow and work.

One Sunday I was speaking at Northbridge in a church some six miles from Sydney. After the service the kindly rector asked me, "Where do you live?"

Laughingly I told him of our dilemma. He nodded slowly, "We may be able to help. There is a lady from my flock who at the moment is in Switzerland and because of war conditions she can't get out. I'm looking after her house. You're the sort of people she would like living there and I would like to have you and yours in the parish. The place is furnished. You can have it for thirty shillings a week on the condition that you're prepared to move at a week's notice should she be able to come back to Australia."

After the service I looked at the house. It was ordinary but there was space. "When could we come?" I asked.

He smiled back, "Tomorrow, if you like."

A week later we were in residence. Schools were near at hand and a bus at the end of the street. There was bush and the harbour within easy walking distance. Again as a family we thanked God.

God seldom blows a trumpet when He is indicating a change of direction in our lives. Most often He indicates the path very quietly. One Sunday after the war was over I spoke in Beecroft, a northern suburb, rich in trees and colourful gardens. Vaguely I remember shaking hands with the people at the church door.

Then came the news that the lady who owned our house was planning to return. Housing was hard to find. The Government had "pegged' prices. Few real estate sales were being made. Again we prayed for our needs. Then I heard of an English minister who was leaving Australia and selling his furniture. I

Home again: with Mary in Launceston, 1942, and the growing family in 1948

The family at Beecroft with Rob, the dog, in 1957

rang, to discover that he had sold everything only hours before. "However," he said, "I may be able to help. I will ring you back." He did. "Are you interested in a house-full of furniture and that includes the house?"

"Indeed I am. Tell me more about it."

"Not long ago you spoke at Beecroft and you helped an engineer named Hugh Braga. He came from Hong Kong and he's going back there very shortly to help in rehabilitation. He says there is nobody he'd rather have take over his home than you."

Next day we went as a family to a delightful street in the richly timbered suburb of Beecroft. The house was exactly right, and in a lovely bush setting. The smiling faces of the family gave me my answer. The furniture was beautiful, made by Chinese craftsmen from teak which had come in large part from old ships which had been dredged up from the bottom of Hong Kong harbour.

Hugh Braga told me the pegged price plus a valuation of the furniture was a figure close to three thousand pounds. He made it clear that the price was strictly according to regulations. I thanked him and said we certainly would buy, although I could not even pay a deposit of three thousand shillings.

But three days later I had the money – every penny of it. An elderly lawyer, Octavius Cowley by name, whom I consulted, both advanced the required sum and undertook the conveyancing for nothing.

That evening came a phone-call. "Doctor, I'm ringing to let you know that the good lady who owns your house is definitely leaving Switzerland and she will want possession of her home in three weeks' time."

When she came back we were happily living in our new house – the first house which had ever been our own. Mary loved it, the children loved it and it suited me splendidly.

To me that house was a clear indication of what God can do when you pray. The owner had wanted the deal completed in seven days. Within five days I had been offered the whole sum at absurdly low interest.

Just beyond our house was a reserve – the bush, we called it – with gum trees, wattles, ferns beside the creek, small orchids, Christmas bush and a score of evergreen shrubs. A place where birds sang and nested and the sun was greeted and farewelled by the laughter of kookaburras. There were fairy wrens, magpies and spur-winged plover. Swallows nested under the bridge. We were not far from the railway line. It was the day of the steam train and, being on the main northern route, powerful locomotives thundered their way up the hills out of Sydney. Many of these snorting monsters were the very engines that I had watched as a small boy.

I enjoyed Beecroft. However, after we had lived there for some ten years a fly appeared in the ointment. Asthma made itself felt. It was a half-mile walk to the station and when, as my family laughingly put it, Dad's breath came in short pants that was a long, long walk.

The inability to breathe is not a happy experience. When I went away for a few days I could breathe, when I came back I sneezed and wheezed. To me it was clear that something radical had to be done. Routine medication was falling far short of the mark.

We had been working for a long time in preparation for the coming of television to Australia. Clifford Warne and Graham Wade had both gone overseas to see, study and take part in the arts and crafts of television. We now needed a place to serve as a cross between workroom and studio. The only way to start the ball rolling when something new, like television, appears over the horizon is to push it yourself. Very many are interested. Still more say at length and loudly that something needs to be done. However, until they see definite results they are unwilling to help.

One Saturday morning Clifford, Graham and I sat down to discuss all angles of the situation. "We need a big place along a road that more or less threads up the television channels," said Clifford.

"Why don't we have a talk to Bill Harbour?" suggested Graham.

I did. Bill is a builder, an ex-missionary and a capable, jovial man with considerable foresight. I summarised what was in our minds.

Bill thought for a moment. "Realise that houses are hard to find and houses with vacant possession are rare. But I think I know exactly what you want. I've been building a house for a lawyer on Epping Road. He's selling his old house and it's big. Now although he's had a For Sale notice up for three weeks nobody has come along willing to pay what he wants for the place. I think that if he liked you, you could buy for about eight-and-a-half thousand pounds."

"Bill, what do you think our present house is worth ?"

He paused, "I would say seven-and-a-half. Here I'll give you his number. Ring him up."

I did so and the answer came back briskly, "Can you be here in half an hour?"

I could. I groped for a tie to grace the khaki shirt that I was wearing and found my hand touching my old school tie. I put it on, drove to the address and rang the doorbell.

A smiling elderly gentleman opened the door. "Come in, Dr. White. I have just been talking to Bill Harbour about you." His smile broadened as he saw my necktie. "You went to Sydney Grammar School, did you?"

"I certainly did."

He gripped my hand. "So did I. It's a fine school. Now come and see the house."

I looked at the large, roomy house in what I estimated to be about an acre of land planted with trees and a fine collection of shrubs. He opened the door. "It became too big for us but we like it here. There's space to think and it's reasonably close to the city – nine miles from the front gate. The bus passes the door. For all that, you might be right out in the country."

What I liked about it was that it must have been designed by an architect who had asthma. There wasn't a dust trap in the whole of the place. No picture rails or turned up edges. The floors were all polished wood. There would be plenty of room for the family and any other radio, television or audio visual ideas that I might have. I posed the big question.

"Eleven thousand five hundred is my basic figure," he replied.

The corners of my mouth turned down. "Mr Jones, I've been wasting your time. I can't match that. Bill Harbour tells me that my present home is worth seven thousand five hundred pounds. I can muster another thousand but that's far short of your figure."

As he closed the front door he said, "I'm sorry about that, I would like to have had you for a neighbour. Actually there are a number of Italian families coming into this area, market gardeners mainly, and I'm not keen for our house to be occupied by a large number of people, particularly children. We like a quiet life."

I drove quietly home and asked God to guide us about our future and especially about my asthmatic problem.

Early that evening the telephone rang. "Jones here," said the voice. "My wife and I have been thinking about your offer for our property. We've decided to accept it. Will you ask your solicitor to contact me?"

Somewhat breathlessly I thanked him and rang off. I hadn't made an offer. I had stated facts but after considerable discussion with the family and many visits to number 113, Epping Road, North Ryde, we moved.

House-moving is always an ordeal. Leaving friends and neighbours is a wrench. But we did it and settled in well. Then it was that I realised fully my sharpness as a businessman! Not only had I bought a house in an acre of land but I had also purchased two paddocks beside it, not realising that they were included in the sale. For some thirteen years we lived happily there – years full of activity and interest. Both David and Rosemary married. Our television dream had come into reality and professional facilities were available. My radio studio which took over the garage (and relegated the car to the car port) had been used hard and successfully.

Then the house was too big for Mary and myself, and her health was deteriorating. The Water Board had put two huge pipes, eight feet in diameter, through the middle of our two acres. The Electricity Authority had high tension wires over the top of the land; and then the Main Roads Board informed me that they would be taking a strip forty feet wide by three hundred feet long to enable the road in front of us to be turned into a six-laned highway. Already traffic noise was uncomfortably distracting.

We prayed that God would show us what to do and where to go. In quick succession three offers came our way to purchase our land but all fell through. Mary's health made it obvious that we needed to move and to do so swiftly. Another offer came – a good one. We accepted it and the usual legal machinery was put under way. We needed a new house. I rang up a Christian estate agent. The first day we went out together I saw six houses but none of them fitted our needs. The second day I said to him, "We've started this the wrong way. Let's stop under that gum tree and ask God to guide us to the house in which He wants us to live." We did so.

The agent looked at me and smiled. "I've been in this game for a long time and that's the first time that has ever happened to me." He looked beyond the gum tree. "There's an interesting place down here."

We drove into a quiet little crescent. It was planted with shapely trees of many varieties and shades of green. We stopped outside a white cottage. Behind it were some tall, picturesque gum trees with the softness of jacarandas beneath them. There was a small, trim garden with many roses and a maple tree on the westerly side. There was a friendliness about the house brought out by shrubs and evergreens and a bush with red berries clipped to grow against the white wall. When the front door was opened, at once I had the feeling that this was the right place. It exactly fitted our needs. Fifty years old, it had recently been modernised and had about it cupboards and doors exactly where I wanted cupboards and doors. The lead-light windows each gave a picture of garden or a view of this green and pleasant suburb. I was delighted, thanked God, and wrote a cheque for a deposit.

When I was signing documents regarding our old house I discovered that it was to be bulldozed and probably turned into a parking area. I put in a plea for my favourite shrubs. "Take what you like," said the negotiator. "Take the house as well if it's any good to you."

My signature was hardly dry on the documents before I was ringing up those who could best use building materials of this sort. The Saturday after we moved, some three dozen experts and enthusiasts from Scripture Union descended with lorries, crow-bars, pinch-bars and a variety of hammers, and in three hours our house was a mere shell. Lorries were driving to camp sites north and west of Sydney loaded with timber, stoves, cupboards, iron piping, doors, windows and all sort of fittings. People from a local church lifted tons of crazy paving to put in paths near their Sunday School building. Another church sent a bulldozer to dig up camellias, azaleas, magnolias, flowering trees and a variety of ornamental pines. At sundown it was a sorry sight but nothing had been wasted. Instead, thousands of dollars' worth of valuable material would be put to good use. All of this gave me intense satisfaction. I hate to see waste.

As I write I am looking through a wide window of our Lindfield house at flowering azaleas with their wonderful tints. There are bulbs growing happily, and near to our letterbox is an Australian red bottle brush, some flannel flowers and other native plants. It's a very satisfying house and after seven years of occupation its charm has deepened.

Chapter Sixteen:

Radio to Television

"WE HAVE THE FIRST RADIO IN THE STREET," SAID A SCHOOLfriend of mine. "Would you like to listen to it?"
I could not get there fast enough. From one chimney to the other was a length of copper wire attached to china affairs that looked like cotton reels. "That's the aerial," he told me, "and there's a wire leading inside to the set." This was a cardboard cylinder wound with insulated copper wire. He pointed to a mounted fragment of silver-lead ore. "That's the crystal." A very thin coiled wire was above this. "That's the cat's whisker." He made various adjustments and then, smiling, handed me the head phones.

My mouth dropped open as I heard a voice saying with great clarity, "This is station 2FC, Sydney, Farmer and Company." Then came music. It was astonishing. Much as I would have liked to listen on and on I dragged myself away from the first radio set I had ever heard or seen. My twelfth birthday was close. For thirty shillings I bought the parts required to build one of my own. An aerial dangled from our chimney to a gum tree and I spent hours listening, sometimes going to sleep with the headphones on.

One notable day I tiptoed over the carpet of radio studio 2BL, Broadcasters Limited, Sydney, and saw the mystic device, the microphone, hanging from the ceiling.

Three years later mother purchased, second-hand, a two-valve set with a loud speaker that looked like the outgoing end of an outsize in trumpets. We not only listened to a variety of Sydney stations, but also to Melbourne and Brisbane, each five hundred miles away. It seemed incredible. What a tremendous opportunity to talk to a huge number of people all over the place at the one time.

It was not until just before going to Africa that I faced a microphone and had the uncomfortable experience of hearing my own voice. I was talking to the women's session on 2GZ, Orange, a country station with a wide coverage. The announcer, a very kindly individual had said, "Before we go on the air, realise what you're doing. You're talking to women doing their housework or sitting down and having a cup of tea. Visualise them. Talk to them. Smile at them. They'll hear the smile in your voice. Take them into your confidence. Never, whatever you do, put on an assumed or professional voice. Above all things you must keep people from turning you off; and the surest way to make them go for the knob is to be unnatural or pompous. Be as relaxed as you can. Keep your nose a hand span from the mike and don't move your head around or rustle paper."

These were golden words and I followed them faithfully as I told of the job that lay ahead in Africa.

Four years had gone by. Africa was far away. I was walking along one of Sydney's crowded streets when my arm was gripped by a muscular man who said in a beautifully modulated voice, "Dr. White, I presume." I recognised him as the manager of 2GZ, who had arranged for me to be interviewed years before. "Have a cup of coffee with me, doctor. I've been reading your book and have a few ideas."

We talked hard, drank two cups of coffee and walked down to the radio station. "There is no time like the present. Have a talk to the women's session again. Many of them will remember you. Tell them about babies for two shillings a time and twins at three shillings. Make it live like you did in that Doctor of Tanganyika book – even more intimate still if you can. Talk to people about people." Apparently he listened to that broadcast for afterwards he was waiting for me outside the studio. "Can you do another one next week, doctor?"

"Yes, I can indeed; but I'll script it next time."

He nodded, "Tell you what: why not do a month of them and we'll change the time so that you can reach the whole family."

I did. Again he was there as the studio door opened. "Shall we see you again next week, doctor?" When I nodded, he said "It's going well. You're on the air from the Blue Mountains

Radio to Television 163

and down the South Coast. I've had a word to 2KA, Katoomba, and 2WL, Wollongong."

I didn't see him again until I had recorded script number thirteen. "Three months," I thought. "They'll round it off now." But no. The manager asked, "How are you going for material, doctor?"

"I've hardly made any inroads into it so far."

He laughed, "Well, carry on."

Now it appeared that my secretary had typed an extra copy of the broadcast scripts. This she took to Sunday School and read to the children there. Another Sunday School teacher, Joan Bates, worked for the advertising manager of Reuters. She took several scripts to work and showed them to her boss, E. J. Caldecoat, who was a Christian. "Where did you get these?" he asked. "They're different."

"They're good," said Joan. "They're written by a doctor who worked in Tanganyika."

"I want to see him," said E. J. Caldecoat.

The message was relayed and I went to Reuters. With me I took a Doctor of Tanganyika book and, following what I had learned from George Dash, autographed it. I soon found myself talking about the broadcasts, their three months on the air, on three stations.

"When do you make your next recording?" asked my new friend.

"Tomorrow at ten thirty."

"I shall be there if I may."

He sat in a quiet corner of the studio and listened. When it was all over, Caldy, as he liked to be called said, "This broadcast needs wide distribution and I know all the advertising and radio boys. This is my special game. I have it at my fingertips. You make the broadcasts and put everything you know into the writing and the recording and I will see that they're spread through Australia."

Two weeks later we were on the air in northern New South Wales and from Brisbane up to the Great Barrier Reef.

Next came a message, "Go down to Melbourne. I think I have a good nibble from there. Take six recordings and this letter." I looked at a Reuters' envelope addressed to Mr. Sid Kemp.

I travelled second-class and sat up all night. Mr. Kemp was a top executive of a network of Victorian stations. He listened to me, looked at the Doctor of Tanganyika book and said, "Caldecoat says there's no money in this, but I take it that if we can raise some it would do a lot of good." Later in the morning he introduced me to others. They listened to the recordings and then took me out to lunch and asked many and pointed questions. "The decision about going on air is not mine," Mr. Kemp told me later, "I'll be in touch."

I visited bookshops, autographed several hundred books and in due course spent another uncomfortable night sitting up in a crowded carriage on the five-hundred mile journey back to Sydney. First thing, I went to Reuters to report progress and found an excited Caldy. "I've just had a telegram from Sid Kemp. We're on Melbourne, Warragul, Warrnambool, Shepparton and Mildura and he's making contacts with the radio people in Tasmania. That's fourteen stations."

Tasmania came to the party. That made twenty.

A week went by. I was busily writing a script when Caldy rang up. "Drop everything and come down here. I have an important man from Western Australian radio."

And so it was we were on Perth, Merredin and Katanning. Adelaide followed and before the first year was over Jungle Doctor was being aired in Australia from high north to deep south, from the East Coast to the Indian Ocean.

Writing those scripts was not just telling a story. I would pray that God would help me to produce a living picture. I wanted people to meet my African friends, to feel the opposition of the witch doctor and to share in the struggle to show a better way than medicine man could offer. I tried to draw word-pictures of the way in which our African staff handled things, their sense of humour, their love for God.

I used dialogue and a spice of African language and twist of phrase like, "*Kah!* Great one, I have no joy in my jaw." "*Kumbe!* There is a restless snake within me, I can hear its voice."

There was fun and adventure. The perpetual battle against the *dudu*, the insect, and all varieties of tropical diseases. There were the occasional uncomfortable experiences with large creatures. The man who was bitten by a hippo, and the woman who was savaged by a rhino's horn, and the damaging hostility of the claws and teeth of lion and leopard. I tried to convey the emptiness that came with tragedy, the deep frustration I felt when people came in too late, or worse, those who came in time, but for whom no drugs were available. There were those whose lives could have been saved by a more experienced surgeon.

There was the triumph of vaccination over smallpox and the great satisfaction when the antibiotics became available for the battle against pneumonia and germs generally. There was so much to tell.

As I wrote scripts I used the stories in talks and sermons and with deep satisfaction week by week felt that as I faced the microphone I was talking to a vast audience.

Two years later Caldy informed me, "We've established a record: thirty-six stations for three years. We've dropped off three and we've picked up six. Wouldn't it be a wonderful thing if we stayed on them for five years?"

Unfortunately he didn't see it happen, for he died a few months before Jungle Doctor Broadcasts had their fifth birthday. I shall always remember Caldy as a wide-awake Christian, grasping opportunity and eager to use his experience for the Kingdom of God. His work in master-minding the launching and maintenance of the broadcasts was monumental.

About this time I hit on the idea of a Jungle Doctor Rally. To be invited into people's homes via the radio was splendid, but to meet them face to face was better still. Clifford Warne helped me greatly. His puppetry and ventriloquism gave a splendid lift to proceedings. People rocked with laughter at the antics of Toto the monkey and the problems of Boohoo the hippo. Graham Wade would grip attention with his lightning sketches. We held packed meetings in Sydney and from time to time in Melbourne, Adelaide and large provincial cities and country towns. Always I told a story with a punch in it, sometimes showing a filmstrip or film according to what had been produced that year.

When we could, we introduced missionaries home on leave or Africans studying in Australia. We took care to talk about books and broadcasts. Always we evangelised and enthused but we aimed to entertain as well. Some of the children and young people whose faces I had come to recognise year by year are these days active in God's front line.

In 1954 we featured the fact that the broadcasts had been on the air for twelve years and had reached a peak throughout Australia on forty stations, as well as overflowing to New Zealand, the Philippines and Equador.

Another "twelve" was *Jungle Doctor Goes West*, the twelfth book of the series. There was a special meaning to this title, I told them. The broadcasts were and would continue to be right up to date. Four years before I had arrived in East Africa with the first tape recorder to enter the country. I had brought back unique tapes of singing, drums and special African dramatic sound. This was ideal for both feature and background in the Jungle Doctor Session. It had not been easy however. We needed electric power to drive the recorder. We had borrowed a "home light" device which produced what was wanted but also what we could well do without – the explosive noises of a two-stroke engine. To reduce this to a minimum I bought a lead, fifty yards long, dug a hole and put the generator in it, covering the lot with an ancient blanket.

This tape had been used over and over again. I promised my audience, "Before our next Jungle Doctor Rally I'm going west, across the Indian Ocean, with a new clockwork-powered recorder that will make the broadcasts sparkle. So keep on listening and ask other people to listen as well."

At this stage surveys showed that half-a-million people a week were listening to our broadcasts in Australia alone.

I duly went to Tanganyika and collected all kinds of music and sound, folk songs, camp singing, work songs, and the vocal skills of tribal musicians. We turned on a special party – a *sikuku* – featuring goat stew. Hundreds turned up. I recorded from sunset till midnight. Home-made instruments, guitars, *kudu* horns, drums of all sizes and shapes with tremendous variety of rhythm, all went on tape. I recorded a thunder-storm, the sound of African agriculture, the special noises that water-carriers made, and the encouraging "Push!" noises made by the helpers when a car is being coaxed out of a bog.

To me a special highlight was one night when we climbed up a huge tree and lay flat on a platform above the only waterhole for miles. First we recorded the evening chorus of birds and the

Return to Tanganyika: greeting an old friend: "Bwana, do you remember the day on safari when you gave me that injection with a big, blunt needle?"

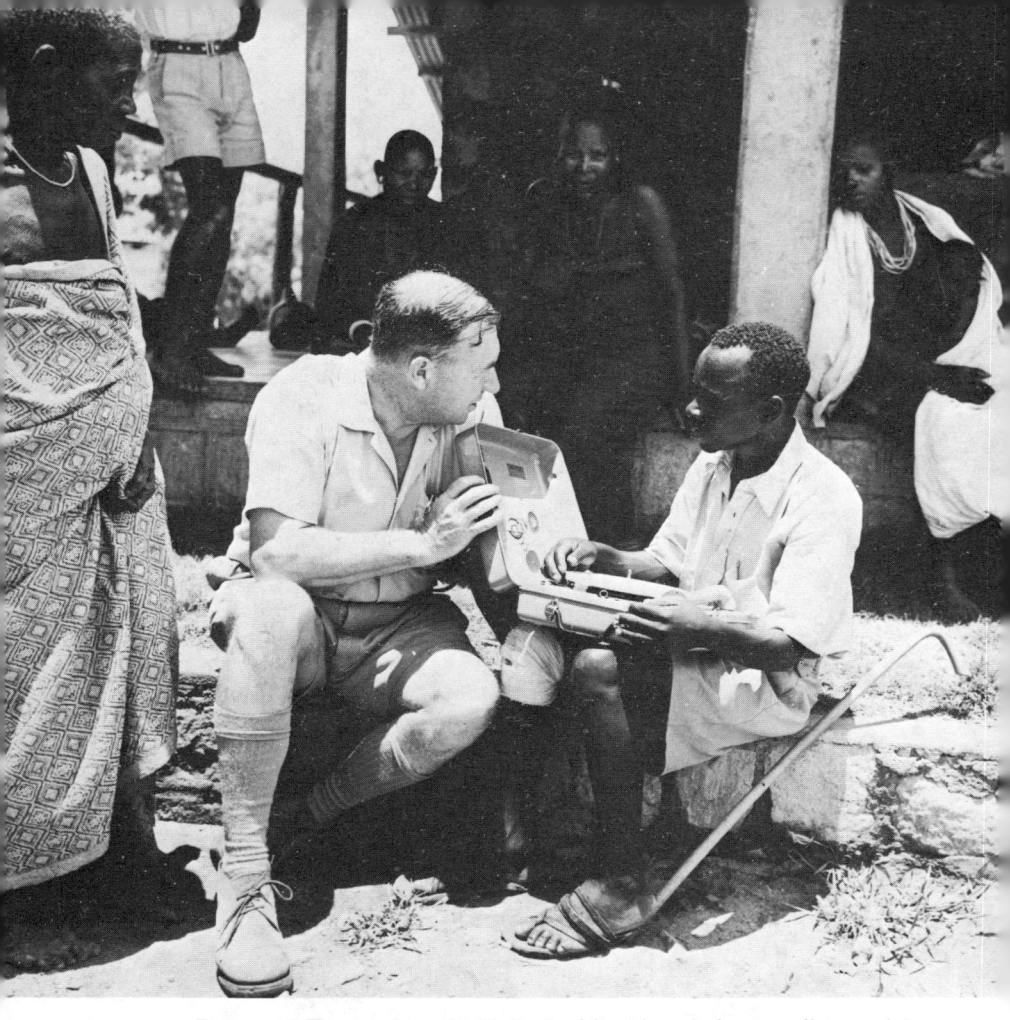

Return to Tanganyika: Danieli, the blind hospital evangelist, explains how he plays Gospel recordings on a gramophone, while old Sechelela looks on

chatter of monkeys and baboons. After dark came the sounds of lions, hyaenas and jackals, the hooting of owls and, in the very small hours, the arrival of over fifty elephants. They looked ghostly in the moonlight and moved their huge frames soundlessly. However, after drinking, they trumpeted and squealed magnificently. It was tremendous as batch after batch of unique sound came safely through my eager microphone. On this safari much colour-film was taken. We were seriously preparing for the days when television would come Australia's way.

One June morning I rang the manager of station 2GZ, Orange. "Mr. Ridley, I just wanted to let you know that today is the thousandth broadcast of Jungle Doctor and to thank you for all that you've done over the years."

"Congratulations," he said, "I had the feeling at the beginning that something like this would happen. How many stations are you on now?"

"Forty-one in Australia and dotted round the other continents, from Luxembourg in French, from Okinawa in Chinese, from the Philippines in Nepali, Bengali and Hindi, from Bangkok in Thai. From Seattle, Washington, Ecuador, Monrovia and Kenya, it's in English."

"This must be the widest distribution of any broadcast ever to originate in Australia," he said. "And have you any more material ?"

"Plenty, I'm just getting my second wind."

It is hard to realise how much work and behind-the-scenes activity goes into a broadcast. Each of those scripts took at least four hours to write, put in background music, rehearse and record.

Sid Russell was the man who was the panel operator and whose skill kept our recording equipment at top pitch. He produced and insisted on top quality. Bill Harbour, builder, missionary, and most helpful person generally had constructed a studio for us under his house. Here Sid and I worked for hours one or more nights a week not only doing Jungle Doctor broadcasts but a weekly C.M.S. Newsreel – a twenty-minute news, music and missionary affairs programme. There were a number of times that midnight struck before the programme was completed, but Sid never complained. He is a very capable and kindly man who helped me for seventeen years. During this time he won the hand of Beryl Cleaver, another of my splendid secretaries.

On the twenty-first birthday of the broadcasts, new maturity came to the series. A change had to come into radio with television so we reduced the stories from thirteen minutes to ten and sharpened them up by putting in more sound and song.

In mid-1967 we had been on the air for a quarter of the century and were beginning to show a few wrinkles. I had received a number of very kind letters from the stations saying, "We are reluctant after all these years to take Jungle Doctor off our schedule but in view of the changing face of radio we are dropping your programme as from. ..."

As I write this, thirty-four years from the time the first broadcast was made, you may still hear Jungle Doctor from Hobart.

Does anyone ever listen? For years there was hardly a town in Australia out of sound of the broadcast on medium-wave transmitters; also there were the short-wave broadcasts. Ossie Emery, the photographer, was driving on the road from Alice Springs to Darwin and listening to HCJB, the voice of the Andes, from Quito in Ecuador, when on came the Jungle Doctor theme. "Strike a light," said Ossie. "It's hard to dodge that blighter!"

I was in Tanganyika at Kilimatinde on the edge of the Great Rift Wall. The African nurses had a short-wave radio and were twisting the knob. Startlingly loud came the sound of drums, then the well-known theme, and we sat listening in a Jungle Hospital to a story of happenings in a ward that we could see through the window. To me the fantastic thing was that I sat there in the middle of Africa listening to my own voice, recorded in Australia, and broadcast from Asia.

One day, driving from Sydney to Melbourne I had the misfortune to crack the cylinder-head of my 1936 model Chevrolet. This occured in a picturesque town called Avoca, some seventy miles from the southern capital. We managed to reach a garage and approached a cheerful-looking mechanic. "I'm on safari and seem to be in great trouble. Can you help me?"

He looked at me hard. "Say that again."

I did.

A smile spread all over his face and he pitched his voice in a deep African tone, "*Kah*, Bwana, old Sukuma, the car, has no joy. Dr. White, I'd know your voice anywhere. Of course I'll fix her but come first and meet my family. They've always wanted to meet Jungle Doctor. Stay and have lunch with us."

Thank you, Bill Williams.

This year I was in a T.V. studio, part of the audience of a top line show called "This is your Life." The producer had rung me earlier. "The man on our show tonight, Graham Irvine, is quite a character. He's one of the top men in World Vision – you know, those folk who fight famine and look after orphans all over the place. I hear that his life was changed when he was a teenager through listening to one of your Jungle Doctor broadcasts." Some time before Graham had told me how he had committed his life to God as a result of listening week after week to stories that told about the only answer to the sick soul.

A letter from a young Singapore Chinese leader had much the same to say. I have his letter in front of me. "Before I became a Christian, when I was studying in Australia, I heard your broadcasts. This started a work of God in my soul. Sunday by Sunday I listened to Jungle Doctor and the message was working within my soul. One day you brought me to that point when I knew I needed to come to Jesus Christ and that day I asked Him to be my Saviour."

It has been one of the great encouragements of my life to hear that sort of statement in all sorts of places from all kinds of people. Time, effort, wear-and-tear; all are worth it to help people to know Jesus Christ, to become a member of His family, and grow up in that family.

Having a place in radio was good but television was a different matter. My efforts to interest people received either the order of the moist blanket or, what is equally hard to take, polite interest and utterances like, "It's ten or more years away. Let's concentrate on the things we have on our plate now." I had heard the same thing said in a slightly different way twenty years before when Jungle Doctor broadcasts were being discussed. I had addressed a committee regarding broadcasting. It was the few who were interested and concerned. It was the few who realised the potential but, fortunately, the few were prepared to act.

We were a loosely-knit team, each with his own contribution to make. The time came when the whole concern took to itself the name of Pilgrim Design and later Pilgrim International. I found myself in the position of Chairman of Directors. On occasions I would wield the baton but the first violin in this audio-visual, advertising concern was undoubtedly Roy Baxter. His wife Jill had been my secretary in the early 1950's. Roy was an accountant who before becoming a Christian had set his sights on being a bookmaker. He would have been a very successful one. Business, finance, planning, looking into the near and far future – these were Roy's special talents. Clifford Warne with his abilities in front of camera, microphone and audiences was on the board of Pilgrim, as was Graham Wade with his artwork, ideas, story-telling and lightning sketching. Inevitably he would cover his agenda paper with pictures of the conspicuous anatomy of those at the meeting!

A camera to Ossie Emery was an extension of his eye and his sense of humour. He has a sensitivity about his work blended with robust common-sense which makes many a sparkling film and T.V. show possible with a mini budget. For years Harry Rogers' pencil and brush and general artistic skill made many things possible, including a puppet film of the Goat who wanted to become a Lion. Others have linked up directly or indirectly including Jean-Luc Ray from Switzerland with his nimble camera.

Early in the 1950's the adventure really started. Clifford had been staff-worker with Scripture Union in the audio-visual field. He had finger puppets, glove puppets, shadow puppets and marionettes. We acquired top quality ventriloquial material. Clifford's particular joy was Dudley, created by London craftsman, Davenport, who also produced monkey puppet, Toto, with moving eyes, ears and lips, and Suku the parrot. And then other jungle puppets appeared: Boohoo, the hippo, with moveable mouth, Crunch, the crocodile, and Waa, the hornbill.

One day Graham, who was spending his weekends commencing a church in a new area, came up with the idea of filmstrips and dashed off a dozen pictures in brilliant colour. They were finished just before I set out on a round-the-world trip to try to see how we could grasp a slice of the television pie.

In Chicago, I was stopped in the street by a well-dressed individual who asked, "Sir, would you like to go on a coast-to-coast television show, 'Welcome Traveller'?"

I grinned at him, "How did you pick me as a visitor to the United States?"

"Your walk, your clothes, the way you look at things and now I've heard you speak I would say, 'Welcome Sydney, Australia'."

"You're exactly right." I went with him and they interviewed me thoroughly prior to the show, which was to go on that evening. The obviously experienced young American who sat opposite me asked, "What is your work?"

"I am a doctor."

"What sort of a doctor?"

"A medical one."

"That's swell. Where do you work?"

"In Australia and in East Africa."

There was a sudden change in his expression, "You're not a medical missionary are you?"

"Yes."

There was resignation in his voice. "Then I suppose you'd like to give a testimony to our coast-to-coast audience of twenty-seven million people?" A tight smile came round his lips. "Do it in fifteen seconds and you're on."

"Fair enough." I prayed a short explosive prayer and this is what came into my mind. "I've known *about* God all of my life but I didn't know *Him*. One day I realised exactly who Jesus Christ is, and what He's done for me. I asked Him to forgive me and let me become one of His family. Then I found that the entrance fee into the Kingdom of Heaven was nothing, but the annual subscription was all I had."

He stood up, saying, "That's swell, you must write that out for me."

The same evening I was able to tell this to the vast audience, as well as highlights of working in a mission hospital in Africa. Incidentally, they presented me with five-hundred dollars' worth of surgical instruments and a pair of gold cuff-links with compasses in them.

That day I learnt a great deal about television from the inside and was determined to find out more. I went to a hospital in Boston with an international reputation for its treatment of rheumatic diseases. When the clinic was over I hurried back to my hotel and watched television till midnight: news, children's sessions, sport, a film – the lot. The next day I was due in Toronto. When I arrived I pulled every string available to me and was allowed into the control room to see the production of the children's programme of the Canadian Television Service. The number of people involved, the skills required and the cost took my breath away.

I thought it was vital that Clifford Warne and Graham Wade should see all that I had seen and more. There were special Christian Television courses in New York. I had an entry into television in England, Canada, and the major networks in the States. Arriving back in Australia I worked very hard and earned all I could and made available to my friends enough to pay their fares.

In 1956 Graham and Gwen Wade and Clifford and Doreen Warne set out – the Wades going east and the Warnes going west. If ever there was a spartan round-the-world safari it was that. Sometimes two meals a day was the rule and accommodation was the cheapest available. Graham and Gwen travelled through Holland, Belgium and Germany on push-bikes. In Germany, Graham illustrated the first edition of *Unter dem Buyubaum*, the German counterpart of *Jungle Doctor's Fables*. In East Africa he filled his head and sketchbook with pictures and ideas. Out of that Safari came illustrations for the Jungle Doctor adventure series, and the line drawings for *Jungle Doctor's Progress* and *Jungle Doctor Panorama*. Always Graham captured the atmosphere of a situation.

In Tanganyika Clifford's conjuring was received with awe. He might well have been placed very high in the ranks of the magicians if he had not made it very clear that it was all fun and that he was not working in with the spirit world. Both my friends squeezed every drop of usefulness out of their travels, with Clifford succeeding in appearing before T.V. audiences of the three great American networks.

When television came to Australia we were ready for it. We visited one station with a huge suitcase full of puppets and ventriloquial apparatus and a folder with pictures of Clifford appearing overseas. It was no little satisfaction to realise that

Running a mission at Wanganui, N.Z., with Rosemary and David, 1963 (*above*) and (*below*). With Rev. Dan Mbogoni (Daudi of the books) at the opening of the new Mvumi Hospital, 1967

Television: (*above*) "Meeting Point" programme with William Purcell, BBC Midlands Regional Religious Organiser. 1967. (*below*) With Clifford Warne and "Toto", the TV puppet

we had suprised the station's executives. So thoroughly was this done that for a record thirteen and a half years Clifford appeared as a conjuror and ventriloquist on the children's sesssion of Channel 7 in Sydney. He became seasoned in television technique and script-writing. People in the street nodded to him and made jokes about his clown puppet, Gus. All this time ideas and material were being built up and advances made with scripting.

I flew to England to help launch *Jungle Doctor Panorama*. Howard Mudditt had a contact with the B.B.C. and I was invited out to lunch with Bill Purcell, their Midlands Religious Organiser. In the middle of the soup he asked me, "How did you become a Christian?"

I put down my spoon. "If I tell you that you won't let me near a T.V. camera."

His eyes gleamed. "Nevertheless, tell me."

I told him the story that I told earlier in this book about the Bishop and the stinking polecat. I finished up, "That was the start of it all."

He leaned forward. "Would you say that if I put you on "Meeting Point"? It has eight million viewers every Sunday evening."

"Put me on camera and try to stop me!"

He smiled, went to the telephone, rang through to London and was back in a few minutes. "You're on. Sunday, 4th July."

I wrote the script. The B.B.C. man didn't touch it with his blue pencil but, pointing to the last hundred or so words, said, "That is not a very forceful way to wind up. You're a forthright type. Finish in a forthright way."

I thought at once of the Great Wall fable story. We could use the filmstrip for visuals. He was delighted. "They'll run this show later on in Australia and New Zealand."

On that occasion I spoke to more people than the sum total of all I've ever spoken to from pulpit or platform.

That telecast was directly linked with the writing of this book. Two separate publishers buttonholed me in England and said, "Write it just as you told it on Sunday. Tell about the things that happened to you: love, adventure, tragedy, medicine, the ordinary things, the funny things. ... A book like that could be worth writing."

Chapter Seventeen:

Fables

ANIMAL STORIES HAVE ALWAYS BEEN A DELIGHT TO ME. As a child I made myself a pine-needle nest in the grass under a wattle tree. Here I would curl up in the shade and read the first monkey stories I'd ever met: "The Adventures of Fitzey, the Marmoset", in *Little Folks*.

Again and again I read them and made up many more of my own. I was nine – an age when imagination is at its peak. Imagination is brought to life by sound. There was bird song and the busy hum of bees in the yellow blossom above me and an undercurrent of wind in the branches. The fragrance of wattle and gum trees provided a rich memory background. Here I read Uncle Remus and came to know Brer Rabbit and Brer Fox. What a wonderful day it was when I found Kipling! He held me spellbound with the Just-So stories, Kim and the Jungle Tales. I read every book I could lay my hands on that told about dogs, horses and kangaroos, the farmyard, the forest, the bush and the jungle.

Especially I looked forward to Wednesdays and the arrival of *Tiger Tim's Weekly*. Comic or cartoon books, call them what you will, have a magnetic appeal and this does not always stop at childhood.

As a choir-boy I felt indignant when our minister read the Bible in a dull voice, each word falling with the monotony of a dripping tap. Why should he make a great story and a wonderful happening sound so uninteresting?

I read about the ark and measured out its length in the cow paddock. I saw how high it was and in my mind could see the whole structure – so different to the toys and many of the picture books. Noah must have been an excellent zoologist. There could never have been a dull moment in the ark. I read and thought out how David fought the lion and the bear. Balaam and his ass were intriguing. Then there was the donkey's jawbone that Samson used so effectively. I didn't care much for Samson. I thought that his trick with the foxes was a very shabby one. I chuckled when Jesus said it was easier for a camel to go through the eye of a needle than for a rich man to enter the kingdom of heaven. This was a picture as sharp as the point of the needle. Again, how tremendously clear it was when Jesus spoke of those who strain out a mosquito but swallow a camel. I was not particularly drawn to camels after one had spat accurately at me on the notable occasion of a circus coming to Bowral.

As a child I was greatly impressed with the way that Jesus chose again and again to have some object, person or activity at hand when he made his point. There was Caesar's head on the coin, the child who sat on his knee, the wheat, and the sower. He talked of sheep, fig trees, weeds, lamps, bread and fish.

The only king of ancient history I could ever visualise was Herod. Jesus said, "Go and tell that fox...." Fox-like faces were well known to me.

Tucked away in my head, somewhat untidily, were file upon file of magnificent animal stories. I had been in Africa about six months and was beginning to get my tongue round the Chigogo language. My target was to help men's bodies and to use the parable of sickness and its cure to explain how Jesus frees us from the disease of our soul. I had spent a lot of time preparing my first talk in a language other than English.

The first time Jesus preached he talked about repentance. So did John the Baptist and so did Peter who produced a splendid punchline: "Now you must repent and be converted so that your sins may be wiped out."

I tried to talk about repentance to a ward-full of sick African men and boys. I had asked my friend, Dan, to stand by to help me. I felt that the words were coming quite fluently, although it was clear that Australian thoughts were being translated into an African language. Everybody seemed to be listening when a deep sigh came from a boy with a broken leg. This was echoed from the other end of the ward.

I felt a touch on my shoulder. Dan said to me softly, "Stop now, Bwana. This is *mabulibuli du* — only smoke, and steam."

Do you really understand what you are trying to say?"

"Of course, I do."

"Well, what is repentance?"

I tried to look intelligent, then stumbled and stuttered, "Repentance is — um, eh, well...."

He grinned. "It is not clear in your mind, and how can you make anyone understand what you don't grip firmly with the hand of your mind?"

Later with a dictionary and a commentary, we found that to repent meant "to think again" or "to change the mind."

Dan thought for a while, then smiled, "We have a way in this country of telling stories and making people see the whole thing in their heads."

"Do this tomorrow, Dan, but let me be there so that I may learn." I was intrigued next morning when he told the tale of a monkey who went out on a limb and started to cut through it. Again and again giraffe advised him to change his mind about what he was doing and where he was cutting. The advice became more forceful and then parrot added his voice, "Change your mind. Change your direction. Go to the safe side — the trunk side." Again and again the words, "Change your mind. Change your direction." He told the story dramatically and every eye in the room was on him. They certainly understood what repentance was and the need for it, and I had discovered a new way of making abstract words and long theological terms understandable. My target now was to present the great facts of Christianity in a way that everybody could understand.

In the hot African evenings I listened to stories that had been passed down for centuries in the tribe. I absorbed the way they were told, the colour and the vigour of it all. Hunters told me of their adventures, as did a snake catcher who not only sent creeps up my spine but showed me the art of catching snakes and relieving them of their poison.

On my way back from Africa, in Colombo, I was asked to talk to a Church Missionary Society Girls' School. It was explained that half the school would go out before I started to speak because they came from Buddhist families. Working on the principle that no one is suspicious of a storyteller I told, African fashion, how little leopards become big leopards. There was a hum of excitement amongst those who were in the assembly room. Then there was laughter. Heads appeared at the windows and before long girls tiptoed into the room and the back seats began to fill up. All this time the story went on and little leopard grew bigger and bigger even though he was only fed on porridge. His teeth grew and his claws grew. The suspense of the story held them. Thirty years later a lady from Sri Lanka told me she still remembered that little leopards become big leopards and big leopards kill; also that little sins become big sins and sin always kills. "And what about the great hunter ?" I asked her. "He was wounded," she replied, "so that those of his village might go free."

Back in Australia I had a handful of stories that I used regularly when asked to give a brief talk to the children. If I wanted to speak about the New Birth, I told the story of the Goat who wanted to become a Lion. If Justification by Faith was the subject the story of the Monkey who tried to lift himself out of the mud by his whiskers was told. To illustrate the various aspects of Temptation my listeners heard the Small Wisdom of Feeding Vultures. One of the favourites was the Great Wall that appeared through the jungle, which made it clear that sin separates us from God and that we cannot get through that barrier by anything we do ourselves.

The factor above everything else that gave the fables a world coverage was my meeting with Clifford Warne. I have always been interested in rugby football. On that particular Saturday it was the semi-finals. I had planned to go and was excited about it. The phone went and Mary answered it. "It's Faith Terry. She wants us to go to a special meeting at the children's home she runs and wonders if you would tell them an African story. Also there is a seventeen-year-old who heard you speak once before and he very much wants to meet you."

Inside me flared hostility. Why should they pick this day of all days? I looked at Mary. She really wanted to go and wouldn't say so. So often I went to meetings or committees or on interstate visits when there was no opportunity for Mary to come. She would go to the football because I enjoyed it, but here was a function she really wanted to attend. Trying to keep disappointment out of my voice I asked, "What time do we leave?"

Mary's face lit up, "Oh, you'll go. I thought you wanted to go to the football. I hardly liked to suggest...."

I prayed a short prayer, "Lord, what's it all about?"

Mary was radiant, and told me a lot of stories about Faith and her family, the Begbies, whom I respected tremendously.

We arrived. I found myself facing twenty twelve-year-old girls and a very neat young man. Would I tell them a story? Certainly. I told them the story of the monkey who got into the bog and tried to lift himself out by his whiskers. They listened well. This always makes it easier for a speaker. Then the young man who had been introduced to me as Clifford Warne, gave a conjuring display. His patter was good and full of laughs. I regarded myself as tolerably capable in conjuring but my eyes opened wide as trick after trick, well beyond my capacity, was performed. Then Clifford produced a pack of cards and asked me to select four. I did. They were alphabetical cards and he placed them one above the other and proceeded to give a small talk using these letters as an acrostic. He did it extremely well. Later I said, "Clifford, you ought to be on radio, not working as a clerk in an airline." His eyes lit up. "Would you like me to see what I can do?"

"There's nothing I'd like more."

A month later he was an announcer and running the children's session on the country radio station, 2NZ, Inverell.

Looking back, how glad I am to have missed that football match! Clifford Warne went on to do great things. He has been one of my closest friends and together we have worked on all manner of ventures.

One hot summer's day when we were on a family holiday at Ballina in northern New South Wales, I was relaxed, sitting in the shade and watching the water of the river sparkle. Soldier crabs walked importantly about on the sand. Seagulls flew overhead and crows jeered from a dead tree. It was an ideal situation for writing, and I felt the ink stirring in my blood. I rigged up an ancient tape recorder and told myself the fable stories that I had used over and over again on three continents. When they were on tape I listened to them back again and again, making notes and alterations.

That afternoon's work was the foundation-laying of *Jungle Doctor's Fables*, a book which was to develop in many

Fables

different directions. The individual stories were put through a careful series of filters before I ventured to send the book to The Paternoster Press.

When they were typed out I asked a primary schoolboy to read them. He did and in a good round hand wrote at the bottom of each what he felt. Some were classified as "good," some "very good" and one only merited "very fair."

I played them to Clifford Warne, who is in the habit of calling me "chief." He listened to them carefully, read and polished the typescripts, and adapted them for puppet plays.

My amusing artist friend, Graham Wade, who was later to illustrate the book, drew sketches and sequences, and put on paper the early stages of a comic-strip book and the roughs of flash cards, or a flash-book, used in modern teaching methods.

All three of us started using the stories widely in speaking to people of all ages. Later we compared notes on audience reaction.

Five fable books have been written since then, and from them have come filmstrips, comic books, flash-books, television and radio programmes and cassettes and, latest of all, two-and-a-quarter-minute stories for "Dial-a-Story" on the telephone in New Zealand and Victoria. One or more fables have appeared in seventy-one languages. Writing these books is not without cost. While writing *Jungle Doctor's Fables* I lost the art of putting my head on the pillow and going quickly to sleep. Insomnia comes to the head swirling with ideas. When writing a fables book (or an autobiography for that matter) my mind is in a turmoil with phrases, words, matters I want to express clearly and pointedly, and sleep retreats.

The time required for these small books is out of all proportion to the number of words in them. Let me tell you of the events that led up to the publishing of *Jungle Doctor's Hippo Happenings*.

One miserable night allergy was on the rampage in my system. I lay propped up in bed with a small leather suitcase on my knee. My eyes were itchy and red. My nose was running. I sneezed and wheezed and breath came only in short pants. Self-pity surrounded me like a patch of dank fog. Idly I wrote about a Hippo who sneezed and wheezed and itched, who complained in a loud, sad voice and wanted all within earshot to share in his woe. Boohoo, the Hippo, was born that night. A small smile found its way to the corners of my mouth. I was that Hippo. His moods were my moods. His miseries were mine. As I looked at myself from Boohoo's angle I decided that there was need for a change of thinking. Almost at once the allergy started to lose its grip. *Jungle Doctor's Hippo Happenings* was undoubtedly launched that night but it took five years to get him ready to take his place in the bookshops.

Nine times the script went back to the typewriter. My habit was to correct the roughs in red, then blue, then green and finally black. We tried the stories out on audiences of all ages. We used them on radio and television and were more than encouraged. Publishers, artists, booksellers, teachers, parents – all have read the stories and given their ideas and comments which helped considerably, and then it was finished. However, I decided to read it just once more under circumstances which inevitably seemed to sharpen my wits – the upstairs front seat of a double-decker bus. It was a sunny, windy day. As I had ten minutes to wait, I walked briskly up the road clutching a manilla folder with Hippo in it. As I topped the hill a wild gust hit me. I tripped and lost my grip of the folder. To my horror a snow storm of paper went swirling up the main road, under the wheels of cars and trucks. Some pages flattened themsleves against the fence. Others shot up into the air like kites. I chased those precious papers, which represented years of work, grabbing them and thrusting them back into their folder. People stared at me. I was red in the face, perspiring and feeling a complete goat. Forty minutes later and two miles further on I picked up the last page of Fable Book number four.

When a manuscript is parcelled and posted there is a sense of great relief. Then, almost reverently, I place the notes, jottings and earlier typings of the book into my largest waste paper basket. But this is only the beginning of the end. In due time come the page proofs. These are given complete priority. Everything is dropped to correct them and airmail them back at the first possible moment. Then comes the great day when the new book – the finished article – arrives. There have been years of work in it but it can be easily read in half an hour.

Jungle Doctor's Hippo Happenings had arrived in Sydney.

Fables

There was an eye-catching window display in a large book shop. I stood in an inconspicuous spot admiring the whole set-up and thinking how well a window full of Hippos looked. As I did so I heard this gem of dialogue. A man whom I do not remember meeting was talking to the salesman. He was holding up a copy of *Hippo Happenings* and saying loudly, "This Jungle Doctor man, Paul White, I know him well. These books are no trouble to him. He just sits down and writes these things as they come into his head."

Actually the battle for the right word and the appropriate phrase breaks out again and again even though the book is finished. The stories need to be scripted differently for their audio-visual cousins. This is a considerable and exacting task but, I believe, a small one when compared with translating into another language. This I have never done. I raise my hat to the noble army of linguists who have translated one or more of the fables into seventy-one languages; some of them people I know, others whom I have never met, from all points of the compass. What a task is theirs when they are faced with little verbal twists that add a smile or a special meaning to the English but are untranslatable, as they stand, into another tongue. Take for instance the punchline of the last fable in the Hippo book, "What's the good of having all the worms in all the world if you finish up a dead duck?"

Even the titles have their difficulties. *Jungle Doctor's Monkey Tales* is smooth going in English but in no other language. I was delighted when I found the German publisher had come to light with a title with rhythm in it, *"Von Affen, Giraffen und anderen Tieren."*

In our sitting room is a bookcase. One whole shelf contains books for which I am responsible. The right hand end contains the forty that so far have been published in English, the other end the translations starting with Arabic and ending with Zulu. Of these languages there are only three that I can read with any degree of ease. In some, like Vietnamese, Lao and some Indian languages the European style is followed, but many others like Chinese, Urdu, Arabic and Hebrew run back-to-front from my way of looking at things. I know these are Jungle Doctor Books only by the pictures that are in them. It is an odd situation to find yourself looking at a volume you have written but which you cannot read.

Sometimes I stand looking at these books and quietly pray for the people whose country I have never visited, whose script I cannot read, and yet in God's goodness I have the chance to pass on the Good News by means of an animal story. There have been many letters from a wide variety of places telling of the use of the stories and pictures. One came from a Professor of Pharmacy at a Japanese University, Dr. Sakaguchi. He wrote, "A young couple from Australia, Mr. & Mrs. Ken Ridley, came to take up residence in the small house my family had used as a temporary refuge when we lost our Tokyo houses during the war. I had been a keen student of English for years, and when the Ridleys agreed to my request and began to teach me English conversation I was overjoyed. I believe God used this to draw me to Himself.

"At about this time I was also reading for practice in English the book, *Jungle Doctor's Fables*. Such was the challenge within it that before I had finished reading this book I had accepted Jesus Christ as my Saviour."

Professor Sakaguchi later translated this book into Japanese and it went through a number of editions.

I hope you will have a look at these fable books. To me they represent the most important work of my life. C. S. Lewis said, "If you want to say something important, write a children's book."

Chapter Eighteen:

Bathrooms

I HAVE ALWAYS BEEN INTRIGUED BY BATHROOMS.
In our old family home at Bowral the bath was a noble, high vessel, of a length to be satisfying even to Goliath. It was made of solid cast-iron and painted with partial success with white enamel. The hot water came from three large kettles heated over the fuel stove and when all three had been poured in, the bath had absorbed most of the heat. This meant a hasty bath in an inch or two of tepid water – a thing of little comfort to a small boy, but at least it minimised the frequency of the ordeal.

We moved, and had a really white, ordinary-sized bath, but still hot water came from kettles. It was possible now to share four inches of really warm water with sundry celluloid birds and animals. And there was a shower too, a lovely thing in the very hot weather, but a nuisance as a general rule, for it dripped coldly and left a brown stain which called for the regular use of Old Dutch Cleanser.

Our migration to Sydney was a further step forward. We had a bath-heater – a splendid idea – as much hot water as you wished – in theory, that is. According to the instructions, "run the water slowly, then insert a lighted match in aperture A, turn on gas to the required level and regulate water-flow to obtain desired heat." Turning on the water was all right, but inserting the match and turning on the gas was quite different. The gas tap was stiff and turning it on was no easy matter. The match would burn down. The gas would turn on hurriedly. This would produce surprising explosions, loud enough to excite the neighbours' interest, because the window had necessarily to be open at least four inches at the top. I was well aware of the danger of carbon monoxide.

The luxurious streak in my nature called for a hot shower. I talked mother into purchasing a dozen feet of stout cord, a strong screw-in hook, a galvanised pulley and a noble device known as a bush shower. The container held three gallons of hot water, a plug at the bottom opened into a bowl-shaped device suitably perforated, and when you pulled the string the hot water came down. Cease pulling for some such purpose as groping for the soap, and the water stopped, pull again and there you were until the three gallons ran out. I derived high pleasure from this ingenious machine, but on the other hand our bathroom had a lead-lined floor with no neat little plug-hole to let the water run out. There was a mop, however, in the corner of that bathroom and somehow the satisfaction of a shower was whittled away by the need to wield this unaesthetic household aid.

As a fully-fledged but wholly inexperienced doctor I found a new concept in bathrooms in hospital. For the first time in my life water, H and C, was available at the turn of a tap in the one place at the one time. Hot showers are a magnificently relaxing invention. After an exacting all night of medical emergencies there is considerable solace and some wakefulness to be found under the hot shower. With warm water cascading over weary muscles I have philosophised about motor-bikes and those who fall off them in the early hours of the morning. I have assured myself that nothing can be more thoughtless towards the comfort of an inexperienced casualty-surgeon than asking him to deal with a fractured leg in the hour before dawn.

All hospitals, however, are not the same. In my final year as a student I had worked in another and smaller institution as a resident medical student. The doctor in charge was a lady who lived in a flat two storeys above the quarters of mere men.

In this hospital the hot water was turned off at 7 p.m. on the grounds of economy. At 6.45 I would three-quarters fill the bath with extremely hot water and I looked forward to soaking in it at about 10 o'clock when the temperature would be ideal. The lady doctor upstairs was not of provident mind, and I was amazed and horrified some days later to see her dressed in a striking bath-robe making her way into our bathroom, some half-an-hour before I had even thought of doing so. When this series of events recurred night after night my mind slipped smoothly into gear. I went to the dispensary and came back with a small bottle. With the help of a ladder I interfered with the light globe and satisfied myself that adequate illumination for anyone to find their way about came in through the high-up window which fronted the main road. Now the lady was a blonde – ash blonde I believe is the term. I drew the water, poured in the crystals from my little bottle, reminding myself that this was my bath and I could do with it what I wished. I then sat down to read the distilled wisdom of Sir William Osler, whose writing of clinical medicine is literature as well as science. Footsteps came down the stairs, the lady tripped past my door, flicked down the bathroom light-switch, grunted when nothing happened, then closed the door gently and locked it firmly. I was delighted to hear splashing sounds, picked up the empty bottle that had held the crystals and read with satisfaction the words "Gentian Violet," and I thought what a delightful shade of purple it produced and how relatively permanent the colouring was and, after all, how was I to know that anyone was going to steal my bath-water?

As events turned out the lady did not appear in public for four complete days!

In Africa we had the different situation of having no taps at all. A local craftsman, however, combined a bucket, the rose of a watering-can and a contrivance for regulating the flow of water, to make a jungle shower-bath. When the water had to be carried in kerosene tins from wells a mile away, a two-gallon bath was an expensive luxury, but a delightful one nevertheless. The water was so carefully husbanded that every drop of bath-water irrigated our paw-paws and tomatoes *via* a pipe carefully shielded with wire to keep out both reptiles and insects.

I imported a chip-heater for immediate heating of water in the hospital. This functioned perfectly. The same could not be said for one erected in a beach cottage in Australia. Dressed in my bathing costume I proceeded to stoke this contrivance. Water ran a little spasmodically from its spout, the chips and newspaper in its interior burnt happily and noisily and there came the characteristic panting, throbbing noise from its internal workings. I turned on the tap for the water flow, but as something seemed to be blocking the pipe, I beat a hasty retreat.

I was not quick enough. Before I reached the door there was a loud explosion. The pipe that led to the roof burst wide open. I was showered with soot, and emerged from the bathroom somewhat confused and heavily patterned with black in a way that caused the family to have near hysterics.

In Canada I had two adventures separated by a matter of days, and each associated with children of tender years. In one home in which I was a guest I was apprehensive to find that there was no means of locking the bathroom door. I was in the middle of a shower when the door opened wide, and the four-year-old son of the house stood in the middle of the doorway solemnly inspecting me. Not knowing how to start a conversation I continued with my shower. His voice came clearly both to me and to those in the house generally, "I guess you're fatter than my Daddy."

Sitting in the lounge of a friend in Toronto, Ontario, and talking over weighty matters, our discussions were interrupted by my host's five-year-old daughter, walking regally and unclad down the stairs, a dripping nightdress under her arm. She paused and said, pointing an accusing finger at each of us in turn, "You, or you, or you, didn't put the lid down and I fell in."

Bathrooms are useful and intriguing, but they always contain an element of danger.

Chapter Nineteen:

A Time to Play

SOME THINGS SEEM TO BE TIED UP IN OUR GENES. Hamilton Hume, great-great-uncle, was quite an authority on the birds of the Australian bush, while great-great-grandfather, Walter White, was an inveterate traveller, book-writer and apparently a lover of cricket. This particular chapter is the sort of Saturday afternoon of this book. I'm relaxing, chatting about the outdoor things.

Let me lift a little from Walter White's "A month in Yorkshire" written over a century ago. Incidentally, great-great-grandfather was assistant secretary of the Royal Society in Somerset House. But back to cricket – 1862 vintage:

> I saw a cricket-match. As well might one hope to be merry at a funeral as at a game of cricket improved into its present condition, when the ball is no longer bowled but pelted, and the pelter's movements resemble those of jack-pudding; when gauntlets must be worn on the hands and greaves on the shins, and other inventions are brought in to deprive the pastime of anything like enjoyment. That twenty-two men should ever consent to come together for such a mockery of pleasure is to me a mystery. The only saving point attending it is that it involved some amount of exercise in the open air. Sympathise with modern cricket if you can.

Even more interesting than to find that one's great-great-grandfather was knowledgeable in the matter of cricket, is to find that he was a Christian. He talks of John Wycliffe, and says:

> Wycliffe died faithful to the truth for which he had dared to live. He bequeathed that truth to us and with God's blessing we will keep it alive and unblemished, using it manfully as a testimony against all lies and shams, whatsoever and wheresoever they may be found.

Cricket has always been one of the great joys of my life. I started off playing in the cow-paddock with some lads who lived near our home at Bowral. Singing in the choir involved practice on Tuesday afternoons. Before the music we played cricket, using for a wicket the pile of bricks, which was the foundation for a small tank, behind the church. It was here that I learned the art of bowling off-breaks and had the considerable pleasure of being told that I was a "good bowler" by the boy who was to do mighty things in Australian cricket, Don Bradman.

At Roseville I found a number of lads of my own age and of like mind. We played on a concrete wicket in the local park with a kerosene tin for a wicket. Then at school I had again the opportunity of playing cricket, with considerable satisfaction but moderate success. My broken and somewhat boomerang-shaped right arm was a nuisance when it came to football, but a distinct advantage in playing cricket; although I have the uncomfortable feeling that if anyone had really analysed my action I would have been called a "chucker."

It was always exciting to go to the Sydney Cricket Ground, sit on "the Hill" with my packet of sandwiches and bottle of tepid lemonade and watch a Sheffield Shield or Test match. If you wanted to see cricket and cricketers you had no choice but to go to the ground. These days commentators discuss and explain the wiles of the bowler and the mistakes of the batsmen. In the pre-radio and T.V. era a solitary schoolboy needed to watch closely and figure out these finer points of the game. I learnt much from watching men like Charlie Macartney, Alan Kippax, and the great Englishmen, Hobbs, Sutcliffe and Hammond. However I didn't succeed in infusing their skills into my personal performance. I followed with keen interest the activities of my fellow-chorister, although I have not had the opportunity of speaking to him since the days when we sang together.

Cricketers have coloured my life. The only Test players that I have known personally are Christians. Two of them, Englishmen John Dewes and David Sheppard, came to Australia in the same team. I met them when they spoke at Crusader and I.V.F. meetings. My personal prayer for them was that their cricket would be a positive witness for Jesus

A Time to Play

Christ. Unfortunately they didn't score heavily but their activities certainly made an impact among the schoolboy population of the time.

Then there was Brian Booth and the man who helped him into the Kingdom of God, Roy Gray. Roy is a most interesting personality. He was a Sergeant-Major in the army and at the same time a very forthright Christian. On one occasion he was instructed by the Colonel of his regiment to fall in the troops and march them to church. When they arrived they found that the Chaplain was not there and to the amazement of both troops and Colonel the service and the sermon were undertaken by the Regimental Sergeant-Major. Roy was a first-grade cricketer who believed in action, be it in the matter of Christian activity or in cricket. He hit the ball and hit it hard. One of Sydney's newspapers had offered fifty pounds to the first-grade cricketer who scored fifty runs in the fastest time each week. Roy reached his half-century in thirty-seven minutes and won the prize but requested that the money might be sent to me to be used in the hospital in Tanganyika. He was well aware that there was a newspaper story in this. Not only was his cricket written up, but so was the story of the hospital in Africa and what it was all about. Considerable interest was stirred up.

Roy Gray was a man who would talk to people freely, openly and happily about his Lord, Jesus Christ. One of those to whom he spoke was fellow-cricketer from the St.George Cricket Club in Sydney, Brian Booth. Brian has been one of the outstanding cricketers in Australia, playing in a way which exactly fitted in with his witness. Incidentally he was an international hockey player as well. I prayed regularly for Brian that his cricket would be a blessing to other people. One day while gardening and listening on a transistor radio to his progress towards a hundred in a Test at Brisbane, I prayed that he would be helped in his concentration. He was, and scored one hundred and twelve runs. In writing of Brian's retirement from representative cricket a well-known sporting journalist calls him a Test batsman of elegance and humility.

David Sheppard came out again to play cricket for England when he was an ordained clergyman, and there were a string of stories told about his activities. But I remember his coming to my home and having a meal. We discussed the strategy of producing a book with Christian implications at the time when he was in the public eye with a cricket bat in his hand. He did that in a book called *Parson's Pitch*. When a man's cricket, his sport, is a part of his seeking first the kingdom of God, it can produce results for that kingdom.

It's a strange thing, but if you say you're interested in birds, such is the slang of the moment that a grin breaks over your listener's face. He raises his eyebrows but before he can think of anything sufficiently witty to say, I add, "Ornithology is a tremendous hobby." For me that means not only looking at the feathered creatures but listening to their song.

For as long as I can remember places have been anchored in my memory by the birds I saw and heard there. As a very small boy I was thrilled to see a Red-capped Robin which frequently sat on the fence post, the Willy Wagtail that, as I went to sleep, produced its call of "sweet-pretty-creature" outside the window, and the Jackie Winter – that nimble flycatcher, with its song of "peter-peter-peter." There was the Peewee or Mudlark which was completely unafraid and moved expectantly within feet of my father's spade as he dug the vegetable garden. I would wake to the carolling of the Magpie which somehow always reminded me of a policeman, with its busy walk and expectant eye. Its music at dawn and dusk, especially when there is a background of wind through pine trees, is a delicacy to my ear.

When I reached an age in which tree-climbing was within my scope, Parrots took on a new interest, as did Swallows. In gum trees I found nests with the eggs of the Crimson Rosella and the Eastern Rosella. What magnificent colours these birds wore! I had no realisation then that there were fifty-seven varieties of Parrots in Australia, each of them literally a gem of colour. I did recognise, however, the number of calls that these birds made. The warning call was obvious, but as you sat in the shadow and listened and watched there were bell-like notes, an amusing chatter, and the sounds of fight. The Eastern Rosella, whose colours are more brilliant the closer you are to the coast, has had twenty-seven different, separate sounds recorded and classified, and when all is said and done there are only twenty-six letters in the English alphabet!

Bowral, the town of my boyhood, had a number of English

A Time to Play

shrubs and trees. One picturesque road, half-way up The Gib, had tall pine trees near the fence, which was of mellowed gum tree slabs. On it grew lichen and that red growth of a tiny plant which at the university I discovered was haematococcus – sonorous and imposing word, I thought. But the dictionary took the gloss away when it said this meant "red little round thing."

There were hawthorn and bracken fern and lilac and daffodils and violets and comfortable grass to lie in and listen to the song of the Thrush. How I liked Thrushes, grey and fearless, with an eye that was completely friendly. There was a sound which I learnt to mimic though I do not remember seeing the songster. I now know he is the Rufous Whistler. The whole of Australia benefits from his delightful notes. Sometimes on Saturday afternoons I obtained permission to go and see the cricket on the Bowral oval and with considerable pride watched Don Bradman, a boy of twelve, playing first-grade with the men. I would stop from time to time to look up into the gum trees at the Soldier Birds that produced their own variety of sound, not so much music as noisy comment. And then there were Crows, jeering, noisy and somehow threatening.

There was a gap in my ornithological findings when I left the country for the city. My researches were more into the activities of birds which I regarded as vandals. Sparrows made their nests in our chimney and Swallows built in a corner of the verandah, while Starlings preferred the roof and left their tale behind them. As I searched for information as to how to deal with these intruders I found that in England they were called Lousy Jacks. Mother didn't think this was quite nice.

Years later, one hot Christmas day, I was in the local church – a fine edifice – five seats from the front of the left-hand side. In the middle of the first hymn I was intrigued to see some tiny, crawling beasties moving over the pages of the hymnbook. An inquisitive finger informed me that they were bird lice. More and more of them kept dropping. It was a very hot day. I had no coat and I could see them landing on my white shirt. As soon as the sermon was over, and I hasten to add, after the collection, I hurried from the building, ran home and spent a long time under a hot shower. It gave me pleasure to ring the local minister and inform him that from my own personal observations, St. Alban's, Lindfield, was lousy! This produced a profound silence and I went on to say that the nest of the offending bird was to be found above the fifth seat on the left-hand side.

Many of the birds in Sydney are imports. Starlings we've met. Sparrows we've met. There was the Indian Turtle Dove which would perch near our chimney-pot and fill the house with its soothing note; and then there was the perky little Indian bird, the Crested Bulbul.

No bird flies into my memory to accent university or hospital years, but going overseas I met Crows, strangely raucous in Ceylon, even more so and quite multitudinous in Bombay. They were there again in East Africa and are noble scavengers, thorough and capable. Birds of a like ilk were the Vultures that circled high when some creature had died in the thornbush jungle. Above the East African towns and market places circled Kites. Weaver Birds built their nests, close as home units, in the thorn-trees, sometimes killing the tree by their sheer weight of numbers. A score of families were represented and colours from brilliant crimson to bright yellow merged with the browns and olives and greys of their feathers.

The great drama came with the arrival of the Sacred Ibis after the rains when crops were sprouting and the caterpillars appeared in their hordes. Out of nowhere came thousands upon thousands of these great birds. I was told that no one would in any way assault them: they were the defenders of the crops – good friends. Once I saw a plague of locusts. The Ibis worked with tremendous efficiency to such a degree that they could barely rise off the ground, so full were their crops of the invaders. I was intrigued to find that the African farmers were prepared to spend the night driving off the hyaenas for whom the glutted birds were an easy prey.

There were the Egyptian Geese that flew over in formation at sunset, gaggles upon gaggles. There were the slow-flying Golden-crested Cranes, the national bird of Uganda. A dozen of them in a leafless baobab tree against the brilliant sunset was a picture not to be forgotten.

With the coming of tape-recorders I had a new way of expressing my hobby. Bird photography is an expensive game and as a photographer I was never highly successful, but collecting bird sound was a different matter. Equipment became more

A Time to Play

sophisticated, lighter, and battery-powered. Tape has the great advantage of re-use. If you don't like a run you can go back to where you started and do it again. I was interested but not really enthusiastic until one notable day. Driving along the banks of the Hawkesbury River, some thirty miles north of Sydney, I stopped every now and then to record a bird sound. There were Honeyeaters, Butcher Birds and Wonga Pigeons. It was all fun, but nothing was outstanding. Then up a narrow, gravel road, with mountain rising steeply on one side and gully falling sharply on the other, I heard a Butcher Bird sing more loudly than I had ever heard one do so before. I slid the car into the side of the road, grabbed the recorder, turned it on and with my eyes standing out recorded bird after bird at high volume and great clarity. There were flocks of Rosella Parrots, the Eastern Whip-Bird, a Grey Thrush, the Butcher Bird, and then a note I had never heard before, rising to a crescendo and falling away, powerful, resonant, striking. Then, to my disgust, a large truck ground its way past. I was choked in dust and the machine had to be turned off.

It took a good minute for that smelly horror to drive out of earshot. But the bird went on. It added Gill Bird, Friar Bird, Black Cockatoo and others that I did not recognise and then a unique song. Car after car passed me, again and again I switched the machine off and on. I found a place where I could put an arm round a strong sapling and hang out over the forty-foot drop. Beneath me there were tree ferns, dense scrub and a quiet pool of water. On the other side of the gully were sandstone caves crested with gum trees. It was a magnificent sounding-bowl for that master of mimicry and music, the Superb Lyrebird. In size it is similar to a Pheasant, its tail second only to a Peacock's. There it was beneath me going through its display routine, on its mound – a cleared area amongst the ferns. I listened entranced for forty minutes while it went on, traffic or no traffic. This was a golden nugget of bird sound. The singing of that bird created a new facet in my life.

Lyrebirds sing in the winter. I was in the New England National Park at the edge of the Great Dividing Range. The East Coast of New South Wales was visible for a hundred miles. This was the highest peak of the range and a spot frequented by Lyrebirds. You could hear them deep down in the valley in the day-time. It was a cold and frosty morning. In the dawn light I could see icicles hanging from the eaves of a hut. Outside there was music — a Lyrebird again, rich in mimicry but with a fantastic song of its own. I had found out that Lyrebirds have their own key melody according to their habitat and here was the sound of flute music. I grabbed the recorder and the microphone, rushed outside in my pyjamas, taking no notice of the frost, and set up to record. I stood amazed at the music. There were three birds. Suddenly I was conscious of the temperature. I had been standing in that chilly dawn unaware of anything but bird sound. With feet cold beyond belief I hobbled inside the hut, lit the stove, had a hot shower, cooked breakfast — and still they sang on and on and on. Twice I changed tapes. There was an hour and a half of bird sound such as I did not believe possible. Tape-recorders and carefully labelled boxes are in front of me. This is such fantastic bird song that I am making cassettes of it for such as appreciate this kind of music. How I would have liked to play this to Mozart, Bach and Telemann; and I smiled to think what Haydn would have done with it.

You become aware of birds and their voices when you watch international cricket. On Brisbane Cricket Ground you hear the Fig Bird. From Sydney and Melbourne comes the melody of the Indian Myna, while everywhere you have Silver Gulls by the score, not only watching but going fearlessly into the middle of the ground. With them occasionally is Willy Wagtail and Peewee.

I look at a heap of tapes in my cupboard. One is labelled "Birds and Bells." There is the Bell Miner, a small canary-sized, olive-coloured bird whose sound is a tinkle which Paganini would have enjoyed. Inland is the Crested Bell Bird with a variety of bell-like notes. Lyrebirds' small friend the Yellow Robin, has his own small bell.

Another mimic and an altogether amazing bird is the Bower Bird. The male Satin Bower Bird in beautiful deep blue plumage, skilfully constructs a bower from carefully selected sticks. He decorates it with blue articles, be they flower, cloth, toothbrush, or varied bits and pieces of plastic. I stood at the edge of the rain-forest and watched him display in his bower and then depart. A few moments later the Regent Bower Bird,

A Time to Play

beautiful with his black and gold and a touch of red on his brow, came bringing a yellow plastic teaspoon which he deposited amongst the blue and proceeded to do his own display in the borrowed bower. All went well for some half minute and then with a noise like an angry cat the Satin Bower Bird was back, the Regent put to flight, and the yellow spoon tossed out.

There are Kingfishers: the tiny Blue – a rarity, the Azure, that beautifies so many rivers. The largest Kingfisher is the Kookaburra, the Laughing Jackass of the Southern States. He chuckles, laughs and includes snakes in his diet. His cousin is the Blue-Winged Kookaburra, who can also laugh but has the most fantastic jeer for the notes of his Southern relatives.

It is a magnificent way of relaxing to walk through the bush and listen to the sound of Cuckoos, Whistlers, Warblers, the harmony of small birds and the concerto of the bush at sunrise and sunset. There is nothing more peaceful to a busy mind than to sit back and to listen to a dawn chorus of birds. All cannot do it: few have the opportunity of hearing the birds at the right time, still fewer have a means of recording it. Men who know and love birds have been a joy to meet. The doyen is A. H. Chisholm, once the editor of one of Australia's great newspapers, now in his middle eighties – a keen observer and storehouse of a wealth of information.

Gardening I enjoy, although I am not very good at it. Shrubs seem to grow and flower whatever I do. The fence is covered with passionfruit vine. People admire the variety of flat stones that ornament the garden. I move them from place to place to discourage the weeds. Time needs to be made to watch the football. I am amongst the many who must deny themselves the delights of crowded roads, long queues and hard seats at the football grounds. Let there be no mention of wet days and water filling shoes and running down the neck! I have to content myself with lying on my bed and watching the action on a colour television set which was presented to me. I believe wholeheartedly that there should be a time to play.

Chapter Twenty:

Mary

WE WERE IN BED. MARY HAD BEEN LISTENING ON THE RADIO TO A talk about cancer of the breast and wanted to know more about it.

"It's not a difficult matter to examine a breast clinically," I told her. "You need to keep your hand flat against the ribs. You can find all sorts of lumps and bumps if you pick up breast tissue between your fingers."

"Show me," she asked.

I demonstrated on her left breast and did it thoroughly, explaining each step.

As I kissed her good night she said, "It's very good to know there is nothing there."

Christmas time that year I had been invited to speak for the International Fellowship of Evangelical Students at Urbana, Illinois.

Two weeks before I was due to leave and a month after our in-bed discussion, Mary came to me and said quietly. "I have a lump in my left breast."

She had. A hard, moveable swelling the size of a marble. My heart sank. Here was an ominous condition. Of one thing I was sure: a month before that lump wasn't there. We prayed together and asked God to show us what to do and to help us whatever happened. In a short time Mary went to sleep. I lay listening to the wind in the pine tree over the way. Sleep didn't come. I set out to plan what would normally be done under the circumstances.

There was a kindly and competent surgeon whom I knew well. He would take the matter over from there. Next day I took Mary to see this surgical specialist. His rooms were just down the street from mine. I went back to my own rooms and worked. It was important to act normally.

In the early afternoon I was seeing a patient and the telephone rang. I heard the crisp voice of the surgeon saying, "I'm afraid we must face it, Paul. Your wife's condition is malignant."

He went into technical detail to which I listened mechanically, but I had the feeling of being struck on the back of the head. Death seemed to come at me from the corner immediately ahead. The doctor's calm voice told me of the arrangements he had made for surgery. In as level a tone as I could manage I thanked him and put down the receiver and then tried to concentrate on a full afternoon of medical work.

There are times when medical knowledge is a handicap. This was one of them. That afternoon five cancer cases came to my notice and in each case there was the grim overtone of tragedy. The door closed behind my last patient. I put my head in my hands and wordlessly was in God's presence. Then came the thought, "The peace of God which passes all understanding will keep your heart and mind in the knowledge and the love of God."

How my heart needed keeping! It was heavy and bruised. How my mind needed keeping! It teemed with ominous statistics which shouted, death! death! death!

"Father," I breathed, "thank You for the knowledge that You are almighty and thank You for Jesus who helps me to understand You and thank You for His resurrection which takes the sting out of death."

Mine was a lesser Calvary that evening. Quietly I prayed for the life of the one I loved and as I did so the words came to my tired mind – Jesus' own words in Gethsemene, "Father, if it is your will let this cup pass from me, nevertheless not my will but yours be done."

As I walked down the street the lights of the city came on in a blaze of colour. I dodged through a maze of traffic but still His voice came, "Think in terms of eternity not of time. Your apprenticeship ceases when you pass through the small gate called death."

Days later I sat outside the operating theatre. The surgeon put his hand on my shoulder, "It was what we thought."

And the next day the telephone rang. This time it was the pathologist. Two words hit me, "Undoubtedly malignant."

What should I do now? Scripture after Scripture ran through my mind, "The prayer of faith shall heal the sick." And of course I had prayed and I had followed through the accepted routine for cancer of this variety. The operation had been skilfully performed but what now? My place was to accept what God gave, to thank Him for whatever He permitted and to keep on living my life close to Him.

Jesus had only three years of public ministry. This was the way God planned things and His healing and teaching and His training of men had only started when He was thirty. I thought that if I had been organising Jesus' time on earth how differently I would have planned it. But God had said, "My thoughts are not your thoughts neither are your ways my ways." And again I prayed, "Father, Mary's life means more to You and to Your kingdom than my wishes. If You want her now You know best but if the plan allows for her to stay, how greatly I want her. Nevertheless, Father, not my will but Yours be done."

There was no voice, no miracle, but there was deep peace in my heart.

Mary lay in hospital. She put her hand on mine as I sat beside her and said quietly, "You must go to that conference in America, Paul. How often we've said we must live our lives seeking first God's Kingdom. Perhaps our attitude to this crisis can underline to some of those students how important the missionary job is."

I could only nod. Her voice was only a whisper, "If they realise what it cost us for you to go...." Again I nodded.

A week later, not far from the windy city of Chicago I stood in front of an auditorium crowded with undergraduates and graduates. Most parts of the world were represented and certainly all states of the U.S. I told them what had happened, what Mary had said, and of how the challenge of the words of St. Paul had lifted my thinking. "I urge you to preach the word of God," he had written. "Never lose your sense of urgency in season and out of season. Prove, correct and encourage, using the utmost patience in your teaching. Stand fast in all that you're doing, meeting whatever suffering this may involve. Go on steadily preaching the Gospel and carry out the full commission that God gave you." Timothy 4, verses 1 to 5.

That was 1955. To this day I know of no direct result of that talk, but both Mary and I recognised our responsibility and carried it through.

I am well aware that God is able to do the miraculous. After all He made us and as I see it, why should it be unduly difficult for Him to intervene in any situation or circumstance He chooses? He had done it before.

But I feel that it should be remembered that much of the healing arts and skills have been made clear to man's mind over the years. I see it as a clear indication for people to avail themselves of the routine, well-accredited ways of medicine. I had thought of this at length before I had studied and practised medicine. For a large slice of my life I had sought to do my part in fighting against suffering, weakness and death.

When we had come back from Africa the warning had been that there was every likelihood of more episodes of the depressive psychosis. This is exactly what happened. One or two attacks occurred yearly.

There are two main varieties of depression – the built-in sort called *endogenous*, arising from inside, and *exogenous*, caused by outside events. Mary suffered from the first. It's a grim experience to see attack after attack occurring in one you love.

Mary told me that it was very much more shattering to suffer from it. She said depression would descend on her without warning: a sense of impending doom, of being crushed into the ground, of fear – paralysing fear. She felt cut off from other people and from God. Prayer was impossible except clutching desperately, vaguely, wordlessly. Depression can become an illness. Medical help has progressively become more effective and may be essential.

Back here in Australia in the mid 1940s advances had been made and hospitalization was readily available. All of this helped but it did not dispel the great cloud which would come down not only on Mary but on our whole home when depression struck. Ordinary living suddenly took on new unshapely proportions. Being cook, housemaid and laundryman and trying to take a mother's place cut sharply across my work of making broadcasts, giving talks, writing scripts and my annual book. Apart from this, to boil the pot I was working part-time in medicine. The children were splendid. Earlier on they had gone to stay with my mother but so often the unexpected had occurred. Once it was measles and on the next visit mumps.

In these times of stress I did not want to let my own personal heartbreak involve the children or show negatively as I met and worked with people. Doing my everyday medical work then and many times since I would be told of similar circumstances in other homes. Often what was said would be qualified with, "But doctor, you can't really understand. No one can unless they've gone through it."

Sometimes it would help greatly to tell that I had travelled that road and to me faith in God had made all the difference.

When an attack occurred I had to take Mary to hospital. The drive through the suburbs, over the Harbour Bridge and through congested city streets was a special ordeal. Time moved bitterly slowly. Delays were frequent. The traffic lights seemed always to turn red as I arrived at them. Mary sat there bolt upright, silent, looking straight ahead, almost spastic, a fixed, vague look on her face.

These journeys to me were drawn-out, grey and desperate. But unlike the days in Africa they were not weighed down with apparent hopelessness. There was the knowledge that treatment would succeed and that the drive home – it might be in a matter of days or at the worst weeks – would be with a relaxed Mary taking an interest in what she saw and heard. A Mary who talked and smiled. Those journeys back from the hospital seemed no distance at all.

The attacks became less frequent and less severe and, after her breast operation, for no clinical reason of which I am aware, they stopped altogether.

For ten years life moved on, full of action, interest and happenings. We moved to the North Ryde house. It had a big colourful garden. The door-bell and telephone were always ringing. David and Rosemary negotiated their teens constructively and happily. Higher education brought new friendships and interest to life. I wrote in a newsletter, "Mary is a stalwart helper in all that goes on. Her support and understanding make it possible for so much, which otherwise couldn't be attempted, to be done." And there *were* a host of activities.

We were a contented, busy family, in step and in harmony. Holidays were fun and relaxing.

Then one day when her fifty-fourth birthday was in sight, I was aware of trouble. Slowly, so very slowly, as to make me wonder if I was observing accurately, Mary lost abilities. Her writing became slower and, as week followed week, less distinct. Counting up small change started to be a problem and would be done inaccurately over and over again. Keys and locks became a puzzle as did telephones and switches and then she found it beyond her to put a coat on a coat hanger. Cooking was not possible but she could still peel vegetables. Then an election occurred. The voting was too much for Mary and there was a scene at the polling-booth. At this stage I called for help.

Ross is a close friend, an active, cheerful Christian and a most capable psychiatrist.

He went into the situation carefully and advised clearly, honestly and with great kindness, "You're facing a Presenile Dementia. Mary will go downhill inevitably and progressively. Medically we can do little." He paused. "Now let's switch to my other patient. You." He sat back in an armchair. "Listen, Paul, you've been a busy, outgoing boy for a long time. Doctoring, talking to people about God, counselling students – do you remember the chats we used to have in the train when I was a medical student? You've run conferences, houseparties, preached, written, broadcast, and all the time it's been giving out and giving out. You've had the wear and tear of Mary's recurring depressions and the suspense of never knowing when another balloon might go up." He leaned forward, "You think you're a tough cookie. You're not, you know. Make no mistake, the next year or two are going to be rougher than you think. Mary has the endogenous variety of depression but I don't see how *you* are going to dodge the exogenous form." He went on to give me sound and practical advice.

As I said good-bye at the gate I thought what a wise and helpful person he was, but I didn't take seriously what he had said about "hit-you-from-outside" depression.

A year went slowly by. Mary lost skill after skill and ability after ability. Reading was beyond her. She could not sign her name. Taps would be turned on and on and on, producing flooding and acute distress. She couldn't find her way around the house, then came the heartbreaking day when she didn't recognise me.

Ross came and his quiet voice said firmly, "Mary must go to hospital now. If you hadn't been a doctor and reasonably capable with a broom and saucepan you'd have had to take this step many months ago."

Hospital beds for this condition are rare. Two months earlier I had talked the matter over with the matron of a church geriatric hospital; a place where all the facilities were available.

Without my knowing it, Ross had again and again made inquiries, but the reply had been – no bed available.

That dark day I walked sadly and tiredly about the house. The time had come when nothing I could do would bring even a flicker of joy or even consolation. I prayed, "Please Lord, help me." Some hours later the phone rang and the matron's kindly voice said, "We have a bed today."

God's timing was exact.

To see Mary leave our home with finality was worse than any funeral.

To visit the hospital to be unrecognised and to see the features and hands I loved wilted and purposeless was beyond words. I found it too hard to face people in the lift so I used to walk down the stairs. One particularly upsetting day I bumped into a white-dressed figure, mumbled an apology and stumbled on. My arm was gripped and I was forced to show my tears. It was the matron. She too had travelled this road and understood it only too well. She sat down in her office and spoke quietly and firmly, "You mustn't keep coming here. You're doing nothing to help. If your wife comes back into awareness, I'll let you know."

"I can't abandon her, Matron. We've shared life for thirty years together."

"You're not abandoning her. You've shouldered every responsibility for years and done everything in your power."

"Of course, I love her. But now...."

"Now leave her to us. You have work to do. Don't tear your life apart to do what you think people expect you to do."

That day, that wise experienced Christian woman did a most important thing for my life and mind. Ross said the same thing, even more forcefully. However I struggled against it.

Stress always accentuates physical troubles. My old enemy asthma crept up on me and attacked. Doctors never expect to find themselves in the business end of an ambulance or to find their name on the chart above a hospital bed. But it happens!

I lay propped up in bed with medication flowing down a tube into a vein and an oxygen apparatus making it somewhat easier to breathe. I wondered vaguely if this was the take-off for the great safari. I prayed, "Lord, whatever happens, please help me to be useful to someone."

Late at night a nurse adjusted the inhaler and said, "Dr. White, I believe you are a Christian." I nodded. "Can you tell me how to become one?" Again I nodded. "Well, will you?"

I panted. "Could you – possibly – wait – till – tomorrow. I'm – a bit – puffed – "

She said quietly, "I'd rather you told me tonight. You see, you're on the danger list."

I explained the Way to her more slowly than I have done it before or since. I told her, with the feeling that there was a lot of life still to be lived.

Six weeks later, somewhat battered I was again doing my routine-work. It was far from easy to keep moving even in a lower gear. The year was running out. This would be Mary's second Christmas in hospital. These had been long, sad months of vagueness and unawareness of people and places.

In August, in the hope of bringing a few moments of joy, Rosemary had visited her with her new-born daughter. Mary had always greatly loved babies, but she neither recognised her own daughter, nor noticed baby Karina. Leaving the ward and hospital on days like that left us stunned and sick. We reminded ourselves that Mary's life had been in the hands of her Lord since she was a small girl. Her life here had been quiet and purposeful and utterly unselfish, but the matter that counted was that her life did not end with the wearing out of her body.

Christmas day came and went. Two days later the matron rang, "Come and see your wife today."

Mary was in a bed with guard rails. She was deeply unconscious. Life had seeped away over five long years leaving the merest shadow of the girl I had loved for more than half of my life. The next evening Mary moved forever out of the grey cloud.

The mist from that cloud remained dank and chill, the road seemingly empty. As I saw it the thing to do was to keep on in the centre of the track, walking purposefully, although, as Ross had prophesied, the going was steeply uphill.

In early January I had promised to give the Presidential Address at the Fellowship of Evangelical Students' Conference. I was determined to do this since everyone of the thousand or more students who were coming to the Australian National University at Canberra would at sometime come head on into tragedy. While still in the valley of shadow I could perhaps help some of them by sharing what I had found out.

It takes months and often years for many people to be free from the depression that results from circumstances. But even that grey mist can be turned to a positive purpose. Being aware of the geography makes you useful as a guide and also as a map-maker.

Mary and David, 1959

With Ruth in Switzerland, 1973

Chapter Twenty One:

Secretaries and More

I SHALL ALWAYS BE GRATEFUL TO HAZEL HOPKINSON. SHE WAS one of ten competent women, the noble platoon of secretaries, without whom I would not have done so many things. They turned odd, mis-spelt pieces of paper into spotless pages of typescript. They protected me from the telephone, made sure I kept appointments and that I did not arrange to speak at two places at the same time. On occasions they were firm and insisted that I kept the "IN" tray empty. They brewed countless cups of tea and did jobs that were far outside the demands of duty.

Hazel was a woman of courage and determination. As a child a detonator accident had robbed her of her left hand. She was a competent stenographer and a trained artist. Hazel had decided that she wanted to write books herself, to make simple what many found difficult. To do this she worked part-time while she matriculated and later gained her Arts degree with honours. For years she was the keel of the Jungle Doctor ship and we sailed smoothly forward.

One day she came beaming and brandishing the morning paper. "I've graduated and can get a job in the Education Department."

My heart sank.

For months I tried to be my own secretary, making copies of such letters as I wrote, banking, checking pass sheets, paying bills and sending receipts. I did all of this, or at least part, in my own peculiar way. I followed Hazel's two-year-ahead schedule of sending tapes to various radio stations, wrapping the boxes in corrugated cardboard and then in brown paper, tying carefully with thin string, then labelling. I put my best efforts into this but inevitably the end-result was unsatisfying. I have always been conscious of my shortcomings in any form of handcraft. Week followed week. Things became more untidy, more jumbled, until a state of hopelessness loomed.

I sent out an S.O.S. "Hazel, help. Chaos approaches. Do you know anybody? Can you find somebody who would be able to give a helping hand? Mary has lost more ground. The "IN" tray overflows. You know only too well what can happen in the White's house."

Efficiently and promptly came the reply. "I do know someone. You may remember her. She called for me in the car one day – Ruth Longe. She's doing an Arts degree at Sydney University, part-time, and has been offered a job there in the Anthropology Department. She might come."

She did. And arrived in a battle-scarred Morris Minor which she drove with considerable competency. Quietly she took over all the things I couldn't do properly. She knew how to keep books, typed well, and I was amazed that she could deal with the unusual words that cropped up in medical letters. She laughed when I mentioned this. "I did three years of nursing before a generation of boils drove me to book-keeping."

Mary was delighted to have laughter in the house again, and to hear the piano. Sometimes arriving home I was greeted with, "How do you like my hair? Ruth washed and set it," or "We've been making an apple pie."

University lectures were so happily placed that Ruth could hold the fort while I was away at my medical practice and I could keep the home fires burning while she left to study Greek. My inabilities had been so many; what a blessèd relief this sort of help was.

But stress mounted, asthma attacked and resulted in some interesting and useful weeks in hospital. Ambulances, uncertainty of life, the modern way of treating asthma, thoughts on the great safari, convalescence and the opportunity of talking to people about God – all this and more flashed through my mind like the pictures of a filmstrip.

There was the exhilaration of going home, walking round the garden and inspecting special roses and wild flowers. The colour and joy faded suddenly when I realised all over again that Mary would never come home from hospital. Fatigue descended, frustrating my determined efforts to pick up sufficient strength to go back to the practice.

"Do half as much as you want to do," was my standing order. Even this was hard going. The routine was maintained only because Ruth was at the wheel. We finished the last of the hospital series of Jungle Doctor Books. It had taken three years.

With difficulty I journeyed to Brisbane to speak for Scripture Union – three talks in a weekend and a flight home. Again that lurking fatigue. Then came great loneliness.

Back at my surgery I contrived to be cheerful and encouraging until the last patient went through the door. Writing reports, answering letters and even driving home was drudgery. Day after day it went on. My clinical work was up to ordinary standard but concentration was bitterly hard. It was so difficult to give to others the support I lacked myself.

Time went by. It dragged. Sickness, stress, tiredness, death – each left its footprint heavily.

One evening the rare urge came upon me to tidy up. In a cupboard were three tarnished cups with my name engraved on them. They were a sorry sight. Beside them was a stout sealed enveloped labelled, POCKET OF ATHLETICS BLUE, and some words from St. Paul, written years before, "Run with your mind fixed on winning the prize – go into serious training. Athletes will take tremendous pains for a fading crown of leaves. Your contest is for an eternal crown which will never fade. RUN WITH DETERMINATION."

My "Blue" had been a very colourful, striped blazer. I took it to Africa with me. There white ants (termites) had wrecked it beyond repair. I had salvaged the pocket with the University badge embroidered on it and sealed it in that envelope. It had been there for years. I tore open the flap. Other insects had been at work. It was in a state of rags and powder. I looked at my once-treasured athletic trophies. Moth and rust had corrupted. I was determined this rust and rot would not happen to me. I would continue to live with determination.

That night in my lonely home, I saw the obvious answer and the complete difference that could possibly come about.

Philip Knight was best man. He whispered to me, "I'm nervous."

I laughed, "I'm not."

"It's all right for you," he replied, "you're only the bridegroom."

Ruth, my bride, looked beautiful. I glowed as I stood in front of the communion rails of our local church and watched her walk up the aisle. When asked, "Do you take this woman to be your wedded wife, to love and to cherish. ..." I answered clearly and happily, "I do."

That day Ruth became an instant grandmother, while I became uncle to twenty more nephews and nieces.

In the rain and chill of early winter we set out on a nine-week honeymoon which would take us north to the Great Barrier Reef. Following the usual pattern of my safaris, since I was President of the Australian Fellowship of Evangelical Students, I planned to visit the Christian students in the universities and colleges north from Newcastle to Townsville.

Zeal was not lacking but commonsense and medical wisdom was in singularly short supply. In the excitement I overlooked medical advice not to go beyond the fringe of fatigue and gave seventeen talks and lectures. These and an assortment of activity saw us return to our new life with me dragging my feet and Ruth more tired than she liked to say.

One morning Ruth drove out of our carport in reverse. The bumper bar caught our neighbour's tap and neatly removed it. I quelled the resultant fountain and did a little rough plumbing to restore matters. The lady-next-door was very understanding. "You're fortunate, my dear, to have a father who can do these practical things."

Now there is a disparity of a mere quarter-of-a-century in our ages, so to clarify the matter I explained that she was not my daughter but my grand-daughter! The lady-next-door had a twinkle in her eye. She saw the rings on Ruth's finger and joined in the laughter.

Laughter, however, became harder to produce those days. Moving back into the old routine seemed dreary, ineffective plodding. Life went on apparently as before but inside me were all the by-products of depression. Three six-hour days as a rheumatologist sapped all my energy. It was possible to concentrate on medical problems and be understanding and a good listener until the last patient had gone. Then came flat fatigue.

To lift my mood was almost physical exertion. If ever a

human mind needed propping up it was mine in those drab, tasteless days. Ruth's were the hands and heart that did it and it cost her very considerably. Together we planned a careful programme of book-writing and production of audio visual aids and records.

David Longe was one of my newly acquired brothers-in-law. He is a skilled broadcaster and public relations man. With his aid a project was put into action that had been hanging fire for years. Ten new filmstrips incorporating all that was up-to-date were produced. They were good – the script, the message, the colour, the humour and the sound. David was enthusiastic. But I walked up and down deep in pessimism, complaining that we'd go broke, that they wouldn't sell. Querulously I asked, would the British market be interested? Would the Americans complain about the Australian accent of the jungle animals?

David laughed. "Why don't you and Ruth start a concern called 'Paul White Productions'? Look at the way things are happening with the books." He picked up two new translations that had arrived by post that day and waved them at me. "And you have those Picture Fables Books on the way." I nodded glumly. He thumped me on the shoulder. "There's an exciting future ahead."

Not long before, a new inhaler for the treatment of asthma had come on the scene. I tried one. Within a minute I knew that I had a new ally in my personal battle for breath. Here was a new boost for my morale. Ruth and I talked about this and many other things till late into the night. Pillow-talk can be very valuable. One of the things we agreed upon was that I should discuss matters with my friend who practised psychiatry.

I did so. I told him about my vulnerability, how easily I became tired, how much harder I found it to deal with difficult people and trying circumstances. I admitted that to speak in public was something I now shrank from and I felt acutely nervous before getting to my feet.

There is something rather special about consulting a friend who listens intently and whose advice you know is considered and good. I reported back to Ruth, "He suggests I reduce the amount of medical work I'm doing and also take a close look at what lies ahead in the matter of books, broadcasting and television. Then I told him about our thoughts for a long safari to see what was offering in Asia, America, Europe and back in Africa. He said it was a good idea as long as I take you with me and don't overdo it."

We prayed about the matter and asked that God would help us to see what he wanted done. An overseas trip meant being away from the practice for some four months. If my medical work was to be reduced or if medicine was to be left behind there was need for someone to take my place. This I regarded as of first importance.

I have found that God's planning is so often well ahead of my asking. Sometime before, a month after my visit to hospital, when I had gone to Brisbane to speak for Scripture Union, one of the people I met was a young physician, David Lind, who took me out to dinner. We talked of many things: God's way for our living, the supremely practical nature of His book and our particular responsibilities as medical men. As we talked shop, I asked if he was interested in rheumatic disease. He was and his conversation proved it. I suggested that he might be interested in joining our group.

Both he and I had regularly prayed about this for over two years.

The possibilities of a long safari started to come into focus. Letters with a direct bearing on the matter arrived in quick succession from the Far East, England and Tanzania. All of these things pointed in the one direction. We planned our itinerary. Then for the first time I heard from the Queensland physician. "I will be free from my current job on April 1st. Could I be of any use to you?"

He could indeed. Our departure date was April 17th. This was the first obstacle removed.

Safaris of the sort we had in mind are costly. I sat down to work out finances. It was not going to be easy. Then quite out of the blue came a letter from an American publisher, saying, "Please find enclosed a cheque for two thousand eight hundred and sixty-five dollars. We were greatly concerned to find that these royalties have been due to you over the last ten years. Changes in personnel must somehow have produced this situation. Please accept our most sincere apologies."

This I gladly did. That money balanced the safari budget.

Vastly encouraged, Ruth and I continued to pray that God would guide us and show us what he had in front of us in 1974 and beyond.

Chapter Twenty Two:

Cars and Dogs

AUNTIE JESS WAS MY FAVOURITE AUNT. SHE HAD A MARVELLOUS sense of humour and the habit of pushing a coin into my hand and smiling with great understanding. Uncle Jack, her husband, was a Presbyterian minister who had what now would be termed a vintage car: a horn with a huge rubber bulb behind it, acetylene headlights, shining brass-work, gear lever and hand brake outside the driver's door. Uncle wore goggles, dust coat, and a cloth cap and I once heard him use words that I did not think were Presbyterian when he had a blow out!

Auntie Jess liked dogs and didn't really mind if Carlo, a black and white semi-retriever, dug a little in the garden. I could talk to Carlo and he listened and licked my face. This, I had been told, was unhygienic but it was very comradely if you were lonely. Also, Carlo did not break confidences.

I've always associated dogs with cars and vice versa. For a long stretch of my boyhood we had neither. Occasionally I was taken for a ride but none of our neighbours had dogs. When I should reach what I believed were called years of discretion I determined to have a dog of my own.

Discretion was late in coming. However, when I was at Ryde Hospital the matron asked me to destroy a large, part-Labrador which was a somewhat persistent visitor to the wards. This large and cheerful dog had been removed by the police twice but his public relations were so good that his life had been spared. The dog had no collar and apparently no owner.

I said solemnly that I would deal with the situation. The matron said, "You'll do it painlessly won't you, doctor?" I said I would.

I borrowed mother's small Austin and took Kim, as I called him, home, all the way giving instructions and advice. Mother saw this big golden dog leap out of her car and was thunderstruck.

"Don't you bring that beast into my..." Kim ran up to her, sat and held out his paw. His eyes spoke volumes. He was rather thin.

"I've been instructed to destroy him," I said in a hard voice.

Mother held the dog's paw. "You're a lovely big fellow," she said. "Paul, I will not allow you to harm him."

"What will I do then, mother? I can't take him back to Ryde and to toss him out of the car on the way — that would not be a right thing at all."

"He can stay with me for a while then and we'll see. What's his name? Kim. That's a good name. You must not come into the house, Kim. Do you hear?" The smiling and tail-wagging was well done.

When I left two hours later Kim was asleep at mother's feet and slept that night beside her bed.

When I married, Kim was reluctantly handed over with a long story of a rose-bush uprooted; but I saw the tears in mother's eyes.

Kim was hit by a car and his foreleg broken. I set it with care, having found to my amazement that dogs need very big doses of morphia to cope with pain. Mary felt that an injured dog required a special diet of mince and breast of lamb. I objected strongly, which ensured the maintenance of the diet.

When David was born, the golden dog was first interested and later very possessive, lying beside the cot and vocally suspicious of visitors, especially several folk who had never impressed me. Privately I congratulated Kim on his discernment.

When we went overseas, mother said, "Of course Kim will live with me." Over a year later one of the saddest letters ever to reach me told of Kim's death under the wheels of a taxi. Mother would never have another dog.

In Africa we had no dog. Rabies was not a rarity. We had a large hare which was most fastidious and well trained. Named Sungura, Swahili for rabbit, he was with us for three years and never once drank water. Grass and cabbage leaves had sufficient moisture. Sungura is a famous figure in folk tables and loosened many an elderly African storyteller's tongue.

My one and only form of transport in Tanzania when I

arrived was an ancient Ford which I called Sukuma, Swahili for push. We had a number of ingenious contrivances that made it go, like a two-gallon tin of petrol clamped on the roof which supplied a gravity feed if all else failed. Hours were lost, frustration was high and life was at risk. I prayed for a new car. There was little money, and that went into the purchase of medicines. It was the time of the Great Depression and the people at home knew little of conditions where we were. I wrote and told them whimsically but without asking for help. Then I did what I have never done before. I ordered a new machine, a Ford with a platform back; one hundred and ninety-nine pounds was the quote.

My friends Dan and Samson were concerned, "But you can't pay for it, Bwana."

"True, but I believe God will supply the cash." Deep inside somewhere west of my stomach was a full confidence.

Time went by. The money did not come. My friends shook their heads. Then just before the war started came a note, "New Ford is ready to be picked up."

We were given a ride into the main town, Dodoma, in a Public Works Department lorry. There was no money in my pocket but that day was mail-day. We went to the Post Office. My African friends were silent and concerned. I was handed a packet of letters: medical advertisements, bills – dull stuff, all except one envelope addressed in the well-known hand of my ex-Sunday School teacher, a prominent businessman in Sydney. I opened it:

DEAR PAUL,

I laughed when I read your letter about old Sukuma and drove to the city in my new car. I was uncomfortable all the way in. Enclosed is a bank draft for two hundred pounds. I hope this will help.

MAURICE HORDERN

Without a word I showed the cheque to my friends. "This is God's work," breathed Dan.

"It's God's timing, too," I nodded.

We sat on the steps of the Post Office and thanked Him, then we strode through that East African town, paid for our new vehicle, filled the tank with fuel with our spare pound and sang all the thirty miles back to the hospital.

Cars and Dogs

Back in Australia, with difficulty and for ninety-one pounds, I purchased a Morris 8/40. We made a pilgrimage in it to the dogs' home where for a small sum you could take your pick of scores of dogs. The whole family attended and by popular vote selected a large black dog that looked kindly but had wandering built in. Sadness was our lot on the fifth day. Bimbo had departed. Extensive searching was ineffective, and a second safari and much more careful selection produced Smokey, a dog of good looks but no genealogy.

For three years he shared the Morris with us and later the four-cylinder non-syncromesh eighty-pound Chevrolet which was definitely pre-war and all the better for it.

Smokey had an inherent dislike for the iceman, who was a notable professional boxer. I reinforced the wire fence I had erected and firmly closed the gate every Tuesday and Saturday. A tick that had dropped from its alternate host the bandicoot – a snouted rat-like marsupial that delights to dig holes in lawns – buried deep into his skin and despite the best of medical and veterinary efforts Smokey succumbed and was replaced by a half-border-collie, half-labrador, selected by myself. Mary liked him and the children slowly accepted him. Rob was fully a member of the household after he had been entered for a pet show in a neighbouring parish. The minister, a man of small stature and mellow voice, announcing the prizes, said, "Now our last award, a highly coveted award, goes to a very good friend of St. Barnabas' church – Best-looking mongrel – Dr. Paul White." This convulsed family and friends for a considerable time.

Rob was an ecclesiastical beast, following us to church. He would sleep on the porch and look coldly on both those who arrived late and made early exits. Rob too was bitten by a tick and early paralysis threatened. At the same time Mary's stepmother was very unwell. In Rosemary's prayers she asked among other things, "And if you must have one of them, God, please take Grannie."

For years he travelled in the car and guarded it faithfully. He approved of my small Singer, but was never comfortable in the back of the very second-hand Vauxhall. He seemed to be aware that I had been taken down. Our first Holden – demonstrator model – pleased him, and he would sit waiting for me in the driver's seat, both paws on the wheel.

At this time I acquired a new and significant number plate for the car – JD-001 – J. D. standing for Jungle Doctor. It was given to me for a birthday present by the Deputy Commissioner of Police, Mr. W. J. Lawrence, who was my friend and patient.

One Sunday I went to speak at his church and on the way home was booked for exceeding the speed limit of 35 miles per hour. The next day I was visited by a policeman who handed me a receipt for a fine which I had incurred but not paid. With it was a hand-written letter from Mr. Lawrence:

DEAR PAUL,
I see you were booked for driving at 42 m.p.h. and that you admitted your guilt. I could not strike your name off the report – that would have been unjust and illegal – but I could and did pay your fine. You will see the analogy clearly.

When we moved to a house with two acres of ground, Rob, who by now was reasonably well on by canine standards, seemed to lose interest in most of life. At sunset when his meal was ready he would emerge smiling and wagging his tail but when he meditated on an empty dish he would become somnolent again. He woke sufficiently to tree the somewhat sour individual who read the electricity meter. This person seemed to take it as a planned insult that the family did not return for some two hours!

As a reward for Rob's faithfulness Rosemary visited the dogs' home and returned with a miniature collie, a lady and permanently childless, whom she called Susie – a small dog with a large heart and considerable charm. Rob was outraged, but the very first evening we found both dogs sleeping, Susie with her head on the less hairy parts of Rob's understructure. Both enjoyed to the full my updated – again demonstrator model – Holden and our second-hand 1937 model Austin 10 UF-820 – alias Uffie.

After many days Rob was too slow in crossing the road. He died with his head on my knee. I'm glad no one saw my tears. He was a dog of great character and kindness. Susie was broken-hearted and grieved for days. Mary gave her considerable tender loving care. The little dog brought us joy for some years and died in the beginning of the dark days when Mary started to lose strength.

Cars and Dogs

A dogless house seemed to be strangely empty. I did not feel like visiting the dogs' home again. One day Mary said, "I want a dog – a bigger one. When you're out I need a companion."

We heard of a brown kelpie, bred in the country as a working dog with all the characteristics and charm of a highly intelligent sheepdog. She was little more than a pup, full of energy and love of mankind. This was somewhat disguised by a conscience-stimulating bark. She had lived with a Canadian geography lecturer and his wife on the foreshores of Sydney Harbour. They told us how this cheerful, medium-sized, brown dog had incurred the wrath of local fishermen by eating their bait. She apparently did not easily learn by experience and returned home not infrequently with her hair wet with salt water having been thrown into the harbour for her sins.

We called her Chibwa – Chigogo for small dog. Mary's eyes would light up when the brown kelpie – Scottish for a sprite – would come to her.

Then one day, she was not. Search parties, telephoning to pounds and municipal authorities produced no results. Days later by a round-about-way came the news she was at the dogs' home! Cutting into my medical work I went and ransomed her to be greeted by the flying dog treatment as she leaped into my arms. This was her last unlawful excursion from our home.

Ruth had not had much experience with dogs, but Chibwa quickly made a track to her heart.

What better company can you have when you're sick than a brown-eyed dog with ears at the alert, sitting there hour after hour? When necessary there is the soft thump of an understanding tail and a nose pushed gently into your hand. She reads the moods and there is no rocketing around or excited barking.

However, if the tune of life is normal the front-door bell is the signal for a wild burst of dog sound followed by a rapturous welcome, paw-shaking and gavotting to her friends and watchful silence for those about lawful business. To those unlawfully inclined I believe could come an ungentle encounter with ivory.

If it appears that we are going out, an intelligent head with pointed ears awaits the magic words, "Out" and "Car." Chibwa is a strong supporter of Volkswagens – after all, she is nearly nine now and so is our VW.

Chapter Twenty Three:

Changing Jobs

It was Sunday afternoon. We had been married a year and were relaxing quietly together in our sitting room.

Ruth had been playing the piano and now we were listening to a Brandenburg Concerto. We had found our tastes in music surprisingly similar. We had spent a lot of time in that room watching cricket and Rugby football on TV. There is a special satisfaction when your wife can really throw a ball and understand the leg-before-wicket rules. My hobby of birdwatching had proved infectious. Ruth is as enthusiastic as I am about the music of the bush and those who produce it. Above me on a ledge were a row of beautifully carved animals. African craftsmen do these extremely well. The room had a strong jungle flavour with prints of David Shepherd's elephants on opposite walls. It was a comfortable room; not luxurious, but a room which I found exactly to my taste.

The music finished. We put on a cassette of a talk by J. O. Sanders on the life of Caleb. "J. Oswald reminds me of Caleb," said Ruth.

I agreed, "Amongst our friends there are some great stalwarts like him." I pressed a switch and we came face to face with a situation that was to change our thinking about the future.

J. O. told how Caleb at eighty-five had no thoughts of retirement and had asked that his share of the Promised Land be hill country, peopled by giants, who were particularly hostile to God. Three times came the words, "Caleb wholly followed the Lord."

I like that word *wholly*. . . .

He chose a sword rather than an armchair in the evening of his life.

We sat quietly for a time, then I said, "We could go to Tanzania. Perhaps I could manage a few years' work in, say, the Leprosy Hospital. My chronic diseases experience would help."

"Wellesley Hannah is planning to go back," nodded Ruth. "In his last letter he said he was retiring early from his job in Victoria."

We prayed together and talked about all angles of the situation. Then we both had a sudden understanding of what this step could mean. We walked around our home and looked at the pictures we had carefully chosen, the bookcases with their choice inhabitants, the piano – we both felt a house without a piano was incomplete. And then there were our records. We would leave this but we felt deep down it would be hard to do so.

"An overseas safari is necessary," I said at last. "We need to be on the spot and see exactly what the present-day conditions involve."

We landed within view of Mount Kilimanjaro. Enthusiasm was high. The picture the country gave was much the same. Herd-boys still drove their hump-backed cattle to pasture. The hills were still outlined with granite outcrops. The thorn-bush jungle was still there. It was refreshing to chat to the local people in Chigogo. They were delighted to hear their own language spoken and I was delighted to speak it. At the leprosy settlement I saw the work and its outreach. But as day followed day I became aware of the frustrations of the ordinary, everyday problems: shortages, delays, unfulfilled promises, bats that got into the roof, catastrophies that could occur to sanitation.

Even with no responsibilities to carry I found myself physically and emotionally unable to deal with life in modern East Africa. I felt this very keenly till I realised that I had asked God for guidance and here it was – stark and real. A closed door.

Ruth and I had travelled with our eyes open through the Far East, North America, Europe and places in between. World travel is no rest cure. After a couple of days to recover we sat down quietly at home and weighed up all we had seen and heard.

There were two paths still in front of us. I could walk back to the old track of Consultant Physician in Rheumatic diseases, doing a little less medicine, while writing as much as possible when energy permitted. That, or a complete change of professions. I went back to medical work. It was uphill. I had lost my zest for it. There was the conflict of medical politics due to trends towards nationalisation. I found it unpalatable and distressing.

For thirty years I had been planning the "end game" of my life and preparing for it. Plans and preparations were in order; timing was the factor about which I had to be sure. Someone of like mind with the medical qualifications was needed now. Again, at the right time, David Lind came to see me. He had found work at the practice congenial while I was away. Already I had discovered that the majority of my patients liked him and appreciated his medical skills. He told me he would be willing to take over from me on January 1st.

And so it was that with Christmas in sight I walked out of my consulting rooms, had a last look at my name on the door, bowed to it, and said to myself, "Your name may be there for a while, Paul White, but the medical phase of your life is over."

It was plain that the thing I could do with the greatest usefulness to God was to change professions. The best use of my time and experience would be through literature and the media, working at it full-time. With the help of translators and experts in all manner of communication areas I could touch millions of people and do it within the limits of my strength and energy. What's more I could do my writing at times when I felt like it — when the words came bubbling out of me.

Unplanned retirement can be fatal. A patient came to see me, rubbing his hands together. "I'm retiring in June."

"Oh, and what are you going to do?"

"Well, I'll paint the house and there are all sorts of repairs about the place that I've wanted to do for years."

"And then?"

"Oh, I don't know...."

He was dead in a year. Again and again this happened. I did not retire.

Our home is in a tree-rich suburb. My table is twelve feet long and looks out on lawn, shrubs, palms and tall evergreen timber. I am surrounded with books, files, recording devices and a battered dictaphone. There are cupboards housing books in various stages of growth and master tapes for the production of cassettes of Jungle Doctor material and of bird sounds. In a book labelled IDEAS are roughs for the next three filmstrips, pages of notes on new fables and comic books.

My target – the final result of prayer and research – is to expand Paul White Productions: books, audio visuals and scripts, and work in front of microphones and television cameras. There is no limit to the possibilities.

In England a publisher put out the staggering request, "Will you write a book on death for six to nine-year-olds?" A little dazed, I agreed; but immediately thought of one on *birth* as well!

Already in a folder were ideas and roughs for a book for young people in which I would share my mistakes and discoveries in practical Christian living. I did, and it is called *Get Moving*. There was this autobiography. At home I had a large box full of diaries and scribblings, columns I had written for a New Zealand paper, articles from all corners of the earth, tapes and letters I had both written and received. It was a mine of material.

Already I had seen international co-editions of the Picture Fable Books in four colours and eight languages. Thousands upon thousands of them. Four books were ready for the market. "Do four more when you arrive home and think of another lot in 1978," was the bones of a publisher's letter.

In Australia Clifford Warne beamed at me. "There are a number of things I want to do for the Church of England Television Society. Some one-minute readings from the Bible with Graham Wade doing some super lightning sketches." These are appearing widely throughout Australia.

Simon, my four-year-old grandson, hearing my voice coming from the television set, ran excitedly to his mother. "Quickly, come and listen. My grandad is talking about my Jesus."

I find myself interviewing and interviewed and taking part in television panels which involve being plastered with pancake make-up at frequent intervals.

In the broadcasting field came requests from the newly formed Anglican Radio Unit to do two-and-a-half-minute scripts for radio in Australia.

Then came a suggestion, "Why not turn the ten-minute broadcast episodes into six-minute cassette stories and then reduce them to two and a half minutes for radio?" Another thought was, "Why not do cassettes of distinctive Australian bird sounds? What about the lyrebird — a marvellous mimic!" Why not? And turn a life-time hobby into bread-and-butter. Far more, it would help the many who seldom see a bird or are conscious of its song, to appreciate something of beauty and interest.

Paul White Productions works with Pilgrim International, Emu Book Agencies, Challenge Films, Church of England Television Society, Anglican Radio Unit, and others with their own contribution of talent. It is a loosely knit team. Each draws on and enriches the other. We work together without friction — not building up our own little empires. The work of the Kingdom is bigger than us all and can absorb our combined skills and more.

As I have been writing this last chapter two "Calebs" have crossed my path. One is E. M. Blaiklock, Emeritus Professor of Classics from Auckland who has been a spiritual leader for half a century. He is a verbal artist and can take the words of Scripture and see them in their rich historical context. His battle ground for God's Kingdom has been his special knowledge of Biblical language and classical history. At seventy-two retirement is not in his vocabulary. On this visit to Sydney, he was coping with a preaching and lecturing programme which would be considered heavy for a man half his age.

In the same weekend I talked with Dr. Denis Burkitt, a man about my age. He is a notable figure in medical research. In East Africa he had shed great light on a cancerous condition named after him, Burkitt's Lymphoma. A humble man, he has the ability to use clear, simple word-pictures to explain both medicine and Christianity. His enthusiasm for evangelism is infectious. Throughout my life it has been a profound encouragement to meet those with the stamp of Caleb upon them.

Through the window I watch the postman loading our sturdy post box. Here can be more adventure. I walk down to collect that mail. Soon Ruth and I will open it with all the anticipation of children with Christmas stockings.

"The funniest thing I've read since Darwin"

LIST OF PUBLISHED WORKS BY PAUL WHITE "ALIAS JUNGLE DOCTOR"

Medical Man or Medicine Man?

I. V. F. Invites a General

Jungle Doctor
Jungle Doctor on Safari
Jungle Doctor Operates
Jungle Doctor Attacks Witchcraft
Jungle Doctor's Enemies
Jungle Doctor Meets a Lion
Jungle Doctor to the Rescue
Jungle Doctor's Casebook
Jungle Doctor and the Whirlwind
Eyes on Jungle Doctor
Jungle Doctor Looks for Trouble
Jungle Doctor Goes West
Jungle Doctor Stings a Scorpion
Jungle Doctor Hunts Big Game
Jungle Doctor on the Hop
Jungle Doctor's Crooked Dealings
Jungle Doctor Spots a Leopard
Jungle Doctor Pulls a Leg
Jungle Doctor Sees Red

Jungle Doctor's Fables Series:

Jungle Doctor's Fables
Jungle Doctor's Monkey Tales
Jungle Doctor's Tug-of-War
Jungle Doctor's Hippo Happenings
Jungle Doctor's Rhino Rumblings

Doctor of Tanganyika
Jungle Doctor's Progress
Jungle Doctor's Panorama

Jungle Doctor Picture Fables Series:
Illustrated by Peter Oram

Donkey Wisdom
Famous Monkey Last Words
Monkey in a Lion's Skin
Reflections of Hippo
The Cool Pool
The Monkey and the Eggs
Monkey Crosses the Equator
Sweet and Sour Hippo

Yacobo in Slippery Places

What's happening to Mother

What happened to Auntie Jean?

Get Moving!

Also in collaboration with Dr. David Britten: The Ranford Series:

The Ranford Mystery Miler
Ructions at Ranford
Ranford Goes Fishing
Ranford in Flames

Selections from the JUNGLE DOCTOR SERIES of books have also been published in the following different forms:

Flash Books:
Safe as Poison   Monkey who Didn't Believe in Crocodiles   Little Leopards   Monkey, the Mirror, and the Red Paint   The Great Wall   The Small Wisdom of Feeding Vultures

Comic Strip or Cartoon Books:
Safe as Poison   Monkey who Didn't Believe in Crocodiles   Little Leopards   Monkey in the Bog   Monkey in a Lion's Skin   The Great Wall   Out on a Limb   The Sticky End   Helpfulness of Hippo

Film Strips, with dramatised sound track:
Fables Series:
Famous Last Words   Donkey Wisdom   Reflections of Hippo   Sweet and Sour Hippo   The Trap   Crocodiles   Vultures   Monkey in a Lion's Skin

Farmyard series:
Simon's Lucky Day   The Dare-Devils   The Rescue Squad   The Great Escape

Cassettes:
Jungle Fables
Monkey Tales
Farmyard Capers

Dramatised Bible Series:
The King Must Die   The Bold Ones   Strange Stories from the Bible   More Strange Stories from the Bible

List of Languages and/or Countries in which THE JUNGLE DOCTOR SERIES or selections from it have been published

AFRICAN
Amharic (Ethiopia)
Afrikaans
Chokwe (Angola)
Cigogo (Tanzania)
Gbaya (Cameroun)
Kilega (Zaire)
Kirundi (Burundi)
Lingala (Zaire)
Nuba Mtns. (Sudan)
Setswana
Sotho
Swahili
Vagla (Ghana)
Zulu

EUROPEAN
Czechoslovakian
Danish
Dutch
Faroese
Finnish
French
German
Magyar (Hungary)
Italian
Norwegian
Portuguese
Spanish
Swedish
Yugoslavian

ASIAN
Arabic
Assamese
Bengali
Cebuano
Chinese
Gujerati
Hebrew
Hindi
Ilocano
Ilongo
Indonesian
Japanese
Kanarese
Lao
Malayalam
Marathi
Oriya
Persian
Pattani Malay
Rumi Malay
Tagalog
Tamil
Telugu
Thai
Urdu
Vietnamese & 3 dialects:
    Radai, Jairai & Koko

OCEANIC
Pidgin
Australian Aboriginal Languages:
    Anindilyaugwa
    Gumatj
    Gapapuynu
    Kuku-Yalanji
    Maung
    Nganyatjarra
    Walmatjari
    Wik-Munkan
South Sea Is. Languages:
    Ellice
    Fijian
    Gilbertise
    Raratongan
    Samoan
    Tongan